FINE BOOKS

BY
ALFRED W. POLLARD

New York

COOPER SQUARE PUBLISHERS, INC.

1964

Originally published by Methuen & Co. Ltd., London
Library of Congress Catalog Card No. 63-20469
Published by Cooper Square Publishers, Inc.
59 Fourth Avenue, New York 3, N. Y.

Lithographed in the U.S.A.
by NOBLE OFFSET PRINTERS, INC.
New York, N. Y. 10003

PREFACE

IF the mere taking of trouble ensured good work, this contribution to the *Connoisseur's Library* should be entitled to the modest praise of being "superior to the rest" of its author's book-makings, since it has been ten years on the stocks and much of it has been written two or three times over, either because the writer's own information had increased or to take account of the successful researches of others. Yet in the end defeat in one main point has to be acknowledged. The book was begun with a confident determination to cover the whole ground, from the beginnings of printing and printed book-illustration down to our own day, and in the case of printing the survey has been carried through, however sketchily. But the corresponding survey of book-illustration ends, with rather obvious marks of compression and fatigue, about 1780, leaving the story of a hundred and thirty years of very interesting picture-work untold. Pioneering is always so exciting that recognition of the impossibility of carrying out the full plan of the book within the limits either of the present volume or of the author's working life was not made without sincere regret. The subject, however, of the abandoned chapter was not only very large, but very miscellaneous, and the survey for it would have had to include at least three other countries (France, Germany, and the United States) besides our own. To one section, moreover, that of illustrations in colour, a separate volume of this series has already been devoted. The author would, therefore, fain console himself with the hope that in one or more other volumes a competent account may be given by some other hand of the wood-engravings, etchings, steel-engravings, and lithographs, with which books have been decorated since 1780. The poorness of paper and print with which these modern illustrated books have too often been handicapped has caused collectors to take little interest in them—it even suggested the unworthy excuse for the failure to write the missing chapter that these are not really *Fine Books*, but only books with fine pictures in them, and so are outside our subject. But both students and collectors have their duties as well as their delights, and in view of the high artistic value of quite a large proportion of these modern illustrations, the preservation of clean and uncropped copies of the books in which they occur and the tribute of careful cataloguing and description are certainly their due.

While the desired completeness has not been attained the ground here covered is still very wide, and for the book as a whole no more can be claimed than that it is a compilation from the best sources—a list of these will be found in the Bibliography—controlled by some personal knowledge, the amount of which naturally varies very much from chapter to chapter. The obligations incurred in writing it have thus been great, and a sad number of these are to fellow-workers and friends— Proctor, John Macfarlane, W. H. Allnutt, Konrad Burger, Dr. Lippmann, Anatole Claudin, and the Prince d'Essling—who have died while the book has been in progress. Among those still happily alive acknowledgment must specially be made to Sir Sidney Colvin for help received from his masterly introduction to the great monograph on *Early Engravers and Engraving in Eng-*

PREFACE

land published by the Trustees of the British Museum ; to
Mr. A. M. Hind for use made of the list of engravers
and their works in the same book ; to Mr. Campbell
Dodgson for dippings into the wealth of information in
his *Catalogue of German and Flemish Woodcuts in the
Print Room of the British Museum* (Vols. I and II); to
Mr. Gordon Duff for help derived from his three series
of Sandars Lectures on English Printing, and to Mr.
Evans for information obtained from his *American
Bibliography*. Among other obligations the chief is to
the writers (notably Mr. H. R. Plomer) of numerous
papers contributed to the *Transactions* of the Bibliographical Society and to *The Library*, and these are
acknowledged with special pleasure.

A. W. P.

CONTENTS

LIST OF PLATES

FINE BOOKS

xiv

LIST OF PLATES

*Engraving of an Author, possibly CAXTON
Presenting a Book to Margaret, Duchess of Burgundy,
prefixed to the Chatsworth copy of the 'Recuyell.'*

FINE BOOKS

CHAPTER I

COLLECTORS AND COLLECTING

FROM the stray notes which have come down to us about the bibliophiles of the later Roman Empire it is evident that book-collecting in those days had at least some modern features. Owing to the abundance of educated slave-labour books were very cheap, almost as cheap as they are now, and book-collectors could busy themselves about refinements not unlike those in which their successors are now interested. But in the Middle Ages books were by no means cheap, and until quite the close of the fourteenth century there were few libraries in which they could be read. Princes and other very wealthy book-buyers took pleasure in possessing finely written and illuminated manuscripts, but the ruling ideals were mainly literary and scholastic, the aim (the quite right and excellent aim) being to have the best books in as many subjects as possible. After printing had been invented the same ideals continued in force, the only difference being that they could now be carried out on a larger scale. Libraries like those formed in the sixteenth century by Archbishop Cranmer and Lords Arundel and Lumley, or that gathered in France by the historian De Thou, were essentially students' libraries, and the books themselves and the catalogues of them were often classified so as to show what books had been acquired in all the different departments of human knowledge. Even in the sixteenth century, when these literary ideals were dominant, we find some examples of another kind. In Jean Grolier, for instance, we find the book-lover playing the part, too seldom assumed, of the discriminating patron of contemporary printing and bookbinding. Instead of collecting more old books than he could find time to read, Grolier bought the best of his own day, but of these sometimes as many as four or five copies of the same work that he might have no difficulty in finding one for a friend ; and whatever book he bought he had bound and decorated with simple good taste in Venice or at home in France. It would be an excellent thing if more of our modern collectors, instead of taking up antiquarian hobbies, were content to follow Grolier's example. Books always look best when clad in jackets of their own time, and this in the future will apply to the books of the twentieth century as much as to any others. Moreover, there is more actual binding talent available in England just now than at any previous time, and it is much to be desired that modern Groliers would give it scope, not in pulling about old books, but in binding beautifully those of our own day.

Grolier found a modest imitator in England in the person of Thomas Wotton, but with some at least of the Elizabethan book-lovers the havoc wrought in the old libraries by the commissioners of Henry VIII and Edward VI provoked an antiquarian reaction which led them to devote all their energies to collecting, from the unworthy hands into which they had fallen, such treasures of English literary and bookish art as still remained. Putting aside John Leland who worked (to what extent and with what success is not quite clear) for Henry VIII, Matthew Parker, Archbishop of Canterbury, was the earliest of these antiquaries, to the great benefit of the libraries of Lambeth Palace and of Corpus Christi College, Cambridge, though as to how he came by his books perhaps the less said the better. Parker was soon followed by Sir Robert Cotton, whose success in gathering books and documents illustrating English history was so great that his library was sequestered and very nearly altogether taken from him, on the plea that it contained state papers which no subject had a right to possess. Owing to the carelessness and brutality of the previous generation, Cotton's opportunities were as great as his zeal in making use of them, and at the cost of his fortune he laid the foundations of a national library. Humbler men imitated him without being able to secure the same permanence for their collections, more especially Humphrey Dyson, a notary, who seems to have acquired early printed books and proclamations, with the same zeal which Cotton devoted to manuscripts. Many of his treasures passed into the hands of Richard Smith, the Secondary of the Poultry Compter, but at his sale they were scattered beyond recall, and the unity of one of the most interesting of English collections was thus unkindly destroyed. Both these men, and some others of whom even less is known, worked with a public aim, and already Sir Thomas Bodley had gone a step further by founding anew the University Library at Oxford on lines which at once gave it a national importance. This it preserved and developed for over a century and a half, and has never since lost, though no national help, unfortunately, has ever been given it, save the right already conceded by the Stationers' Company, of claiming a copy of any new English book offered for sale.

Bodley's munificent donation marked an epoch in the history of English book-collecting because its tendency was to make private book-collecting of the kind which was then admired incongruous and even absurd. When there were no public libraries open to scholars, for a great man to maintain a splendid library in his own house and allow students to read in it was worthy of Aristotle's μεγαλόψυχος, the man who does everything on a scale that befits his dignity. But in proportion as public collections of books and facilities for obtaining access to them are increased, the preservation of a library on a large scale in a private house, where none of the inmates have any desire to use it, becomes an easy and justifiable object of

3

satire. A man without literary instincts who inherits a fine library is indeed in a parlous state, for if he keeps it he is as a dog in the manger, and if he sells it he is held up to opprobrium.

That considerations of this kind were beginning to have weight is shown by the rapidity with which during the seventeenth and eighteenth centuries one private collection after another drifted into public ownership. In some cases there were intermediate stages. Thus Archbishop Usher's books were not bequeathed to Trinity College, Dublin, but were purchased for it by the subscriptions of the soldiers of Cromwell's army in Ireland. The manuscripts of Sir Simeon d'Ewes remained in the possession of his family for nearly a century, were then purchased by Harley, and came to the British Museum with Harley's collection. Stillingfleet's manuscripts were in the same temporary ownership; his printed books came to Dublin through the public spirit of Archbishop Marsh. So again Bishop Moore's books were purchased for the University Library at Cambridge by George I. Thus even when a collector was not inspired by, or could not afford to indulge, public motives, respect for his memory or desire to benefit an institution often brought his books to a safe haven. But more often the munificence was personal and direct. For some cause not quite easy to see the flow of benefactions to English libraries has dwindled sadly of late years,[1] so that journalists with short memories write of gifts and bequests to American libraries as if they were unprecedented. Even of late years, however, the foundation of the John Rylands Library, Chancellor Christie's gifts and bequest to the Victoria University, the Sandars legacy to the University Library, Cambridge, and Mr. Alfred Huth's bequest to the British Museum of any fifty books it might choose to select from his fine collection, show that the stream is not quite dried up, while for nearly two centuries

---

[1] Even Mr. Carnegie will only help to found new libraries, not to make old ones more efficient.

4

and a half from the foundation of the Bodleian it ran with splendid freedom. Thus Archbishop Williams gave noble gifts of books to S. John's College, Cambridge, and to the Chapter House Library at Westminster Abbey; Selden's books enriched the Bodleian; Laud was a generous benefactor alike to the Bodleian, to S. John's College, Oxford, and to the library of Lambeth Palace; Sir Kenelm Digby gave both to Bodley and to Harvard; Ralph Sheldon benefited the Heralds' College; Pepys (through his nephew) bequeathed his collection to Magdalene College, Cambridge; Archbishop Marsh founded a library at Dublin; Richard Rawlinson gave his manuscripts to the Bodleian, and Harley arranged that his should be offered to the nation.

The example of the men who bought under the influence of an intention to bestow their books on some public institution naturally affected others, and was responsible for a good deal of rather haphazard collecting in the eighteenth century. The private modern library was often confused with the antiquarian collection, and the antiquarian collection itself was seldom dominated by any central idea. Yet collectors who devoted themselves to one subject and knew thoroughly well what they were aiming at were already coming into existence, and these also, when their work was done, were inspired by an honourable ambition to preserve it intact, and so the libraries were once more enriched. Thus Garrick, guided by his professional interest, devoted himself to early plays, and bequeathed his collection to the British Museum. Malone bought the books which were useful to him as a student of Elizabethan literature, more especially of Shakespeare, and bequeathed them to the Bodleian, while Capell left his similar collection to Trinity College, Cambridge. The library of Natural History books brought together by Sir Joseph Banks and bequeathed by him to the British Museum is another example of well-defined collecting, though of a different sort. Among men who were not themselves specialists the vogue lay in

5

the direction of first editions of the Greek and Latin classics and of a few Italian and English authors of special merit, together with books illustrating the history of printing down to about the year 1480 or 1485. The early classics seem to have been the indispensable element in any collection of the first rank, and they appear with monotonous regularity in the libraries of George III, of the Rev. Clayton Mordaunt Cracherode, and of Thomas Grenville, which all three passed to the British Museum ; in the Spencer Collection, now in the John Rylands Library, Manchester; and in the Sunderland Library, sold at auction in 1881-3. When these prizes were secured the collector seems to have felt himself free to follow his individual taste in supplementary purchases, and the Grenville Library is a fine proof of the broader interests of its possessor. Two notable collectors, Heber, the last of the great book-gluttons, and William Henry Miller, founder of the famous Christie-Miller Library at Britwell, cut themselves free from the cult of the *editio princeps*, the latter (despite a taste for modern Latin verse) devoting himself to English poetry, while Heber added to this the literatures of France, Italy, and Spain.

Despite the exceptions we have mentioned, in almost all of the collections of the early years of the nineteenth century two different ideals were combined : the student's ideal of the best books in the best editions, and the antiquary's ideal of the books by which the history of printing and its kindred arts could be most vividly illustrated. The combination is still common, for one of à Beckett's comic histories (though I am not prepared to assert that this is a "best book") still figures as the first entry in many sale catalogues which contain also incunabula assuredly not bought for their literary interest. It is more easy to defend such a medley on the ground of sentiment than of logic. Whoever uses books has reason to be grateful to the men who invented or diffused the art of printing, and may be interested in learning something about them. Yet it can hardly be denied that to collect various kinds of books from an antiquarian, æsthetic, or any other well-defined point of view, not directly literary, is an independent pursuit in its own right, just as to collect old or beautiful china or silver is an independent pursuit, whether or no the china or silver be used for eating or drinking from. It will be said, of course, that on this view books are no better than china (or postage stamps), and there are indeed some strange instances of men who have fallen below their possibilities and have collected books, and not without success, despite a most amazing indifference to their contents. This reduces the joy they can get from their hobby to the bare pleasure of collecting for the sake of collecting, an ignoble delight in indulging acquisitiveness, redeemed to some extent by the higher pleasure of overcoming difficulties and observing the rules of the game. But the ignorant book-collector, until he has educated himself, is like a rose-fancier who cannot distinguish one odour from another. By the time they attract the collector books have become, or are on the road to becoming, so precious that their primary usefulness has to be left dormant. To use them constantly for our daily reading would approach the fault which the Greeks called ὕβρις, the arrogance which makes a man esteem himself so highly that he thinks nothing too good for his own use. But even when this limitation is recognized, for those who can appreciate them they preserve all the associations of their primary use, and it is because these associations are so delightful and so various that the bookman claims that his form of collecting is the best of all.

What then are the associations and qualities which give books value in the eyes of a collector? We may answer the question negatively in the first instance by reducing to their proper importance the two qualities which are popularly supposed to be the most attractive to the book-hunter—rarity and age. If a book is otherwise uninteresting, what is it the better for being rare? In passing it may be noted that unless a book is interesting for other reasons its rarity is necessarily an unknown quantity. Sir Sidney Lee's Census of the extant copies of the First Folio Shakespeare, a comparatively common book, but of supreme interest for its associations, is a striking example of the zeal with which every discoverable copy of a valuable book is now hunted down. Those whose business it is to gather such information can tell in the case of dozens of books of much less importance exactly how many copies have been discovered and in whose possession they remain. But in the case of a book of little interest the most that can be said is that it is "undescribed," and it may be "undescribed" not in the least because it is really rare, but because no bibliographer has troubled himself to make a note of it. Were some real point of interest discovered in it the chances are that the attention thus attracted would speedily bring to light other copies, as in the case of the school magazine to which Mr. Kipling was found to have contributed. Of this the first set catalogued sold for over £100, with the result that so many others were unearthed that the price speedily sank to less than as many shillings.

Granted, however, that it could be proved that a dull book is not merely undescribed, but absolutely, what so few works are, unique, in what way does this make it of interest to the collector? A great library might buy it for a trifle out of compassion, or under the idea that its registration in a catalogue might help to piece out a genealogy, or that it might count as another unit in statistics (a poor reason), or justify its purchase in some other haphazard way. But considerations of this kind, such as they are, cannot affect private collectors. A really dull book is merely a nuisance, and whether only one copy of it, or many, can be proved to exist, nobody wants it. If this be so we are justified in saying that, although as soon as a book is found desirable for any other reason its rarity becomes of paramount importance in determining its price, Rarity by itself is of no interest to collectors.

The attractiveness bestowed by Age cannot be treated quite so summarily, because although the same line of argument can be followed, it has to be helped out by an explanation arising from a particular case. No collector would value a dull sermon printed in 1800 any higher than a dull sermon printed in 1900, and if we go back two centuries instead of one, in the case of a book printed in London its value is none the greater for the extra hundred years. If, however, the sermon chanced to have been printed in 1700 in some provincial town, its age would distinctly be an element of value. Down to 1693 printing was only permitted in London, Oxford, Cambridge, and (after the outbreak of the Civil War[1]) at York. When the restraining Act was dropped in 1693 printing made its way, not very rapidly, into one provincial town after another. Hence a dull sermon with a provincial imprint may be dear to the heart of some local antiquary as the first-fruit of the press in his neighbourhood.

If we go back another sixty years from 1700 we reach another typographic zone, as we may call it, within which some slight interest attaches to all examples of English printing, for the end of the year 1640 is the limit of the special catalogues of early books published by the British Museum, the Cambridge University Library, and the John Rylands Library, Manchester. The first and last of these have indexes of printers; in the second the primary arrangement is typographical. Thus all books which are old enough to have been printed before the end of 1640 are thereby invested with some slight interest solely as products of English presses. When we get back to before 1600 we are in the period covered by the different editions of the *Typographical Antiquities* of Joseph Ames. When we go back another hundred years we are within the fifteenth century; printing has been introduced into England for less than twenty-five years, and the smallest fragment of a book from one of the early presses at work at Westminster, Oxford, St. Albans, or the City of London, is esteemed as of interest and importance.

[1] During the Civil War itself presses were also set up temporarily at Newcastle-on-Tyne, at Shrewsbury, and perhaps elsewhere.

Thus if we go far enough back Age does add to the interest of a book, but only by bringing it under another influence, that the interest of an English fifteenth century book is due to its importance in the history of printing and not to its antiquity being easily demonstrated by the fact that a contemporary unadorned manuscript of the same work will probably have only a fraction of the value of the printed edition. There are, of course, other cases in which age may be said to have some secondary influence, as in the case of books dealing with social customs, ballads and the like. But here it is still more evident that the social or literary interest is the primary consideration, and that this cannot be created, though it is greatly enhanced, by Age.

Having thus to the best of our ability abated the pride both of Age and Rarity, we come back to our original question as to what are the qualities and associations which give books value in the eyes of a collector.

The only good qualities which a book can possess in its own right are those of strength and beauty of form. Everything else about it is inherent in no single edition, though association of ideas may give greater dignity to one edition than to another. Type, paper, ink, presswork, the arrangement of the page, and also (though not quite in the same way or to the same extent) the illustrations, are all part and parcel of the book itself, and may be combined, at least so bookmen believe, in a really beautiful unity. No doubt as to this students run some risk of losing their sense of proportion. I myself am conscious, for instance, that I have looked at so many fifteenth century woodcuts, as compared with other works of art, that I distinctly overrate them. Mr. Robert Proctor, who knew more about fifteenth century books than any other man has ever known, or is ever likely to know, once said to me in all seriousness, that he did not think he had ever seen an ugly one. Allowing, however, for this very human tendency to set up our own esoteric standard, there yet remains a more generally recognizable beauty of form which some books possess in a higher degree than others, and to collect such beautiful books independently of any other kind of attraction would be no unworthy pursuit. As a matter of fact, bookmen are more inclined to make beauty of form a secondary consideration to which, as to age and rarity, they pay attention, but without adopting it as the basis of their collection.

As a secondary consideration the attention collectors pay to beauty can hardly be exaggerated in respect to the condition of copies, the ratio of an unusually good to an unusually bad copy of the same book, even if the bad copy have no leaves actually wanting, being often as ten to one. The unusually bad copy, indeed, would often have no selling value at all were it not that it may be useful to students and so win a purchaser at a small price. The collector should leave it severely alone, partly because such "working copies" are the rightful perquisite of poor scholars, partly because, as he presumably buys books for his pleasure, he defeats his own object if, except in the case of the very rarest, he buys copies at which he cannot look without regretting that their head-lines are cut off or the paper rotten through bad cleaning. Mr. Frederick Locker recorded in his catalogue that his copy of Blake's *Songs of Innocence and of Experience* had been cut down by a previous owner to the dimensions of the old covers of a washing-book. I think it was his chivalry, his piety toward Blake's memory, that induced him to rescue it from this dishonour. Had he bought such a poor copy simply because it was cheap, he would have fallen far below his standard as a collector.

Putting on one side beauty of form, the interest of books in the eyes of a collector lies in their associations, historical, personal, or purely literary. For reasons touched on already but which we may now consider more fully, among historical associations those connected with the history of printing fill a very large place. As we have said before, the invention of an art by which books were so greatly cheapened and multiplied was an event of almost unique importance in the social history of Europe, and everything which throws light on the first discovery, on the manner in which it was carried from one country and city to another, and on the methods and lives of the early printers, is of interest, and in its degree and measure, of importance. Moreover, just as foxes are hunted because they show such good sport, so these early books are collected because the study of them combines in a singular degree the charms of scientific and historical discovery, with all sorts of literary, social, and human side-interests. The claim which Henry Bradshaw put forward that antiquarian bibliography must be studied scientifically has been perverted by the unwise into the assertion that bibliography is a Science, or as they are sometimes pleased to put it, an Exact Science, till sensible people are wearied of the silly phrase. But the claim itself is absolutely true, and the gifts which enabled Mr. Proctor to classify, exactly or approximately, any fragment of early printing according to its country, place, printer, and date, if employed on any other field of scientific inquiry would easily have gained him a Fellowship of the Royal Society, besides the European recognition which, in his own small field, was already his before he died.

A large proportion of early printed books are without any indication whatever of their place of origin, printer, or date. The dates are obscured by the quickness or slowness of individual printers in adopting various improvements—sheet-numbering, leaf-numbering, printed capitals, titlepages, methods of imposition, etc.—which thus become uncertain and delusive landmarks. The place of origin is obscured by the existence of almost identical types in different cities and even in different countries. A fortiori the identity of the individual printer may baffle research from types being transferred or copied in all but one or two letters of the fount, which thus become the sole means of differentiating them. As helps the bibliographer has, in the first place, such a classification of the two or three thousand fifteenth century types as he is able to carry in his head. This, in proportion to its completeness, enables him to narrow down the field to be investigated. Some small typographical peculiarity, the way in which the illuminator or rubricator has filled the blank spaces, the note which by good fortune he may have appended in this or some other known copy saying when he finished his work, similar notes by early purchasers which occasionally give the date of their bargain, these and other points may all help forward the happy moment of final identification. Such a hunt as this may sound alarmingly difficult, as if it were all over five-barred gates and inconveniently hedged ditches. But facsimiles and other aids have been greatly multiplied of late years; many a book can be run down and the identification verified in a few minutes, and the possibility of hunting successfully in one's own library presupposes the purchase of many books giving full information as to their origin. These, while offering the means of identifying other books, will themselves raise no questions, so that the collector's life need not be unceasingly strenuous.

The side-interests of these old books are very varied. Many of them, at least to eyes trained to perceive it, are of great beauty. Others, although the half century during which printing was in its infancy produced few masterpieces of literature, have real literary interest. More than any other single event the invention of printing hurried on the transition from the medieval world to the modern, but while many printers in Italy nearly ruined themselves by the zeal with which they helped forward the classical renaissance, all over Europe the medieval books which were still read were seized on for the press, so that in the books printed between 1470 and 1490 we are presented with a conspectus or summary of medieval literature. Caxton printed the works of Chaucer and Gower and prose renderings of the old romances. The Italian presses were busy with Boccaccio, Petrarch, and Dante. The enormous size of the great Speculum or Encyclopædia of

Vincent de Beauvais did not deter the printers of France and Germany, and the ponderous tomes of medieval theology and law seem to have found a ready market. Above all, the highest skill available in the best equipped workshops was employed almost ceaselessly in the production of beautiful and often magnificent editions of the service-books of the Church for the use both of priests and laity, and it is hardly possible to dabble much in old books without acquiring an interest in liturgiology.

Owing to this fact, that the early presses were so largely occupied with printing the works of the previous three centuries, there is comparatively little human interest in incunabula on their literary side. Instead of authors we have mostly to deal with editors, an assertive and depreciatory race, always vaunting their own accuracy and zeal and insisting on the incredible blunders by which previous editions had been deformed past recognition. We receive, however, no small compensation in the personal details which many of the early printers give us about themselves. Titlepages, though they occur at haphazard in a few books of the early seventies (and there is one still earlier example), did not become common till about 1490, and even twenty years later we find many books still without them. The information which we now expect to find on a titlepage was given in a paragraph, mostly at the end of the book, to which bibliographers have agreed to give the name "colophon," from κολοφών, the Greek for a "finishing stroke." As we have already noted, in many books no information of this kind is given, but when printers, or their proof readers or editors, took the trouble to write a colophon at all, they had no reason to confine themselves to the severe brevity and simplicity of statement which marks the modern titlepage. It was in colophons that editors cast stones at their predecessors, or demanded sympathy for the severity of their own labours, and it is in colophons that we find the expressions of the printer's piety and pride, his complaints of his troubles with his workmen and rivals, his pleas for encouragement, and

14

occasionally, penned by another hand, the record of how he was struck down by death in the midst of his work. I have never heard of any one making a representative collection of books with interesting colophons, but collecting has taken many worse forms.

To lend grace to their colophons, or sometimes as a substitute for them, the early printers and publishers often used a woodcut containing their mark, sign, or device. Like the colophon itself, this was printed as a token of the master's pride in his work and his desire that it might be recognized as his, and many printers' marks are very decorative and even beautiful. Comparatively neglected until recently, within the last few years the devices used in various countries have been almost exhaustively reproduced in facsimile, thus leaving few chances of fresh discovery.

The mention of devices brings us to a very interesting section of early printed books, and one which has attracted only too much attention of recent years, those decorated with the primitive cuts on wood or metal with which fifteenth century printers endeavoured to imitate the glories of illuminated manuscripts, or to increase the popularity of their books with not too critical readers. Occasionally, as in the metal cuts in the best editions of the French Horae, in the Florentine and Venetian woodcuts of the last ten years of the century, and in the best work of other countries, these early pictures possess real beauty. Often they are badly spoilt by the incompetence of the cutters, who were working without the aid of modern gravers or modern methods of preparing the wood. The early German wood-cutters, whilst their outlines are often less graceful than those of their French and Italian competitors, had a special gift for characterization, and the quality of their work is much more uniform, perhaps because even before the invention of printing with movable types they were an organized craft. But in almost all fifteenth century cuts there is a certain naive simplicity which captivates those who allow themselves to study it, until they are apt, as the present writer has confessed is probably true of himself, to rate it too highly. As is the case with the more ambitious artists in oils of the same periods, wherever there was any demand for book-illustrators a local school with strongly marked characteristics at once appears. The work of the Augsburg cutters can be told at a glance from that executed at Strassburg, and the styles predominant at Venice and Florence, at Milan and Naples are all absolutely distinct. With one or two exceptions we know nothing, until after 1500, of the men who designed or cut these illustrations, and (except in the case of those of the Low Countries) hardly any attempt has been made, or seems possible, to subdivide the work done in any given locality so as to group it under individual masters. Otherwise the problems of fifteenth century book-illustrations are much like the problems of the types with which they harmonize so well, and the collector can either devote himself to representing as fully as possible the work done in any single district, or range at large over the Continent (as regards fifteenth century illustrations England may almost be left out of account) and collect a few good specimens of each school.

It has been made a cause of complaint recently against bibliographers that they know more of the work done at any insignificant fifteenth century press than of the history of printing at any subsequent time. It is not easy to coerce men into taking up any sections of a subject beyond those in which they are interested, and the supposed culprits have at least this much justification for their neglect of the later work that very little of it repays examination. Until 1465, save for some possible Dutch experiments, Germany enjoyed the monopoly of printing. From 1465 to about 1530 she shared the primacy in it with Italy, though during most of this period Italy was slightly ahead ; from 1530 to about 1570 France was far in advance of the rest of Europe ; after 1570 there was a higher technical level in the Low Countries than elsewhere, and Plantin and the Elzevirs gained individual reputations. But there was very little good taste even in the Low Countries, and from a typographical standpoint the seventeenth century is a Sahara with hardly any oases. From this wilderness the eighteenth century, under the guidance of France and England, timidly felt its way back to a kind of trim neatness, but the positive experiments of Baskerville and the Didots, and in Italy of Bodoni, were not very exciting, and at present are quite out of fashion. In the nineteenth century the work of the Whittinghams in England deserves more attention from collectors than it has received, and throughout the whole period any one working on historical lines, with the desire to illustrate the vicissitudes of the art of printing and not merely its successes, has an ample field. But for positive excellence, after the period of "origins," the French books of the middle of the sixteenth century offer almost the only hunting ground in which the fastidious collector is likely to find an attractive quarry, and it is no use to try to tell any other tale.

Of the later book illustrations a somewhat better account may be given. Owing to the steady deterioration of paper and presswork, which was the real cause of the typographical decline, woodcuts by the end of the sixteenth century had gone quite out of fashion, the old simple style having been lost and no printer being able to do justice to the finer work on which designers insisted. But copper engravings throve in Germany and the Low Countries, and when the fashion of engraved frontispieces and titles took root in England in the last years of the century it was pursued with considerable success for a couple of generations, while in the eighteenth century the French *livres à vignettes* attained an extraordinary brilliancy and elegance, and Gravelot and other French engravers bestowed some of their skill on English books.

The use of wood, now worked with the graver and no longer with the knife, was revived in England by Bewick about 1784, and was pursued with varying success for over a century, great technical skill and, at least in the

17

" sixties," very fine design being marred by the poverty and often the tawdriness of its typographical setting. Despite these drawbacks, the collectors who are bestowing attention on all this wood-engraved work of the nineteenth century will probably reap their reward.

When wood engraving was killed a few years ago by the extraordinary perfection attained, at a much smaller cost, by the process block, its fate was shared by the line-engraved illustrations which had appeared fitfully throughout the century, and had lingered on in the beautiful work of C. H. Jeens, who died in 1879, and in the use of old plates. As the wood engraving was killed by the half-tone block, so the line engraving disappeared before the photogravure, and the colour processes now being rapidly perfected threaten to reduce all black and white illustrations to unimportance. In so far, however, as the new processes necessitate the use of heavily loaded papers as a condition of their being even tolerably well printed, the least antiquarian of collectors may be forgiven for neglecting the books illustrated by them. Some of them can only be preserved by every plate being backed with sound paper, and a hundred years hence of all this illustrated work, much of it really beautiful, which is now being produced in such quantities, very little will remain. The modern Groliers whom we tried to call forth at the beginning of this chapter will need to be experts both in paper and in leather if they are to leave behind them any permanent record of their good taste. But this is only a crowning proof of how urgently they are needed.

It would be pleasant to glance briefly at some of the more literary considerations which bring books within the collector's scope. But the scheme of this series restricts the subject of the present volume to books which are prized either for their typographical beauty, their place in the history of printing, or the charm of their illustrations. This is in itself so large a field that no more pages must be wasted on introducing it.

CHAPTER II

BLOCK-BOOKS

THE collector of the time of George III, whose heart was set on Typographical Antiquities, and who was ambitious enough to wish to begin at the beginning, must have hungered after a block-book. Even in the days of Bagford, at the very outset of the eighteenth century, interest had been aroused in the block-printed editions of the *Speculum Humanae Saluationis*, so that Bagford himself travelled from Amsterdam to Haarlem on purpose to see a copy of one of the Dutch editions, and set an English wood-cutter to work, with very poor success, to manufacture a bogus specimen of it, wherewith "to oblige the curious." This, with a similar imitation of a page in the *Biblia Pauperum*, was intended to illustrate the History of Printing which Bagford had the temerity to plan, although such of his smaller dissertations as have been preserved show conclusively that he was quite incapable of carrying it out.

The interest thus early shown in block-books sprang from an entirely reasonable, but probably incorrect, view of the part which they had played in the development of printing with movable type. It was known that woodcuts without letterpress were printed in Germany quite early in the fifteenth century, the cut of S. Christopher, formerly in the Spencer Collection, now in the John Rylands Library, bearing the date 1423.[1] On the other hand, printing with movable type was practised at Mainz in the fifties, and about 1461 Albrecht Pfister published at Bamberg several books with woodcut illus-

---

[1] The authenticity of a still earlier date, 1418, on a cut of the Blessed Virgin at Brussels is disputed.

trations and printed letterpress. In the logical order of development nothing could be more reasonable than the sequence:

    i. Woodcut pictures.
    ii. Woodcut pictures and woodcut text.
    iii. Woodcut pictures and text printed from movable type.

Facts, however, do not always arrange themselves with the neatness which commends itself to an a priori historian, and the most recent students of block-books are unable to discover sufficient justification for the early dates which their predecessors assigned to them. On the old theory, in order to put it in front of the invention of printing with movable types, the *Biblia Pauperum*, which appears to be the oldest of the block-books, was placed about 1430 or 1440, and the *Ars Moriendi* and the other chief specimens of block-printing were all supposed to have been produced before 1460, the main period of block-printing thus coinciding with the interval between the S. Christopher of 1423 and Pfister's activity at Bamberg about 1461. Positive evidence in favour of this chronology there was none. It rested solely on the idea, at which bibliographers had jumped, that the block-books were necessary "steps towards the invention of printing," as they have often been called, and on what seemed the improbability that any one, when the art of printing with movable type had once been invented, would have troubled himself laboriously to cut letterpress on wood.

So far from block-printing being unable to co-exist with printing from movable type, it was not till nearly a century after printing had been invented that block-books finally ceased to be produced. The example generally quoted as the latest[1] is the *Opera nova contemplativa per ogni fedel christiano laquale tratta de le figure del testamento vecchio: le quale figure sonno verificate nel tes-*

---

[1] The *Libro di M. Giovanbattista Palatino*, printed at Rome in 1548, is spoken of by Mr. Campbell Dodgson as a "belated specimen" of a block-book. But this was a writing-book, and hardly counts.

tamento nuovo. As its title implies, this, curiously enough, is an adaptation of the *Biblia Pauperum*, which was thus the last, as it may have been the first, of the block-books. It is undated, but has the name of its publisher, Giovanni Andrea Vavassore, who worked at Venice about 1530.

The *Opera nova contemplativa* was from one point of view a mere survival, but Vavassore is not likely to have produced it solely to cause twentieth century antiquaries surprise. He must have had a business reason for having recourse to block-printing, nor is that reason very hard to find. From the frequency with which the early printers changed and recast their types, and the short intervals at which popular books printed with types were set up afresh, it is clear (1) that the type-metal[1] employed was much softer and less durable than that now in use, and that only small impressions[2] could be taken from the same setting up ; (2) that only a small amount of type was cast at a time, and that type was quickly distributed and used again, never kept standing on the chance that another edition would be wanted. Now when we come to the illustrations in printed books, we find the same woodblocks used for five or six successive editions, and then, in many cases, enjoying a second lease of life as job-blocks, used at haphazard by inferior printers. It is clear, therefore, that while it was a much more difficult and laborious business to cut the letter-press of a book on blocks of wood than to set it up with movable types, when the blocks were once made much more work could be got out of them. In a word, in the case of a small book for which there was a steady demand, a printer might be tempted to have it cut as a

---

[1] Numerous references in colophons show that the metal mostly used was brass, e.g. "*Primus in Adriaca formis impressit aenis Vrbe libros Spira genitus de stirpe Johannes,*" and the use of Chalcographi as a name for printers. But there are one or two references to printing "*stanneis typis,*" with types of tin.

[2] Of the first book printed at Venice only 100 copies were struck off, but the number was trebled in the case of its immediate successors. At Rome Sweynheym and Pannartz mostly printed 275 copies, only in a few instances as many as 300. But at the end of the century Pynson was printing at least 600 copies of large books and as many as 1000 of small ones.

block-book for the same reasons as might cause a modern publisher to have it stereotyped. The labour of cutting the letterpress on wood was much greater than that now involved in stereotyping, and the result clumsier. Hence it was only to short books intended for unexacting purchasers that the process was applied and with two or three exceptions it was used only for illustrated books with a small amount of text. But within this restricted field it had its own commercial possibilities, and there is thus nothing surprising in its coexistence with printing from movable type.

When the theory that block-books were "Steps towards the Invention of Printing" is thus opposed by the rival theory that they were forerunners of stereotyped plates, we are left free to consider, uncoerced by supposed necessities, such evidence as exists as to the dates of the specimens of block-printing still extant. Putting aside the late Italian block-book as a mere survival, we find two[1] broadly distinguished groups, one earlier, the dates of members of which can only be conjectured, the other later, several of which can only be definitely connected with the years 1470 to 1473. The characteristics of the earlier group are that they are printed (1) with a watery brown ink; (2) always on one side of the paper only; (3) without mechanical pressure;[2] (4) two consecutive pages at a time, so that they cannot be arranged in quires, but must be folded and stitched separately, and the book thus formed[3] begins and ends with a blank

---

[1] A very small third group, earlier than either of these, consists of woodcuts with manuscript text. The most important of these is a German *Biblia Pauperum* quite distinct from those started in the Netherlands.

[2] Some early woodcuts were printed by pressing the block down on the paper by hand; for the early block-books, however, the usual method seems to have been to press the paper on to the face of the block by rubbing it on the back with a burnisher. The paper was thus quite as strongly indented as if passed through a press, but the impression is usually less even. The friction on the back of the paper often gives it a polished appearance. As long as this method continued in use it was, of course, impossible to print on both sides of the paper.

[3] It is possible that the earliest specimens of block-printing were intended not to be bound in books but to be pasted on walls. In the case of the *Biblia*

page and has a pair of blank pages between each pair of printed ones. This arrangement in some extant copies has been altered by modern binders, who have divided the sheets, mounted each leaf on a guard, and then gathered them, at their own will, into quires. The inconvenient intervention of the blank pages has also sometimes been wrestled with (at an early date) by gluing the leaves together, so that all the leaves, except the first and last, are double, and the printed pages follow each other without interruption. These expedients, however, are easily detected, and the original principle of arrangement is free from doubt.

In the later block-books, on the other hand, we note one or more of the following characteristics: (1) the use of the thick black ink (really a kind of paint) employed in ordinary printing; (2) printing on both sides of the paper; (3) marks of pressure, showing that the paper has been passed through a printing-press; (4) the arrangement of the blocks in such a way as to permit the sheets to be gathered into quires.

In the case of the more popular block-books which went through many issues and editions[1] we can trace the gradual substitution of later characteristics for earlier ones. At what intervals of time these changes were made we have bibliographically no adequate grounds even for guessing. Analogies from books printed with movable types may be quoted on both sides. On the one hand, we find the blocks for book-illustrations enjoying an amazingly long life. Thus blocks cut at Venice and Florence between 1490 and 1500 continued in use for fifteen or twenty years, were then laid aside, and reappear between 1550 and 1560, certainly the worse for wear, but yet capable by a lucky chance of yielding

Pauperum, for instance, the space between the two woodcuts placed on each sheet is so small in some issues that the sheets cannot be bound without concealing part of the pictures.

[1] Different issues are distinguished by the signs of wear in the blocks, or occasionally by their being differently arranged, or with changes made in the blocks. In a different edition we have to deal with a new set of blocks.

quite a fair impression. The fact that one issue of a block-book can be positively assigned to 1470 or 1473, thus does not of itself forbid an earlier issue being placed as far back in the fifteenth century as any one may please to propose. On the other hand, when a printed book was a popular success editions succeeded each other with great rapidity, and one centre of printing vied with another in producing copies of it. The chief reason for the current disinclination to assume a date earlier than 1450 or 1460 for any extant block-book is the total absence of any evidence demanding it. If such evidence were forthcoming, there would be no inherent impossibility to set against it. But in the absence of such evidence twenty years seems an ample time to allow for the vogue of the block-books, and (despite the neatness of the a priori theory of development mentioned at the beginning of this chapter) this fits in better with the history both of printing and of book-illustration than any longer period.

The first attempt to describe the extant block-books was made by Carl Heinrich von Heinecken in 1771, in his *Idée générale d'une collection d'estampes*. This held the field until the publication in 1858 of Samuel Legh Sotheby's *Principia Typographica : the block-books issued in Holland, Flanders and Germany, during the fifteenth century*, a painstaking and well-illustrated work in three folio volumes. The most recent and probably the final treatment of the subject is that by Dr. W. L. Schreiber, in Vol. IV of his *Manuel de l'Amateur de la Gravure sur bois et sur métal au xve siècle*, published in 1902 (facsimiles in Vols. VII and VIII, 1895-1900). Dr. Schreiber enumerates no fewer than thirty-three works as existing in the form of block-books, the number of extant issues and editions of them amounting to over one hundred. Here it must suffice to offer brief notes on some of the more important.

BLOCK-BOOKS

BIBLIA PAUPERUM

A series of forty composite pictures, the central compartment in each representing a scene from the life of Christ, while on each side of it is an Old Testament type, and above and below are in each case two half-figures of prophets. The explanatory letterpress is given in the two upper corners and also on scrolls. Schreiber distinguishes ten issues and editions, in addition to an earlier German one of a less elaborate design and with manuscript text, which belongs to a different tradition. The earlier of these ten editions appear to have been made in the Netherlands. An edition with German text was published with the colophon, "Friederich walther Mauler zu Nördlingen vnd Hans Hurning habent dis buch mitt einender gemacht," and a second issue of this (without the colophon) is dated 1470. In the following year another edition, with copied cuts, was printed with the device of Hans Spoerer.

ARS MORIENDI

Twenty-four leaves, two containing a preface, and the remaining twenty-two eleven pictures and eleven pages of explanatory letterpress facing them, showing the temptations to which the dying are exposed, and the good inspirations by which they may be resisted, and, lastly, the final agony. The early editions are ascribed to the Netherlands or district of the Rhine; the later to Germany. There are also editions with German text, one of them signed "hanns Sporer," and dated 1473. A set of engravings on copper by the Master E. S. (copied by the Master of S. Erasmus) may be either imitations or the originals of the earliest of these *Ars Moriendi* designs. (See Lionel Cust's *The Master E. S. and the Ars Moriendi.*) The designs were imitated in numerous printed editions in various countries. In addition to a copy of the edition usually regarded as the earliest extant, the British Museum possesses one with the same characteristics, but of a much smaller size (the blocks measuring 137 by 100 mm. instead of 226 by 162), and from this, as much less known, a page is here given as an illustration.

CANTICA CANTICORUM

Sixteen leaves, each containing two woodcuts, illustrating the Song of Songs as a parable of the Blessed Virgin. Produced in the Netherlands.

APOCALYPSIS SANCTI JOHANNIS

Fifty leaves, or in some editions forty-eight, showing scenes from the life of S. John and illustrations of the Apocalypse, mostly with two pictures on each leaf. The early editions are assigned to the Netherlands, the later to Germany. A copy of the edition regarded as the fourth, lately sold by Herr Ludwig Rosenthal, bears a manuscript note, most probably as to the writer, just possibly as to the book, entering the household of the Landgrave Heinrich of Hesse in 1463.

SPECULUM HUMANAE SALUATIONIS

Scenes from Bible history, arranged in pairs, within architectural borders, with explanatory text beneath. No complete xylographic, or block-printed, edition is known, but twenty leaves printed from blocks are found in conjunction with forty-four leaves printed from type, and have not unreasonably been held to prove the previous production of a complete block-printed edition now lost. In like manner, the fact that two different types are used in different parts of a Dutch printed edition has encouraged Dr. Hessels to believe that this "mixed edition" should be regarded as proving the production of two complete editions, one in each type. On this theory we have (1) a hypothetical Latin block-printed edition ;

III. ARS MORIENDI, BLOCKBOOK, c. 1465

INSPIRATIO CONTRA VANAM GLORIAM

(2-4) three Dutch editions, each printed in a different type; (5) a Latin edition, entirely printed from type ; (6) a Latin edition, printed partly from type, partly from some of the blocks of No. 1. The copy of this "mixed Latin edition," as it is called, in the University Library at Munich, is dated in manuscript 1471, and the hypothetical complete block-printed edition may be as much earlier than this as any one pleases to imagine. But other bibliographers recognize only four editions and arrange them differently.

ANTICHRISTUS

Thirty-eight leaves, with two pictures on each leaf, illustrating the Legends relating to the Coming of Antichrist, and the Fifteen Signs which were to precede the Last Judgment. The text is in German, and the block-book was executed in Germany, probably about 1470.

FRANCISCUS DE RETZA. DEFENSORIUM INVIOLATAE CASTITATIS VIRGINIS MARIAE

Sixteen leaves, mostly with four pictures and four pieces of explanatory letterpress on each leaf, concerning marvels in the natural world which were supposed to be equally wonderful with that of the Virgin Birth, and therefore to render faith in this easier. Unfortunately the marvels are so very marvellous that they do not inspire belief, e.g. one story relates how the sun one day drew up the moisture from the earth with such rapidity that an ox was drawn up with it and subsequently deposited out of a cloud in another field. One edition was issued by a certain F. W. in 1470, another at Ratisbon by Johann Eysenhut the following year.

JOHANN MÜLLER (JOHANNES REGIOMONTANUS). KALENDER

Thirty-two leaves, containing lunar tables, tables of the eclipses for fifty-six years (1475-1530), other astronomical information, and a figure of the human body with notes of the signs of the zodiac by which it was influenced. Composed by the famous astronomer, Johann Müller, and sold by Hans Briefftruck, probably Hans Spoerer, about 1474–5, at Nuremberg and elsewhere.

JOHANN HARTLIEB. DIE KUNST CHIROMANTIA

Forty-four figures of hands, with a titlepage and page of text and a printed wrapper. Early issues are printed on one side of the paper only, later on both. The printer appears to have been Jorg Schaff, of Augsburg, and the date of issue about 1475. The date 1448 found in the book is that of composition, and it probably circulated in manuscript for many years before being printed.

MIRABILIA ROMAE

A German guide-book for visitors to Rome. Ninety-two leaves, printed with black ink on both sides of the leaf, with only a few illustrations. It was perhaps first published to meet the rush of German pilgrims to Rome at the Jubilee of Pope Sixtus IV, 1475. The blocks were probably cut in Germany, and the printing done at Rome. Some of the ornaments are said to have been used in type-printed editions by Stephan Plannck. This suggests that the book may have been published by his predecessor, Ulrich Han.

In addition to these block-books of Low Country and German origin, mention must also be made of a very curious Italian one, a *Passio domini nostri Jesu Christi*, fully described by the Prince d'Essling. The copy of this at Berlin contains eighteen leaves, and was probably executed at Venice about the middle of the fifteenth century. Some of the blocks were subsequently used (after a scroll at the foot had been cut off) for an edition of the *Devote Meditatione sopra la Passione del Nostro*

Signore (attributed to S. Bonaventura), published at Venice in 1487 by Jeronimo di Sancti e Cornelio suo Compagno, and a page from this is reproduced as a frontispiece to our chapter on Italian Illustrated Books.

Mention has already been made of the *Opera nova contemplativa*, an adaptation of the *Biblia Pauperum*, printed as a block-book at Venice about 1530.

The only extant French block-book, if it can be called one, is that of the "Nine Worthies" (*Les Neuf Preux*). This consists of three sheets, the first showing three heathen worthies—Hector, Alexander, and Julius Cæsar; the second, three from the Old Testament— Joshua, David, and Judas Maccabæus; the third, three from medieval romance—Arthur, Charlemagne, and Godfrey of Boulogne. Under each picture are six lines of verse. These three triple woodcuts, with the woodcut text, are assigned to about 1455.

No English block-book has yet been discovered, nor is it in the least likely that one ever existed, though there are a few single woodcuts.

Block-books possess two permanent attractions in addition to their supposed historical importance in the development of the invention of printing on which doubt is now cast—the attraction of popular literature and the attraction of the illustrated book. As we have seen, it would not have been worth any one's while to cause a block-book to be laboriously engraved, or cut, unless a large and speedy sale could be expected for it. The most famous block-books are nearly all of a religious character, and they prove a widespread desire for simple instruction as to the incidents of the life of Christ and the events in the Old Testament history which were regarded as prefigurements of them, as to the dignity of the Blessed Virgin and the doctrine of the Virgin Birth, as to the end of the world and the coming of Antichrist, and as to the spiritual dangers and temptations of the dying and the means by which they might be resisted.

As early specimens of book-illustration the value of the block-books varies very greatly. The majority of them are more curious than beautiful, but the pictures of the *Cantica Canticorum*, the *Speculum Humanae Saluationis*, and the *Ars Moriendi* have all very great merit. The tall, slender figures in the Song of Songs have a charm as great as any Dutch book-illustrations of the fifteenth century ; the cuts of the *Speculum* are full of vigour, while the serene dignity of the scenes in the *Ars Moriendi* illustrating the Inspirations of the Good Angel is as impressive as the grotesque force used in depicting the diabolic suggestions. If we must grant, as the weight of authority now bids us, that these woodcuts are copies from the copper engravings of the Master E. S., it can hardly be disputed that the woodcutter was the better artist of the two.

The block-books are a striking example of the difficulty of gleaning where the earlier collectors have reaped, a difficulty to which we shall often have to call attention. They vary greatly in positive rarity. Of the *Biblia Pauperum* and *Ars Moriendi*, which in their different issues and editions enjoyed the longest life and early attracted attention, Dr. Schreiber (if I have counted rightly) was able to enumerate in the one case as many as eighty-three copies—many of them, it is true, mere fragments—in the other sixty-one. Of the *Apocalypse* fifty-seven copies were known to him, of the *Speculum* twenty-nine, of the *Antichrist* thirteen, of the *Defensorium* twelve, and of the *Mirabilia Romae* six. But of these 261 copies and fragments no fewer than 223 are recorded as being locked up in public libraries and museums, the ownership of thirteen was doubtful, and only twenty-five are definitely registered as being in the hands of private collectors, viz. of the *Apocalypse*, eight copies or fragments ; of the *Biblia Pauperum*, six ; of the *Speculum* and *Ars Moriendi*, four each ; of the *Defensorium*, two ; and of the *Cantica Canticorum*, one. The chief owners known to Dr. Schreiber were the Earl of

Pembroke, Baron Edmond de Rothschild, and Major Holford, to whom must now be added Mr. Pierpont Morgan and Mr. Perrins. No doubt the copies in public institutions are much more easily enumerated than those in private hands, and probably most of the untraced copies are owned by collectors. But when allowance has been made for this, it remains obvious that this is no field where an easy harvest can be reaped, and that the average collector may think himself lucky if he obtains one or two single leaves. The last great opportunity of acquiring such treasures was at the sale in 1872 of the wonderful collection formed by T. O. Weigel,[1] at which the British Museum bought a very fine copy of the first edition of the *Ars Moriendi*, the first edition, dated 1470, of the *Biblia Pauperum*, in German, a block-book illustrating the virtues of the hymn *Salve Regina*, and the compassion of the Blessed Virgin, printed at Regensburg about 1470, besides fragments and woodcut single sheets. The foundation of the Museum collection of block-books had been laid by George III, added to by Mr. Grenville, and completed by a series of purchases from 1838 to this final haul of 1872, since when there have been few opportunities for new acquisitions. It is now quite adequate for purposes of study, though not so rich as that of the Bibliothèque Nationale at Paris.

[1] Since this was written the interesting collection formed by Dr. Schreiber himself has been dispersed.

CHAPTER III

THE INVENTION OF PRINTING—HOLLAND

UP to the year 1465 only one firm of printers evinced any appreciation of the uses of advertisement. In 1457 Johann Fust and Peter Schoeffer, of Mainz, set their names at the end of the liturgical Psalter which they were issuing from their press, and stated also the date of its completion, " In vigilia Assumpcionis," on the vigil of the feast of the Assumption, i.e. August 14th. Save in the case of a few unimportant books this preference for publicity remained the settled practice of the firm until Peter Schoeffer's death early in the sixteenth century, and later still when it was in the hands of his son Johann. With other printers at first the tendency was all the other way. Albrecht Pfister placed his name in one or two of the handful of popular illustrated books which he printed at Bamberg about 1461. No other book before 1465 contains its printer's name, and both at Strassburg and at Basel the practice of publishing anonymously continued in fashion throughout the 'seventies—in Strassburg, indeed, for the best part of another decade.

While printing continued mainly anonymous chroniclers took no note of it, but in the ten years which began in 1465 the progress of the art was rapid and triumphant. Printers, mostly Germans, invaded the chief cities of Europe, and boasted in their books of having been the first to practise it in this place or that. Curiosity as to the beginnings of the invention was thus aroused, and from 1470 onwards we meet with numerous attempts, not always accurate, to satisfy it. The earliest of these attempts is in a letter from Guillaume

Symois ar moit? mamona breuiae solem?
anois nsto breuis cu dembe sydois vt vis
P subesite breue facit o. canop? dabo teste
A sopu retrahas europa siue piropu
Vt placet e canoph? ysop? q iuge debes
O sup r breuias. sephora teste tibi sumas
Deriuatiua pala pduc patet ecce sonorus
Nois obliquos qd i or sit iuge. sed arbor
Et meor et rethor castor seu marmor z eq
Corripue suos. sed logis adde palor
Et queda propria sut obliqs breuiada
Nas facit os oris q dat or et vs breuiam?
O sup s loga. sicut testat alosa
T subesite dubis o longa sicut azotu
Que componitur discreta mete notent
O sup v raro. sed compositiua notato
Ante b corripis v. sz demit inde saluber
v e ptrahunt quies a l vm subit a vs
Cetera corripies. sed polluce tibi temas
Manduco iuges fiducia consociato
Ante d loga mes v. sz pecud retrahat
Sre g longa fit v. tu hic tibi coiuge depta
Sugo pducis sed sanguisuga breuiabis
O sup l breuia geculus adulor adempta
Que declinabit tibi tercia loga notabis
Nr oia sed sabulon breuiat hercule iucto
Dijs sotular socio specular breuiabit origo
Obliqs breuies vt psulis et nebulonis
Dabim? sup m. tibi loga. sicut alume
Cotumax incolumis demis z autumo iugis
P sup n loga tibi sit p teste lacuna
P supra p breuies. sed copositiua notali

IV. EARLY DUTCH PRESS

ALEXANDER GALLUS. DOCTRINALE (3ª)

Fichet, a Professor at the Sorbonne, who was mainly responsible for bringing the first printers to Paris, to his friend Robert Gaguin. This is contained in one copy of the second Paris book, the *Orthographia* of Gasparinus Barzizius, printed in 1470, Fichet having a fondness for giving individuality to special copies by additions of this kind. In this letter he speaks of the great light which he thinks learning will receive from the new kind of bookmen whom Germany, like another Trojan Horse, has poured forth.

Ferunt enim illic, haut procul a ciuitate Maguncia, Ioannem quendam fuisse cui cognomen bonemontano, qui primus omnium impressoriam artem excogitauerit, qua non calamo (ut prisci quidem illi) neque penna (ut nos fingimus) sed æreis litteris libri finguntur, et quidem expedite, polite et pulchre. Dignus sane hic uir fuit quem omnes musæ, omnes artes, omnesque eorum linguæ qui libris delectantur, diuinis laudibus ornent, eoque magis dis deabusque anteponant, quo propius ac presentius litteris ipsis ac studiosis hominibus suffragium tulit. Si quidem deificantur Liber et alma Ceres, ille quippe dona Liei inuenit poculaque inuentis acheloia miscuit uuis, hæc chaoniam pingui glandem mutauit arista. Atque (ut poeta utamur altero) prima Ceres unco glebam dimouit aratro, prima dedit fruges alimenta mitia terris. At bonemontanus ille, longe gratiora diuinioraque inuenit, quippe qui litteras eiusmodi exculpsit, quibus quidquid dici, aut cogitari potest, propediem scribi ac transcribi & posteritatis mandari memoriæ possit.

The good Fichet is absurdly rhetorical, but here in 1470 is a quite clear statement that, according to report, there (i.e. in Germany), not far from [1] the city of Mainz, a certain John, surnamed Gutenberg, first of all men thought out the printing art, by which books are fashioned not with a reed or pen, but with letters of brass, and thus deserved better of mankind than either

---

[1] Dr. Hessels supposes that this phrase indicates the Monastery of Saint Victor, outside Mainz, with which Gutenberg was connected, and that the "report," therefore, can be traced to Gutenberg himself. If so, we have the very important fact that Gutenberg himself claimed to be the inventor.

Bacchus or Ceres, since by his invention whatever can be said or thought can forthwith be written and transcribed and handed down to posterity.

Four years later in his continuation of the *Chronica Summorum Pontificum*, begun by Riccobaldus, Joannes Philippi de Lignamine, the physician of Pope Sixtus IV, who had set up a press of his own at Rome, wrote as one of the events of the pontificate of Pius II (1458–64), how "Jakob Gutenberg, a native of Strassburg, and a certain other whose name was Fust, being skilled in printing letters on parchment with metal forms, are known each of them to be turning out three hundred sheets a day at Mainz, a city of Germany, and Johann Mentelin also, at Strassburg, a city of the same province, being skilled in the same craft, is known to be printing daily the same number of sheets."[1] A little later De Lignamine records the arrival at Rome of Sweynheym and Pannartz, and also of Ulrich Han, and credits them also with printing three hundred sheets a day. Other references follow in later books without adding to our knowledge, save by proving the widespread recognition in the fifteenth century that printing was invented at Mainz; but there is nothing specially to detain us until the publication by Johann Koelhoff in 1499 of the Cologne Chronicle—*Die Cronica van der hilliger Stat Coellen*—in which occurs a famous passage about printing, which may be translated or paraphrased as follows :—

"This right worthy art was invented first of all in Germany, at Mainz, on the Rhine. And that is a great honour to the German nation that such ingenious men

[1] Iacobus cognomento Gutenbergo: patria Argentinus, & quidam alter cui nomen Fustus, imprimendarum litterarum in membranis cum metallicis formis periti, trecentas cartas quisque eorum per diem facere innotescunt apud Maguntiam Germaniẹ ciuitatem. Iohannes quoque Mentelinus nuncupatus apud Argentinam .eiusdem prouinciẹ ciuitatem : ac in eodem artificio peritus totidem cartas per diem imprimere agnoscitur. . . . Conradus Suueynem : ac Arnoldus pannarcz Vdalricus Gallus parte ex alia Teuthones librarii insignes Romam uenientes primi imprimendorum librorum artem in Italiam introduxere trecentas cartas per diem imprimentes.

34

are found there. This happened in the year of our Lord 1440, and from that time until 1450 the art and all that pertains to it was investigated, and in 1450, which was a Golden Year, men began to print, and the first book that was printed was the Bible in Latin, and this was printed with a letter as large as that now used in missals.

"Although this art was invented at Mainz, as far as regards the manner in which it is now commonly used, yet the first prefiguration (Vurbyldung) was invented in Holland from the Donatuses which were printed there before that time. And from and out of these the aforesaid art took its beginning, and was invented in a manner much more masterly and subtler than this, and the longer it lasted the more full of art it became.

"A certain Omnibonus wrote in the preface to a Quintilian, and also in other books, that a Walloon from France, called Nicolaus Jenson, was the first inventor of this masterly art—a notorious lie, for there are men still alive who bear witness that books were printed at Venice before the aforesaid Nicolaus Jenson came there, and began to cut and make ready his letter. But the first inventor of printing was a Burgher at Mainz, and was born at Strassburg, and called Yunker Johann Gutenberg.

"From Mainz the art came first of all to Cologne, after that to Strassburg, and after that to Venice. The beginning and progress of the art were told me by word of mouth by the Worshipful Master Ulrich Zell of Hanau, printer at Cologne in this present year 1499, through whom the art came to Cologne."[1]

[1] Item dese hoichwyrdige kunst vursz is vonden aller eyrst in Duytschlant tzo Mentz am Rijne. Ind dat is der duytschscher nacion eyn groisse eirlicheit dat sulche synrijche mynschen syn dae tzo vynden. Ind dat is geschiet by den iairen vns heren, anno domini. MCCCCxl. ind van der zijt an bis men schreue. l. wart vndersoicht die kunst ind wat dair zo gehoirt. Ind in den iairen vns heren do men schreyff. MCCCCl. do was eyn gulden iair, do began men tzo drucken ind was dat eyrste boich dat men druckde die Bybel zo latijn, ind wart gedruckt mit eynre grouer schrifft. as is die schrifft dae men nu Mysseboicher mit druckt.
Item wiewail die kunst is vonden tzo Mentz, als vursz vp die wijse, als dan

Zell, or his interviewer, ignores the books printed anonymously at Strassburg by Mentelin and Egge-stein, and also the handful printed by Albrecht Pfister at Bamberg; he also is misled by Gutenberg's long residence at Strassburg into calling him a native of that city; in other respects, so far as we are able to check this account, it is quite accurate. It tells us emphatically that "this right worthy art was in-vented first of all in Germany, at Mainz, on the Rhine"; and again, that "the first inventor of printing was a Burgher at Mainz named Junker Johann 'Gudenburch'"; but between these two unqualified statements is sand-wiched a reference to a prefiguration which took shape in Holland in *Donatuses*, printed there before the Mainz presses were at work, and much less masterly and subtle than the books which they produced. He connects no name with this "Vorbildung," and, unhappily, he gives no clue as to how it foreshadowed, and was yet distinct from, the real invention.

Sixty-nine years [1] after the appearance of this carefully balanced statement, the facts as to Dutch "prefigura-tions" which had inspired it moved a Dutch chronicler,

nu gemeynlich gebruicht wirt, so is doch die eyrste vurbyldung vonden in Hollant vyss den Donaten, die dae selffst vur der tzijt gedruckt syn. Ind van ind vyss den is genommen dat begynne der vursz kunst. ind is vill meysterlicher ind subtilicher vonden dan die selue manier was, vnd ye langer ye mere kunstlicher wurden.

Item eynre genant Omnebonum der schrijfft in eynre vurrede vp dat boich Quintilianus genoempt. vnd ouch in anderen meir boicher, dat eyn Wale vyss Vranckrijch, genant Nicolaus genson haue alre eyrst dese meysterliche kunst vonden, mer dat is offenbairlich gelogen. want Sij syn noch jm leuen die dat getzuigen dat men boicher druckte tzo Venedige ee der vursz Nicolaus genson dar quame, dair he began schrifft zo snijden vnd bereyden. Mer der eyrste vynder der druckerye is gewest eyn Burger tzo Mentz. ind was geboren van Straisz-burch. ind hiesch joncker Johan Gudenburch. Item van Mentz is die vursz kunst komen alre eyrst tzo Coellen. Dairnae tzo Straisburch, ind dairnae tzo Venedige. Dat begynne ind vortganck der vursz kunst hait myr muntlich vertzelt d' Eirsame man Meyster Vlrich tzell van Hanauwe. boich drucker zo Coellen noch zertzijt. anno. MCCCCxcix. durch den die kunst vursz is zo Coellen komen.

[1] The first trace of the legend is in a reference to Coster as having "brought the first print into the world in 1446" in a manuscript pedigree of the Coster family compiled about 1559.

Hadrianus Junius, in compiling his *Batavia* (not published till 1588), to write the well-known passage as to the invention of printing, which has been summarized as follows:—

There lived, about 1440, at Haarlem, in the market-place opposite the Town Hall, in a respectable house still in existence, a man named Lourens Janszoon Coster, i.e. Laurence, son of John Coster. The family name was derived from the hereditary office of Sacristan, or Coster of the Church—a post both honourable and lucrative. The town archives give evidence of this, his name appearing therein many times, and in the Town Hall are preserved his seal and signature to various documents. To this man belongs the honour of inventing Printing, an honour of which he was unjustly robbed, and which afterwards was ascribed to another. The said Laurence Coster, one day after dinner, took a walk in the wood near Haarlem. While there, to amuse himself, he began to cut letters out of some beech-bark. The idea struck him to ink some of these letters and use them as stamps. This he did to amuse his grandchildren, cutting them in reverse. He thus formed two or three sentences on paper. The idea germinated, and soon with the help of his son-in-law, and by using a thick ink, he began to print whole pages, and to add lines of print to the block-books, the text of which was the most difficult part to engrave. Junius had seen such a book, called *Spieghel onzer Behoudenisse*. It should have been said that Coster was descended from the noble house of Brederode, and that his son-in-law was also of noble descent. Coster's first efforts were of course very rude, and to hide the impression of the letters on the back, they pasted the leaves, which had one side not printed, together. His letters at first were made of lead, which he afterwards changed for tin. Upon his death these letters were melted down and made into wine-pots, which at the time that Junius wrote were still preserved in the house of Gerrit Thomaszoon, the grandson of Coster. Public curiosity was greatly excited by Coster's discovery, and he gained much profit from his new process. His trade, indeed, so increased that he was obliged to employ several workmen, one of whom was named John. Some say this was John Faust, afterwards a partner with Gutenberg, and others say he was Gutenberg's brother. This man when he had learnt the art in all its branches, took the opportunity one Christmas eve, when all good people are accustomed to attend Church, to break into the rooms used for printing,

37

and to pack up and steal all the tools and appliances which his master, with so much care and ingenuity, had made. He went off by Amsterdam and Cologne to Mainz, where he at once opened a workshop and reaped rich fruit from this theft, producing several printed books. The accuracy of this story was attested by a respectable bookbinder, of great age but clear memory, named Cornelis who had been a fellow-servant with the culprit in the house of Coster, and indeed had occupied the same bed for several months, and who could never talk of such baseness without shedding tears and cursing the thief.

Written nearly a hundred and thirty years after the supposed events which it narrates, this story is damned by its circumstantiality. It is thus that legends grow, and it is not difficult to imagine Haarlem bookmen picking up ideas out of colophons in old books and asking the "respectable bookbinder of great age" whether it was not thus and thus that things happened. Many of the details of the story are demonstrably false; its one strong point is the bookbinder, Cornelis, for a binder of this name is said to have been employed as early as 1474 and as late as 1514 to bind the account-books of Haarlem Cathedral, and in the two years named, and also in 1476, to have strengthened his bindings by pasting inside them fragments of *Donatuses* printed on vellum in the type of the *Speculum Humanae Saluationis*. The fragment in the account-book for 1474 is rubricated, and must thus either have been sold or prepared for selling, i.e. it is not "printer's waste," but may have been bought by Cornelis for lining his covers in the ordinary way of trade. But we have here a possible link between Zell's story of early Dutch *Donatuses* and the story of Junius about Coster and his servant Cornelis, since we find fragments of a *Donatus* in the possession of this particular man.

There were plenty of such *Donatuses* in existence in the Netherlands about 1470. In 1887 Dr. Hessels, in his *Haarlem the Birthplace of Printing, not Mentz*, enumerated fragments of twenty different editions, printed in eight types, of which the type used in the *Speculum Humanae Saluationis* (see p. 26) is one, while the other seven are linked to it, or to each other, in such a way that we may either suppose them to have all belonged to the same printer, or distribute them among two or more anonymous firms. Besides these twenty editions of *Donatus* on the Eight Parts of Speech, Dr. Hessels enumerated eight editions of the *Doctrinale* of Alexander Gallus[1] (another school book popular in the fifteenth century), three of the Distichs of Dionysius Cato (the work from which Dame Pertelote quoted to convince Chantecleer of the futility of dreams), and one or two editions each of a few other works, the *Facetiae Morales* of Laurentius Valla (twenty-four leaves), the *Singularia Juris* of Ludovicus Pontanus, with a treatise of Pope Pius II (sixty leaves), and the *De Salute Corporis* of Gulielmus de Saliceto with other small works (twenty-four leaves). These latter books offer no very noticeable features; some of the *Donatus* fragments, on the other hand, have printing only on one side of the leaf (whence they are called by the barbarous term "anopisthographic," "not printed on the back") and have a very rude and primitive appearance. This may have been caused in part at least by their having been pasted down, and possibly scraped, by binders, for almost all of them have been found in bindings; but it counts for something.

Not one of the books or fragments of which we have been speaking makes any mention of its printer, or of the place or date at which it was produced. A copy of one of the later books, the *De Salute Corporis* of Gulielmus de Saliceto, was purchased by Conrad du Moulin while abbot of the Convent of S. James at Lille, a dignity which he held from 1471 to 1474. The earliest Haarlem account-book which contained *Donatus* fragments was for the year 1474. It is entirely a matter of opinion as to how much earlier than this any of the extant fragments

---

[1] A page from a fragment of one of these in the British Museum forms the frontispiece to this chapter (Plate IV).

can be dated. There is no reason why some of them should not be later.

As to the place or places at which these books were printed, there is no evidence of any weight. But, as has been already said, the whole series can be closely or loosely connected with the types used in editions of the *Speculum Humanae Saluationis*, and in 1481 Jan Veldener, a wandering printer, while working at Utrecht, introduced into an edition of the Epistles and Gospels in Dutch two woodcuts, each of which was a half of one of the double pictures in the *Speculum*. Two years later, when at Kuilenburg, he printed a quarto edition of the *Speculum* itself (Dutch version), in which he used a large number of the original *Speculum* blocks, all cut up into halves, so as to fit a small page. As Veldener (as far as we know) used the *Speculum* blocks first at Utrecht, it is supposed that it was at Utrecht that he obtained them. If the blocks were for sale at Utrecht, this may have been the place at which the earlier editions of the *Speculum* were issued, and thus, in the absence of any evidence which they were willing to recognize in favour of any other place, Henry Bradshaw and his disciples attributed the whole series of editions of the *Speculum, Donatus, Doctrinale*, etc., to Utrecht, about, or "not after," 1471-1474. Bradshaw himself clearly indicated that this attribution was purely provisional. He felt "compelled to leave" the books at Utrecht, so he phrased it, i.e. the presumption that Veldener found the blocks of the *Speculum* there constituted a grain of evidence in favour of Utrecht; and if a balance is sufficiently sensitive and both scales are empty, a grain thrown into one will suffice to weigh it down. It would have been better, in the present writer's opinion, if the grain had been disregarded, and no attempt made to assign these books and fragments to any particular place. As it is, Bradshaw's attribution of them to Utrecht has been repeated without any emphasis on its entirely provisional character, even without any mention of this at all, and perhaps with a certain humorous enjoyment of the chance of prejudicing the claims of Haarlem by an unusually rigorous application of the rules as to bibliographical evidence.

In the eyes of Dr. Hessels, on the other hand, the legend narrated by Junius offers a sufficient reason for assigning all these books to Haarlem, and to Lourens Janszoon Coster as their printer. Dr. Hessels was even ill-advised enough to point out that, as there are twenty editions of *Donatus* in this group of types, we have only to allow an interval of a year and a half between each to take back the earliest very close to 1440, the traditional date of the invention of printing. This is perfectly true, but as no reason can be assigned for fixing on this particular interval the value of such a calculation is very slight.

One result of all this controversy is that the whole series of books and fragments have been dubbed "Costeriana," and the convenience of having a general name for them is so great that it has been generally adopted, even by those who have no belief in the theory which it implies. All that is known of Lourens Janszoon Coster is that he resided at Haarlem from 1436 to 1483, and that contemporary references show him to have been a chandler and innkeeper, without making any mention of his having added printing to his other occupations.

It is difficult to claim more for the story told by Junius than that it represents an unknown quantity of fact with various legendary additions. It is difficult to dismiss it as less than a legend which must have had some element of fact as its basis. In so far as it goes beyond the statements of the Cologne Chronicle, it is supported only by the evidence that Coster and the venerable bookbinder Cornelis existed, and that the latter bound the account-books of Haarlem Cathedral. But no indiscretion of Hadrianus Junius writing in 1568 can affect the credit of the statements made in the Cologne Chronicle in 1499 on the authority of Ulrich Zell, and we have now to mention an important piece of evidence in favour of Zell's accuracy. This is the entry in the diaries of Jean de Robert, Abbot of Saint Aubert, Cambrai, of the purchase in 1446 and again in 1451 of a copy of the *Doctrinale* of Alexander Gallus, *jeté en moule*, a phrase which, while far from satisfactory as a description of a book printed from movable type, cannot possibly refer to editions printed from woodblocks, even if these existed. The *Doctrinale*, which was in verse, was a less popular school-book than the *Donatus*. It is significant that among the so-called " Costeriana" there are eight editions of the one against twenty of the other. Where the *Doctrinale* was used we may be sure that the *Donatus* would be used also, and in greater numbers, so that this mention of a " mould-casted" *Doctrinale* as purchased as early as 1446 is a real confirmation of Zell's assertion. We have no sufficient ground for believing that any of the fragments, either of the one book or the other, now in existence were produced as early as this. It is of the nature of school-books to be destroyed, and every improvement in the process of production would help to drive the earlier experiments out of existence. But taking Zell's statement and the entries in the Abbot's diaries together, it seems impossible to deny that there is evidence of some kind of printing being practised in Holland not long after 1440.

An ingenious theory as to the form which these " prefigurements" may have taken has lately been suggested, viz. that the earliest types may have consisted simply of flat pieces of metal, without any shanks to them, and that they were "set up" by being glued upon wood or stiff paper in the order required. They would thus be movable, but with a very low degree of movability, so that we can easily understand why short books like the *Donatus* and *Doctrinale* were continually reprinted without any attempt being made to produce a large work such as the Bible. It is curious, however, that in the descrip-

42

tion of a "ciripagus" by Paulus Paulirinus, of Prag,[1] "we have a reference" to a Bible having been printed at Bamberg "super lamellas," a phrase which might very well refer to types of this kind, though the sentence is usually explained as referring to either the Latin or German edition of the *Biblia Pauperum* issued by Albrecht Pfister. I think it just possible myself that the reference is really to the Latin Bible known as the Thirty-six Line Bible, which seems certainly to have been sold, if not printed, at Bamberg a little before 1460, and that Paulirinus, having seen books printed "super lamellas," supposed (wrongly) that this was printed in that way. But the statement that it was printed in four weeks is against this.

Whether the Dutch "Vorbildung" of the Art of Printing subsequently invented at Mainz took the form of experiments with shankless types, or fell short of the fully developed art in some other way, does not greatly concern the collector. It is in the highest degree improbable that the claim put forward on behalf of the so-called "Costeriana" will ever be decisively proved or disproved. They are likely to remain as perpetual pretenders, and as such will always retain a certain interest, and a specimen of them always be a desirable addition to any collection which aims at illustrating the history of the invention of printing. Such a specimen will not be easy to procure, because many of the extant fragments have been found in public libraries, more especially the Royal Library at the Hague, and have never left their first homes. On the other hand, the number of fragments known has been considerably increased by new finds. Thus there is no reason to regard a specimen as unattainable.

[1] Et tempore mei Pambergæ quidam scripsit integrum Bibliam super lamellas, et in quatuor septimanis totam Bibliam super pargameno subtili presignavit scriptura.

CHAPTER IV

THE INVENTION OF PRINTING—MAINZ

NO contrast could be much greater than that between the so-called "Costeriana" and the incunabula printed at Mainz. Annually as a small boy I used to be taken to the Crystal Palace, and there a recognized part of the programme in each visit was to spend half an hour in solemnly pedalling backwards and forwards on a semicircular track on a machine miscalled a velocipede. Perhaps these clumsy toys really constituted a definite stage in the invention and perfection of the modern bicycle. On the other hand, whatever may be the historical facts, there is no reason in the nature of things why the modern bicycle should not have been invented quite independently of them. The relative positions of Holland and Germany as regards the invention of printing are very analogous to those of the old velocipede and the bicycle. Even if it could be proved decisively that some Dutch fragment of a *Donatus* was earlier than any experiment made at Mainz or Strassburg, it was at Mainz that the possibility was first demonstrated of producing by print books as beautiful as any written by the scribes, and it was from Germany, not from Holland, that printers carried the art which they had proved to be practicable to all parts of Europe, including Holland itself.

In the development of the art of printing at Mainz three men had a share, though the precise part which each of them played is matter of conjecture rather than knowledge. The first of the three was Johann Gutenberg, the Johannes Bonemontanus whom Fichet, as early as 1470, acclaimed as the first of all men to think out the

44

Incipit racōnale diuinoȝ officioȝ. Pecūqȝ i ecclia sticis officijs.rebȝ ac ōȝmetis ȝsistut. diuinis plena sut signis.atqȝ miste rijs.ac sīngła cele sti sut dulcediē redundātia. Si tñ diligēte habe ant inspectoȝe.q nosit mel de petra

ugē.oleūqȝ de durissimo saxo.qs tñ nouit ozdmem celi ȝ raciones ipius ponet i terra. Scrutatoz quippe maiestatis opprimēt a glia. Si quiȝ puteus altus est.et m q aquā hauriā nō habeo.nisi porrigat ille qui dat omibȝ affluent et nō impropeat.ut mt me dium mōtiū tñseunte.hauriā aquā i gaudio de fon tibus saluatois. Licet igit nō omiū que a maioribȝ tradita sut racō reddi possit. qȝ tamē qd m hijs rōe caret extirpandū est. Id circo ego Guilhelmus scē minatecȝ ecclie sola dei patiēta dcūs Epus pulsans pulsabo ad ostiū.si forte dauis vō apire dignet .ut me introducat rex m cella vinariā.m q michi supnū demōstret exemplar.qd moysi fuit i mōte mōstratū. qtis de sīnglis q m eccliasticis officijs rebȝ ac ōȝme tis cōnstitut.quid sigñicēt ȝ figurēt .eo valea reuelāte clare ȝ apte differē ȝ rōes poñe. q linguas infantū facit disertas.cuius spūs vbi vult spirat.diuidēs sīn gulis put vult ad laudem ȝ gliam trinitatis. Sane hic saċmeta p signis accipim? seu figuris.que hq̄t figure nō sut ututes.sȝ ututu signa.qbus tanqȝ scri pturis vtētes docent . Signoȝ aūt ali sut natura lia.alia poitiua.de quo ȝ quid sit saċmentū dicet m q̄rta parte.sb vij particła canois.sup verbo .misteiū sidei Saċdotes igit et plati ecclie quibȝ datū e no sce misteria. put i luca habet .et saċmetoȝ poztato

printing art, whom the popular verdict has recognized as the inventor, and whom patriotic German biblio-graphers delight to invest with every virtue that distinguishes themselves.

Gutenberg's real name was Gänsfleisch, Gutenberg being an addition to his mother's surname[1] which he assumed for reasons not known to us. He was born about 1400, and just when he attained manhood his family, which belonged to the patrician party at Mainz, was banished and sought refuge at Strassburg. At Strassburg Gutenberg remained till about 1446, and legal and muni-cipal records, so far as we can trust to their authenticity, offer us some tantalizing glimpses of his career there. When the town clerk of Strassburg came to Mainz the exile caused him to be arrested for a debt due to his family, and the matter had to be arranged to avoid a quarrel between the two cities. On the other hand, Gutenberg was himself called to account for unpaid duties on wine, and was sued for a breach of promise of marriage. In 1437 he was the defendant in a much more interesting trial. He had admitted two partners to work an invention with him, and on one of these partners dying his brother claimed, unsuccessfully, to take his place in the partnership. The use of the words "presse," "forme," and "trucken" in connection with this invention leaves it hardly open to doubt that it was concerned with some kind of printing, and loans which Gutenberg negotiated in 1441 and 1442 were presumably raised for the develop-ment of this. About the middle of the decade he returned to Mainz and there also borrowed money, pre-sumably again for the same object.

At this point we are confronted with five fragmentary pieces of printing, all but one of them only recently discovered. The latest of these, according to German bibliographers, is a fragment of an astronomical Calendar in German verse for an unspecified year, which might be

[1] Her maiden name was Elsa Wyrich, but she lived at the Hof zum Gutenberg at Mainz, and the name Gutenberg thus came into the family.

1429, 1448, or 1467, but does not exactly fit any of them ; the earliest is part of a leaf of a *Sibyllenbuch* (originally known as *Das Weltgericht*, because the text of this fragment deals with the Last Judgment). Between these two are placed fragments of three editions of *Donatus*, *De octo partibus orationis*, two found recently in copies of an edition of Herolt's *Sermones de tempore et sanctis* printed at Strassburg [1] by Martin Flach in 1488 and now at Berlin, the third one of the minor treasures of the Bibliothèque Nationale at Paris, where it has lain for over a century. Granting that the Calendar was printed for use in 1448 (it has been argued, on the other hand, that its mention of movable festivals was intended to be only approximate), and that the other four pieces can be proved by typographical evidence to have preceded it, we may suppose the *Sibyllenbuch* to have been printed by Gutenberg shortly after his return to Mainz, i.e. about 1445, or shortly before this at Strassburg.

Soon after the supposed date of the Calendar the second of the three protagonists in the development of printing at Mainz comes on the scene. This was Johann Fust, a goldsmith, who in or about August, 1450, lent Gutenberg eight hundred guilders to enable him to print books, himself, nominally or truly, borrowing the money from another capitalist, and thereby gaining the right to charge interest on it without breaking the canon law. By about December, 1452, the loan was exhausted, and Fust made a fresh advance of the same amount. The inner history of the next four years is hid from us, and the undisputed facts which belong to them have consequently been interpreted in every variety of way that human ingenuity can devise. These facts are that—

(i) Printing was continued with the fount of type used for the Calendar attributed to 1448, fragments of more than a dozen different editions of *Donatus* printed with it

---

[1] It will be noted that this connection with Strassburg offers just a grain of evidence in favour of the *Donatuses* having been printed there rather than at Mainz.

being still extant, also a prognostication, *Manung widder die Durken*, printed in December, 1454, a Bull of Pope Calixtus "widder die Turcken" of 1456, a medical Calendar for 1456, and an undated *Cisianus*, another work of an astronomical character.

(ii) When the pardoners employed by the proctor-general of the King of Cyprus came to Mainz in the autumn of 1454 to raise money by means of a papal Indulgence, valid till 30 April of the following year, they were able to substitute two typographically distinct editions for the manuscript copies which they had previously used, the text of each of these Indulgences being printed in a separate fount of beautifully clear small type, while a larger type was used for a few words. In one of these Indulgences the larger type belongs, with some differences, to the same fount as the books named in our last paragraph. This Indulgence has thirty-one lines, and four issues of it have been distinguished, three of them dated 1454 (the earliest of these being the earliest dated piece of printing) and the fourth 1455. In the other Indulgence there are only thirty lines, the large type is neater, and three issues have been distinguished, one dated 1454, the other two 1455.

(iii) In November, 1455, an action brought by Fust to recover the 1600 guilders which he had lent Gutenberg, with the arrears of interest, reached its final stage. In this suit the third of the Mainz protagonists, Peter Schoeffer, was a witness on the side of Fust, and we hear also, as servants of Gutenberg, of Heinrich Keffer and Bertolf von Hanau, who may apparently be identified with printers who worked subsequently at Nuremberg and Basel. The document which has come down to us and is now preserved at the University Library at Göttingen is that recording the oath taken by Fust, as the successful plaintiff, in order to obtain judgment for the amount of his claim.

(iv) In August, 1456, Heinrich Cremer, vicar of the collegiate church at Mainz, recorded his completion of

47

the rubrication and binding of a magnificent printed Bible in two volumes, now preserved in the Bibliothèque Nationale at Paris, the type of which used to be thought identical with the larger type of the thirty-line Indulgence mentioned above, but is now considered to be only closely similar.

For this last undoubted date of rubrication, August, 1456, German bibliographers have lately substituted a reference to a manuscript date, 1453, in another copy of this printed Bible, now preserved in the Buchgewerbe-Museum at Leipzig, formerly owned by a well-known German collector of the last century, Herr Klemm. While, however, this date appears to have been written at a period approximating to that of the production of the book, its relevance as evidence of the date of printing is highly disputable, more especially as there appear to be signs of erasure near it. Its owner, Herr Klemm, pre-served a discreet silence as to its existence, and it is certainly not obligatory at present to accept it as valid evidence.

In a work which does not pretend to the dignity of a history of printing it is impossible to discuss, or even to enumerate, the different theories as to the events of the years 1453-6, which have been formulated to account for these facts. The edition of the Bible of which Heinrich Cremer rubricated the copy now at Paris is so fine a book and so great a landmark in typographical history, that the desire to regard it as the production of the man who is credited with the invention of printing, Johann Gutenberg, easily becomes irresistible. To refuse to call it the Gutenberg Bible may, indeed, appear almost pedantic, though its old name, the " Mazarine Bible," which it gained from the accident of the copy in the Mazarine Library at Paris being the first to attract attention, still survives, and it is also known among bibliographers as the " Forty-two Line Bible," a safe uncon-troversial title based on the number of lines in most of its columns. Whoever printed it appears to have been possessed of ample means and to have been a master of detail and an excellent organizer. Under the minute examination to which it has been subjected the book has yielded up some of its secrets, and we know that it was printed simultaneously on six different presses, that the body of the type was twice reduced, forty-two lines finally occupying slightly less space than the forty which had at first formed a column, that after the printing had begun it was resolved to increase the size of the edition, and that there is some reason to think that eventually a hundred and fifty copies were printed on paper and thirty on vellum,[1] and that the paper was ordered in large quantities and not in small parcels as it could be paid for. To the present writer it appears that if Gutenberg had possessed the financial means, the patience and the organizing power needed to push through this heavy piece of work in the way described, it is difficult to perceive any reason why the capitalist Fust should have quarrelled with him, or to imagine how Gutenberg exposed himself to such an action as that which Fust successfully carried against him. On the supposition that the Bible was completed in or soon after 1453 the difficulty becomes almost insuperable, for it is inconceivable that if Gutenberg had produced the book within a few months of receiving his second loan from Fust he should not, by the autumn of 1455, have paid his creditor a single guilder, either for principal or interest. After his quarrel with Fust, Gutenberg apparently had dealings with two other men, with Albrecht Pfister who is found in possession of a later casting of the heavier fount of type in which the Astrological Calendar attributed to 1448 had been printed, and with a Dr. Homery. He ended his days as a pensioner at the court of the Archbishop of Mainz, while Fust, with the aid of Peter Schoeffer, whom he made his son-in-law, developed a great

---

[1] According to the excellent *Catalogue raisonné des premières impressions de Mayence* of Mr. Seymour de Ricci, eleven copies on vellum and thirty on paper can now be located, but some of these have only one of the two volumes. The vellum copy belonging to Mr. Robert Hoe sold in 1911 for $50,000.

business. The inventor who lacks organizing power and whose invention never thrives till it has passed into other hands is no unfamiliar figure, and such a conception of Gutenberg perhaps accords better with the known facts of his career than that of a living incarnation of heroism and business ability such as his German eulogists love to depict. According to a theory developed by the present writer in an article in *The Library* for January, 1907 (Second Series, Vol. VIII), though no originality is claimed for it, the key to the situation lies in the assertion[1] made on behalf of Peter Schoeffer that his skill in engraving had enabled him to attain results denied to the two Johns, Johann Gutenberg and Johann Fust.

According to this theory, it was Schoeffer who engraved the two founts of small type used in the two sets of Indulgences of 1454-5, and thus demonstrated that the new art could be applied to produce every kind of book and document which had previously circulated in manuscript. Fust gave him his daughter Christina in marriage, and Johann Schoeffer, the offspring of the alliance, distinctly tells us that this was in reward for his services. From the first, or almost the first, the firm adopted a policy of advertisement which other printers were slow to imitate, the partners giving their names in their earliest colophons and making no secret of the fact that they were using an "adinuentio artificiosa imprimendi ac caracterizandi" which enabled them to dispense with the pen. In 1460, in the *Catholicon* of that year, the work of an anonymous printer to which we shall have to recur (see p. 51 *sqq.*), the invention is distinctly claimed for Mainz, and from 1467 this claim was taken over by Peter Schoeffer, who in the colophons of his subsequent books again and again celebrated Mainz as the city singled out by divine favour to give the art to the world. The fact that for nearly forty years (1460–99) these statements remained unchallenged, and passed into the contemporary history

---

[1] In the verses by Magister Franciscus in the *Justinian* of 1468, subsequently twice reprinted.

of the time, is the strongest evidence in favour of the substantial invention of the art at Mainz that can be conceived. A single reference in 1499[1] to prefigurations of a humbler kind in *Donatuses* printed in Holland and the presentation of a rival theory in 1568 cannot deprive of its due weight the evidence that during all the years when the facts were easily ascertainable judgment in favour of Mainz was allowed to go by default. But the Fust and Schoeffer colophons tell us more than this, for while they make no mention of Gutenberg they never claim the invention of printing as their own achievement. It is clear that Fust could not claim this himself, and while he was alive his son-in-law did not think fit to put forward, or allow to be put forward, any claim on his own behalf. It was only in 1468, when both Gutenberg and Fust were dead, that Schoeffer's "corrector," or reader, Magister Franciscus, was permitted to assert on his behalf, in the *Justinian* of that year, that though two Johns had the better in the race he, like his namesake S. Peter, had entered first into the sepulchre, i.e. the inner mysteries of printing. The claim, thus irreverently put forward, is deprived of much of its weight by the moment at which it was made; nevertheless it can hardly have been baseless.

The desire to credit Gutenberg with some really handsome and important piece of printing has caused his name to be connected with two other large folios, a Latin Bible, of thirty-six lines to a column, printed in a variety of the type used for the *Sibyllenbuch* and the *Kalendar* of "1448," and a Latin Dictionary known by the name *Catholicon*, the work of a thirteenth century writer, Joannes Balbus, of Genoa. The type of the Thirty-six Line Bible passed into the hands of Albrecht Pfister, of Bamberg, who printed a number of popular German books with it in 1461 and 1462. There is considerable evidence, moreover, that a large number of copies of the Bible itself were sold at Bamberg about 1460. The

[1] In the Cologne Chronicle. See *supra*, p. 34.

greater part of the text appears to have been set up from a copy of the Forty-two Line Bible. Where, when, and by whom it was printed we can only guess, but the place was more probably Bamberg than Mainz, and as the type is believed to have been originally Gutenberg's, and there is evidence that Pfister, when he began printing the popular books of 1461–2, was quite inexperienced, Gutenberg has certainly a better claim to have printed this volume than any one else who can be suggested. The Thirty-six Line Bible is a much rarer book than the Forty-two Line, but copies are known to exist at the British Museum, John Rylands Library, Bibliothèque Nationale, and Musée Plantin, and at Greifswald, Jena, Leipzig, Stuttgart, Vienna, and Wolfenbüttel. A copy is also said to be in private hands in Great Britain, but has not been registered. None has been sold in recent times. Besides the more complete copies mentioned above, various fragments have been preserved and some of these are on vellum. The vellum fragment of leaf 204 now in the British Museum was at one time used as a book-cover.

The *Catholicon* is printed in a small type, not very cleanly cut. It was issued without printer's name, but with a long colophon, which has been translated:

By the help of the Most High, at Whose will the tongues of infants become eloquent, and who oft-times reveals to the lowly that which He hides from the wise, this noble book Catholicon, in the year of the Lord's Incarnation 1460, in the bounteous city of Mainz of the renowned German nation, which the clemency of God has deigned with so lofty a light of genius and free gift to prefer and render illustrious above all other nations of the earth, without help of reed, stilus, or pen, but by the wondrous agreement, proportion and harmony of punches and types has been printed and brought to an end.

Upon this follow four Latin verses in honour of the Holy Trinity and the Virgin Mary and the words "Deo Gracias." We can imagine an inventor who, despite his invention, remained profoundly unsuccessful, writing the opening words of this colophon, and it is not easy to see their appropriateness to any one else. It is thus highly probable that Gutenberg set up this book and refused to follow Fust and Schoeffer in their advertising ways. He may even have had a special reason for this, for among the forty-one copies registered (almost all in great libraries) two groups may be distinguished, one embracing the copies on vellum and the majority of the paper copies, the other the rest of the paper copies. The groups are distinguished by various differences, of which the most important is that in the one case the workmen used four and in the other two pins to keep the paper in its place while being printed. An attractive explanation of all this would be that while Gutenberg set up the book and was allowed to print for himself a certain number of copies, there was a richer partner in the enterprise whose pressmen pulled the greater part of the edition. But Dr. Zedler, who has brought together all the available information about the book in his monograph *Das Mainzer Catholicon*, has a different explanation.

In the same type as the *Catholicon* are two small tracts of little interest, the *Summa de articulis fidei* of Thomas Aquinas, and the *Dialogus* of Matthaeus de Cracovia; also an Indulgence of Pope Pius II. In 1467 the type is found in the hands of Heinrich Bechtermünze at Eltvil, who died while printing a vocabulary. This was completed by his brother Nicholas, who also printed three later editions of it.

During the years which precede 1457, Johann Fust and Peter Schoeffer, the one a goldsmith, the other a clerk in minor orders of the diocese of Mainz, are involved in the obscurity and uncertainty which surround Gutenberg's career. Reasons have been offered for believing that it was Schoeffer who designed the small neat types used in the Mainz Indulgences of 1454–5, and that he with his skill and Fust with his money pushed the Forty-two Line Bible to a successful completion. If they printed this, they no doubt printed also a liturgical psalter

53

in the same type, of which a fragment is preserved at the Bibliothèque Nationale at Paris. But we do not touch firm ground until we come to the famous Psalter of 1457, the colophon of which leaves us in no doubt as to its typographical authorship. This runs:

Presens psalmorum[1] codex venustate capitalium decoratus Rubricationibusque sufficienter distinctus Adinuentione artificiosa imprimendi ac caracterizandi absque calami ulla exaracione sic effigiatus, Et ad eusebiam dei industrie est consummatus, Per Iohannem fust ciuem maguntinum, Et Petrum Schoffer de Gernszheim Anno domini Millesimo .cccc.lvij. In vigilia Assumpcionis.

The present book of the Psalms, decorated with beautiful capitals and sufficiently marked out with rubrics, has been thus fashioned by an ingenious invention of printing and stamping without any ploughing of a pen, And to the worship of God has been diligently brought to completion by Johann Fust, a citizen of Mainz, and Peter Schoeffer of Gernsheim, in the year of the Lord, 1457, on the vigil of the Assumption.

Thus in the Psalter of 1457 we have the first example of a book informing us when and by whom it was manufactured; it also illustrates in a very remarkable way the determination of the new partners to produce a volume which should fully rival the best shop-made manuscripts. The effort to print rubrics had already been made in the Forty-two Line Bible, but the red printing was abandoned in that instance as too troublesome. Now it was revived with complete success, and with the printed rubrics came also printed capitals or initial letters in two colours, red and blue, and several different sizes. A good discussion of the manner in which these were printed will be found in the *Catalogue of the Manuscripts and Printed Books exhibited at the Historical Music Loan Exhibition* (1886) by Mr. W. H. J. Weale. In an article in the first volume of *Bibliographica* Mr. Russell Martineau showed that part of the edition was printed twice. When Mr. Martineau wrote nine copies were known, all on vellum, viz. (i) five

---

[1] Misprinted *spalmorum.*

of an issue of 143 leaves containing the Psalms and Canticles only, these being at the British Museum, Royal Library Windsor, John Rylands Library, Bibliothèque Nationale Paris, and Royal Library Darmstadt; (ii) four of an issue of 175 leaves, containing also the Vigils of the Dead, these being at the Bibliothèque Nationale Paris, University Library Berlin, Royal Library Dresden, and Imperial Library Vienna. To these must now be added a copy of the larger issue, wanting five leaves, presented in 1465 by René d'Anjou to the Franciscans of La Baumette-les-Angiers and now in the municipal library at Angers. The distribution of the Psalms in this 1457 edition is that of the general "Roman use," but blank spaces were left for the insertion of the characteristic differences of the use of any particular diocese.

Two years later (29 August, 1459) Fust and Schoeffer produced another Psalter, in the same types and with the same capitals, with twenty-three instead of twenty lines to a page. This was stated in the colophon to have been printed "ad laudem dei ac honorem sancti Jacobi," and was thus apparently commissioned by the Benedictine monastery of S. James at Mainz. Its arrangement is that generally in use at the time in German monasteries. Thirteen copies of this edition are preserved, all on vellum, viz. four in England (British Museum, Bodleian, John Rylands Library, and the Earl of Leicester's library at Holkham), two at Paris, one at the Hague, five in Germany, and one in Mr. Morgan's collection at New York. This last was bought by Mr. Quaritch at the sale of the library of Sir John Thorold for £4950.

Between the production of these two Psalters Fust and Schoeffer printed in the same types on twelve leaves of vellum the Canon of the Mass only, obviously that it might be bought by churches which owned Missals otherwise in good condition, but with these much-fingered leaves badly worn. The unique copy of this edition of the Canon was discovered at the Bodleian Library in a Mainz Missal of 1493 and identified by Mr. Gordon

Duff   It is described by Mr. Duff in his *Early Printed Books*, and by Dr. Falk and Herr Wallau in Part III of the Publications of the Gutenberg Gesellschaft, with facsimiles of ten pages.

In October, 1459, Fust and Schoeffer took an important step forward by printing in small type the *Rationale Diuinorum Officiorum* of Gulielmus Duranti, a large work explaining the meaning of the various services of the Church and the ceremonies used in them. The text is printed in double columns with sixty-three lines in each column, and the type measures 91 mm. to twenty lines. A copy at Munich is printed partly on paper, partly on vellum. All the other forty-two copies described by Mr. De Ricci are entirely on vellum. The book has also one large and two smaller capitals printed in two colours, and the first of these has been reproduced as a frontispiece to this chapter, together with a piece of the neat small type which, by demonstrating the possibility of cheap printing, set up a real landmark.

In 1460 Fust and Schoeffer gave another proof of their skill in their edition of the *Constitutions* of Pope Clement V with the commentary of Joannes Andreae. The text of the Constitutions is printed in two columns in the centre of each page in a type measuring 118 mm. to twenty lines, with the commentary completely surrounding it in the 91 type used in the *Duranti*. Headings and colophon are printed in red, and the general effect is extremely rich and handsome. All the fourteen copies known to Mr. De Ricci are printed on vellum.

In 1461 printing was put to a new use by the publication of a series of eight placards (one in two editions) relative to the struggle between the rival archbishops of Mainz—a papal bull deposing Diether von Isenburg, the Emperor's confirmation of this, papal briefs as to the election of Adolf von Nassau, a petition of Diether's to the Pope, and the manifestos of the two archbishops. All these, and also a bull of the same year as to a crusade against the Turks, are printed in the neat 91 type.

and though we may be struck by the difficulty of reading the long lines unrelieved by any headings, these publications must have been a great advertisement for the new art.

In 1462 the archiepiscopal struggle led to Mainz being sacked, but on 14 August there was completed there perhaps the finest of all the early Bibles, printed throughout in the 118 type, with headings in red and numerous two-line capitals and chapter-numbers in red and blue, though spaces were left for others to be supplied by hand. Three different colophons to this book have been described, and examples of all of these are in the British Museum. Of the sixty-one extant copies registered by Mr. De Ricci at least thirty-six are printed on vellum. The Lamoignon copy bequeathed to the Museum by Mr. Cracherode has good painted capitals added by hand and is a singularly fine book.

The Bible of 1462 marks the close of the great period of printing at Mainz. Whether six, seven, or nine years separate it from the Forty-two Line Bible the time had been splendidly employed. The capacity of the new art had been demonstrated to the full, and taken as a group these early Fust and Schoeffer incunabula have never on their own lines been surpassed. The disaster of the sack of Mainz and perhaps the financial strain involved in the production of the Bible almost reduced their press to silence until 1465, and it was during these years that their workmen are said to have left them and begun carrying the art into other towns and countries.[1] When the partners resumed active work in 1465 they struck out a new line in their *De Officiis* and *Paradoxa* of Cicero, but attained no special excellence in such small folios and quartos. Fust died about this time, and Schoeffer, left to himself, displayed no further originality. The Bible of 1472, save for the absence of printed capitals, is a close

---

[1] It seems reasonable to believe that Ulrich Zell, the first printer at Cologne, who was a clerk of the diocese of Mainz, and Sweynheym and Pannartz, who introduced printing into Italy, owed their training to Fust and Schoeffer.

copy of that of 1462. The Clementine Constitutions of 1460 were reprinted, and similar editions were issued of the Institutes and Codex of Justinian, Decretals of Pope Gregory IX, etc. For his miscellaneous books Schoeffer seems rather to have followed the lead of other printers at Strassburg and Rome than to have set new fashions himself. In 1483 he printed a Breslau Missal, and this was followed by two reprints and editions for the use of Cracow, Meissen, Gnesen, and Mainz itself. He also printed the *Hortus Sanitatis* in 1485, and in 1490 the first of several Psalters in the style of the editions of 1457 and 1459. In 1503 he was succeeded by his son Johann.

About 1476-80 a few unimportant books were issued at Mainz by an anonymous printer known as the "Printer of the Darmstadt Prognostication," from the fact that the first copy of the Prognostication in question to attract notice was that in the Darmstadt library. The books of this press attained undeserved notoriety from the forged dates inserted in many of them about 1800, in order to connect them with Gutenberg.

The work of three other printers, Johann Neumeister, Erhard Reuwich, and Jacob Meidenbach is chiefly important in the history of book-illustration, and will be found mentioned in Chapter VII. The only other Mainz printer in the fifteenth century was Peter von Friedberg, who is chiefly notable as having printed a little series of works by Johannes Trithemius (Tritheim or Trittenheim), the erudite Abbot of Spanheim.

After about 1472 Mainz was easily surpassed as a centre of printing by Strassburg, Cologne, Augsburg, and Nuremberg. But if no book had been printed there after the sack of the city ten years earlier, its fame as long as civilization lasts would still be imperishable.

CHAPTER V

OTHER INCUNABULA

IN August, 1462, the struggle between its rival Arch-bishops led to Mainz being sacked. Very little more printing was done there until 1465, and we need not doubt the tradition that journeymen trained by Guten-berg and Fust and Schoeffer, finding no work for them at Mainz, carried such experience as they had gained to other towns and countries, where they appear, after a few years spent in manufacturing presses and types, in all the glory of "prototypographers."

But even before 1462 two other cities possessed the art—Bamberg and Strassburg. At Bamberg it was practised possibly by Gutenberg, who may have printed there the Thirty-six Line Bible about 1457, certainly by Albrecht Pfister, who is found in possession of the type of this Bible, and may himself have had copies for sale. The books he himself printed at Bamberg are nine in number,[1] and three or four bound volumes seem to have preserved all the remnants of them that we possess, and all of these have found their way to public libraries.

The large and stately folios produced by the early Strassburg printers have naturally resisted the ravages of time better than the Bamberg popular books.

---

[1] Two editions of Boner's *Edelstein*, both illustrated with over a hundred woodcuts, one dated 14th February, 1461 (copy at Wolfenbüttel), the other undated (Royal Library, Berlin); *Die Historij von Joseph, Danielis Judith, Hester*, dated in rhyming verse 1462 "nat lang nach Sand Walpurgentag" (Rylands Library and Bibliothèque Nationale); the *Belial seu Consolatio peccatorum* of Jacobus de Theramo (Rylands and Germanisches Museum, Nuremberg); two issues of a German *Biblia Pauperum* with thirty-four woodcuts (both at the Bibliothèque Nationale, the first also at Rylands and Wolfenbüttel); the same work in Latin (Rylands); lastly two editions of a poem called *Rechtstreit des Menschen mit dem Tode* (both at Wolfenbüttel, the second also at the Bibliothèque Nationale).

Certainly clumsier than the contemporary Mainz books, they yet have a dignity and character of their own which command respect. The first Strassburg printer, Johann Mentelin, was at work there in or before 1460, and was helped during his life and succeeded after his death (1477) by his son-in-law, Adolf Rusch, who never put his name to a book, and most of whose impressions pass under the name of "the R-printer," from the peculiar form of that letter found in one of his types. Mentelin himself did not place his name at the end of a book till he had been at work more than a dozen years; Heinrich Eggestein, who began work about 1464, was equally reticent, and throughout the 'seventies and 'eighties a large proportion of the books printed at Strassburg were anonymous. Heinrich Knoblochtzer, who started about 1476, combines some of the charm of the earlier printers with greater literary interest and the attraction of illustrations and ornamental capitals and borders. Of him we shall have to speak in a later chapter. But after 1485 the bulk of Strassburg printing was dull and commercial.

In the fifteenth century Basel was not yet, as it became in 1501, a member of the Swiss Confederacy, and typographically its relations with Mainz, Strassburg, Nuremberg and other German towns were very close. In what year printing began there is not known. There is no dated book from a Basel press until as late as 1474, but the date of purchase, 1468, in a book (S. Gregory's *Moralia in Job*), printed by Berthold Ruppel, of Hanau, takes us back six years, and it is possible that Ruppel was at work even before this. He is identified with reasonable certainty with one of the servants of Gutenberg mentioned in connection with the lawsuit ended in 1455, and he printed Latin Bibles and other large works such as appealed to the ambition of the German prototypographers.

The second and more interesting Basel printer, Michael Wenssler, seems to have taken Schoeffer as his model, and reprinted many of Schoeffer's editions, follow-

Et hijs ipsis quibus benigne videbitur fieri. et cæte
ris. deinde ne maior sit benignitas . q̃ facultates.
tum ut pro benignitate cuiq̃ tribuatur. id est enim
iusticie fundamentū. ad quam hæc referenda sunt
omnia. Nam et qui gratificantur cuipiam. qd obsit
illi cui prodesse velle videatur. Non beneficia. neq̃ li
berales. sed pernitiosi assentatores iudicandi sunt,
Et qui alijs nocent. ut in alios liberales sint in eadẽ
sunt iniusticia. ut in suam rem aliena conuertant.
Sunt autem multi quidem cupidi splendoris a glo
rie qui eripiunt alijs. alijs largiantur. hij qui arbi
trantur se beneficos in suos amicos visum iri si locu
pletent eos quacunq̃ racione. Illud autem tantū
obest officio ut nichil magis officio possit esse con
trarium. Videndū est ergo ut ea libalitate vtam
que profit amicis. noceat nemini. Quare. l. fille
cæsaris pecuniarum translatio a iustis dominis ad
alienos non debet liberalis videri. Nichil est enim li
berale. quod non idem sit iustum. Alter locus erat
cautionis. ne benignitas maior esset q̃ facultates
q̃ qui benigniores volunt esse q̃ res patiẽ. Primū
in eo peccant q̃ iniuriosi sunt in proximos quas en
copias hijs et suppeditari equius est et reliqui ea
transferunt ad alienos. qn est autem in tali litera
litate cupiditas plerumq̃ rapiendi et auferendi p
iniuriam ut ad largiendum suppetant copie, Vide
re autem licet pleros q̃ non tam natura liberales q̃
quadam gloria ductos. ut benefici videantur facere
multa que proficisci   magis q̃ a
voluntate videantur. Talis autem similatio vani
tati est diunctior . q̃ aut liberalitati aut honestati.
Tercium est propositum. ut in beneficentia delect9
esset dignitatis. In quo et mores eius erant spectã
di in quem beneficiū oferetur a   v   a   c   a   t

ing the wording of his colophons and investing them
with the same glories of red ink. Whereas, however,
from about 1476 Schoeffer's activity was much less conspicuous, Wenssler for the next ten years poured out
edition after edition of all the heaviest legal and theological works, until he must have overstocked the market.
Then he devoted himself almost exclusively to liturgical
printing, but his affairs became hopelessly involved, and
in 1491 he fled from his creditors at Basel, and became
a wandering printer, finding commissions at Cluny and
Maçon, and then settling for a time at Lyon. Many of
the early printers in Italy made this mistake of flooding
the market with a single class of book, but Wenssler is
almost the only notable example in Germany of this lack
of business instinct.

Travelling along the Rhine from Mainz in the opposite direction we come to Cologne, and here Ulrich Zell,
like Berthold Ruppel, a native of Hanau, but who calls
himself in his books a "clerk of the diocese of Mainz,"
enrolled his name on the register of the University in
June, 1464, doubtless for the sake of the business privileges which the Senate had it in its power to confer. The
first dated book from his press, S. John Chrysostom,
Super psalmo quinquagesimo (Psalm li., according to
our English reckoning), was issued in 1466, but before
this appeared he had almost certainly produced an edition
of the *De Officiis* (see the frontispiece to this chapter,
Plate VI), the most popular of Cicero's works in
Germany, which Fust and Schoeffer had printed in 1465
and reprinted the next year. Avoiding the great folios
on which the early printers of Mainz, Strassburg, and
Basel staked their capital, Zell's main work was the
multiplication of minor theological treatises likely to be
of practical use to priests. Of these he issued countless
editions in small quarto, along with a comparatively few
small folios, in which, however, his skill as a printer is
seen to better advantage. He continued in active work
until 1494, gave, as we have seen (Chapter III.), his version

of the origin of printing to the compiler of the Cologne Chronicle published in 1499, and was still alive as late as 1507.

Zell's earliest rival at Cologne was Arnold ther Hoernen, who printed from 1470 to 1482. He may very likely have been self-taught, for his early work is very uneven, but he developed into an excellent craftsman. He is the first notable example of a printer getting into touch with a contemporary author, and regularly printing all his works, the author in this case being Werner Rolewinck, a Carthusian of Cologne, who wrote sermons and historical works, including the *Fasciculus Temporum*, an epitome of history, which found much favour all over Europe. Ther Hoernen used to be credited with the honour of having printed the first book with a titlepage, the *Sermo ad populum predicabilis In festo presentacionis Beatissime Marie semper virginis* of 1470. Schoeffer, however, had preceded him by some seven years by devoting a separate page to the title of each of his editions of a Bull of Pius II (see p. 93), and as neither printer continued the practice these isolated instances must be taken as accidental. In the same book, ther Hoernen for the first time placed printed numbers on the leaves, but this improvement also was not followed up. The third Cologne typographer, Johann Koelhoff the Elder, was the first (in 1472) to place printed "signatures" on the quires of a book, so as to show the binder the order in which they were to be arranged. Hitherto the quires had been marked by hand, and this improvement was not suffered to drop for a time like the others, but quickly spread all over Europe.

At Augsburg Günther Zainer completed his first book, an edition of the Latin Meditations on the Life of Christ taken from the works of S. Bonaventura, on the 13th March, 1468. Though he followed this with three heavy books which had found favour at Mainz and Strassburg, Zainer had the wisdom to strike out a line for himself. Augsburg had long been the chief centre of the craftsmen who cut and printed the woodcuts of saints, for which there seems to have been a large sale in Germany, and also the pictures used for playing-cards. The cutters were at first inclined to regard the idea of book-illustrations with suspicion, as likely to interfere with their existing business. It was decided, however, by the local Abbot of SS. Ulrich and Afra, an ecclesiastic with typographical tastes, that illustrated books might be printed so long as members of the woodcutters' guild were employed in making the blocks. With this as a working agreement, illustrated books greatly prospered at Augsburg, not only Günther Zainer, but Johann Bämler and Anton Sorg (a very prolific printer), turning them out with much success throughout the 'seventies.

At Nuremberg printing was introduced in 1470 by Johan Sensenschmidt, who for a short time had as his partner Heinrich Kefer, of Mainz, another of Gutenberg's servants. Much more important, however, was the firm of Anton Koberger, who began work the next year, and speedily developed the largest business of any printer in Germany. Koberger was able to deal successfully in all the heavy books, which after 1480 other firms found it wiser to leave alone, and seems to have employed Adolf Rusch at Strassburg and perhaps other printers elsewhere, to print for him. He also printed towards the end of the century some very notable illustrated books. Next to Koberger, Friedrich Creussner, who started in 1473, had the largest business in Nuremberg, and Georg Stuchs made himself a reputation as a missal printer, a special department from which Koberger held aloof.

At Speier, after two anonymous firms had worked in 1471 and 1472 without much success, Peter Drach (1477) developed an important business. At Ulm Johann Zainer, a kinsman of Günther Zainer, of Augsburg, began in 1473 by printing illustrated books, which were subsequently taken up in the 'eighties by Leonhard

Holle, Conrad Dinckmut, and Johann Reger, while Zainer himself became a miscellaneous printer. At Lübeck Lucas Brandis produced a universal history called the *Rudimentum Nouitiorum* in 1475 and a fine *Josephus*, important liturgical work being subsequently done by Bartholomaeus Ghotan, Matthaeus Brandiss and Stephan Arndes, similar work being also produced at Magdeburg partly by some of these Lübeck printers. Fine liturgical work was also done at Würzburg by Georg Reyser, who may previously have printed anonymously at Speier, and who started his kinsman Michel in a similar business at Eichstätt. At Leipzig, where Marcus Brandis printed one or two books in 1481, and the following years, a sudden development took place about 1490, and a flood of small educational works was poured out by some half a dozen printers, of whom Conrad Kachelofen and Martin Landsberg were the most prolific. Presses were also set up in numerous other places, so that by the end of the century at least fifty German cities, towns and villages had seen a printer at work. In many of these the art took no root, and in some the printer was only employed for a short time to print one or more books for a particular purpose. But the total output of incunabula in Germany was very large, and leaving out of count the fugitive single sheets, the scanty remnants of which can bear no relation to the thousands which must have been produced, out of about 25,000 different books and editions printed in the fifteenth century registered as extant at the time of writing probably nearly a third were produced in Germany. If, as is likely, a large proportion of the eleven thousand undescribed incunabula (among which, however, there must be many duplicates and triplicates) reported to have been discovered by the agents of the German Royal Commission for a General Catalogue of Incunabula are German, this rough estimate must be largely increased, and it may be proved that Germany was as prolific as Italy itself.

Considerable as was this output of German printing at home, it was probably nearly equalled by the work done by German printers in the other countries of Europe to which they hastened to carry the new art. Turning first to Italian incunabula we find that the first book printed in Italy has perished utterly. The cruel little Latin grammar which passed under the name of *Donatus* had, as we have seen, been frequently printed in Holland and by the first Mainz printers, and there are several later instances of an edition of it being produced as soon as a press was set up, merely to show the printer's types. This was done by Conrad Sweynheym and Arnold Pannartz, the two Germans who began printing at the monastery of Saint Scholastica at Subiaco, some forty miles from Rome, in 1465, or perhaps in the previous year. Being a school-book, the *Donatus* was thumbed to pieces, so that no copy now survives, and it is only known from the printer's allusion to it as the book "*unde imprimendi initium sumpsimus*" in a list of their publications drawn up in 1472. Of the three other books printed by them at Subiaco, Cicero's *De Oratore* has no printed date, but a copy described by Signor Fumagalli bears a manuscript note dated Pridie Kal. Octobres M.cccclxv., i.e. 30 September, 1465, the authenticity of which has, however, been challenged, though probably without good reason. The two others both bear printed dates, the works of *Lactantius*, that of 29 October, 1465, and S. Augustine's *De Ciuitate Dei*, 12 June, 1467. Probably even before this last book was completed the printers were already moving some of their material to Rome, where they found shelter in the palace of Pietro de' Massimi, for their edition of the *Epistulae Familiares* of Cicero was completed there in the same year, probably in or before November. Even so it is not certain that this was the first book printed at Rome, for Ulrich Han, a native of Vienna and citizen of Ingolstadt, whose later work, like that of Michael Wenssler at Basel, shows a tendency to imitate Schoeffer, completed an edition of the

65

Meditationes de vita Christi of Cardinal Turrecremata on the last day of the same year, and Mr. Proctor (after the publication of his *Index*) assigned to Han's press and to an even earlier date than the *Meditationes* a bulky edition of the Epistles of S. Jerome, which must certainly have taken a year to print.

The career of Sweynheym and Pannartz in partnership at Rome lasted but little over six years, their latest book bearing the date 31 December, 1473. Already in March, 1472, they were in difficulties, and printed a letter to Pope Sixtus IV begging for some pecuniary aid. They had printed, they said, no fewer than 11,475 volumes, and gave a list of the different books and of the numbers printed of each. Four of these editions were of 300 copies, the rest of 275, and we can see from the list that there had been three editions of the *Lactantius* and *De Ciuitate Dei* and two each of Cicero's *Epistulae Familiares*, *De Oratore*, and *Opera Philosophica*, and also of Virgil, so that clearly some of their books had shown a profit. But the list is entirely made up of Latin classics, "profane" and theological, and by March, 1472, printing had been introduced into at least ten other Italian cities (Venice, Foligno, Trevi, Ferrara, Milan, Florence, Treviso, Bologna, Naples, and Savigliano), and in most, if not all of these, the one idea of the first printers was to produce as many Latin classics as possible, as though no other firm in Italy were doing the same thing. Unable to obtain help from the Pope, Sweynheym and Pannartz dissolved partnership, the former devoting himself to engraving maps for an edition of Ptolemy's *Geographia*, which he did not live to see (it was printed by Arnold Bucking in 1478), while Pannartz resumed business on a somewhat smaller scale on his own account, and died in 1476.

At Venice, the first printer, Johann of Speier, seems to have had some foreboding of what might happen, and thoughtfully protected himself against competition by procuring from the Senate an exclusive privilege for printing at Venice during the space of five years. This might seriously have retarded the development of the press at Venice. Johann, however, after printing two editions of Cicero's *Epistulae ad familiares* and Pliny's *Historia naturalis* in 1469, was carried off by death while working on his fourth book, S. Augustine's *De Ciuitate Dei*, in 1470, and his brother Wendelin, or Vindelinus, who took over the business, had no privilege to protect him from competition.

In 1470, the way thus being left clear, a Frenchman, Nicolas Jenson, set up the second press in Venice, and by the beauty of his fine Roman type speedily attained a reputation which has lasted to this day. Another fine printer, Christopher Valdarfer, produced his first book in the same year. In 1471 three other firms (an Italian priest, Clemente of Padua, and two Germans, Adam of Ammergau and Franz Renner of Heilbronn) began publishing, and in 1472 yet seven more (three Germans and four Italians). But the pace was impossible, and by this time men were rapidly falling out. As we have seen, Sweynheym and Pannartz, after their ineffectual attempt to obtain a subsidy from the Pope, dissolved their partnership at Rome after 1473, and Ulrich Han in 1471 had taken a moneyed partner, with whose aid he weathered the storm. At Venice Wendelin, after producing thirty-one books in the previous two years, reduced his output to six in 1473, and soon after seems to have ceased to work for himself. Jenson's numbers sank from twenty-eight in 1471-2 to six in 1473-4. Valdarfer gave up after 1471, and is subsequently found at Milan. Other Venetian printers also dropped out, and only two new firms began work in 1473.

At Florence after the first printer Bernardo Cennini and his sons had produced a Virgil in 1471, and Johann Petri of Mainz Boccaccio's *Philocolo* and Petrarch's *Trionfi* in 1472, printing ceased for some years. Presses started at Foligno, Trevi, and Savigliano came to a speedy end. At Treviso, where Gerardus Lisa had published four books in 1471, there was, according to Mr. Proctor, a gap from December in that year till the same month in 1474, though Dr. Copinger quotes one book each for the intervening years.   Only one book was published at Ferrara in 1473.   What happened at Naples is hard to say, since Sixtus Riessinger, the first printer there, issued many books without dates.   At Bologna trade seems to have been stationary.   At Milan, where both Antonius Larotus in 1471 and Philippus de Lavagna in 1472 had begun with extreme caution, there was healthy progress, and these two firms continued issuing editions of the classics, and with the great falling off of competition may have found it profitable to do so.   But of the reality of the crisis in the Italian book trade in 1472-3, although little is said of it in histories of printing, there can be no doubt.   When it was over there were symptoms of a similar over-production of some of the great legal commentaries.   But this danger was avoided.   There was a steady increase in the range of the literature published, and the bourgeois book-buyer was remembered as well as the aristocratic student.   Soon there came a great extension, not only of the home but of the foreign market, and Italy settled down to supply the world with books, a task for which Venice, both from its geographical position and its well-established commercial relations, was peculiarly fitted.   But it is the books printed before 1474 that form the real Italian incunabula.   In the subsequent work within the limits of the fifteenth century Rome took no very important part.   Ulrich Han continued to print till 1478.   Joannes Philippi de Lignamine, Papal Physician and native of Sicily, produced some exceptionally interesting books between 1470 and 1476, and again in 1481-4, and Georg Lauer, who worked from 1470 to 1481, and completed an edition of S. Jerome's Letters, left unfinished by Pannartz at the time of his death, showed himself a good craftsman.   The later printers, especially Stephan Plannck and Eucharius Silber, had some good types, but produced few notable books, the bulk of the Roman output after 1480 being editions in small quarto of official documents and speeches at the Papal Court.

To devise any summary description of fifteenth century printing at Venice is wellnigh impossible. Some 150 firms were at work there; at a low estimate some four thousand extant books and editions must be credited to them, and these embraced almost every kind of literature for which readers could be found in the fifteenth century, and many varieties of craftsmanship. From a decorative point of view, the firm of Erhard Ratdolt did exceptionally good work, and it is also remarkable for specializing mainly on astronomy, mathematics, and history. Liturgical printing began somewhat late (there seems to have been a prejudice against printed service books in Italy, and I can remember none printed at Rome); in the fifteenth century Johann Hammann or Herzog and Johann Emerich were its chief exponents. Franz Renner produced chiefly Latin theology, a department much less predominant at Venice than in Germany. Several firms, e.g. Jacques Le Rouge, Baptista de Tortis, Andreas Torresanus (father-in-law of Aldus and a very fine printer), and Georgius Arrivabene devoted themselves like Jenson first mainly to Latin classics and then to law; others, such as Filippo di Pietro mingled Latin and Italian classics. Filippo's kinsman, Gabriele di Pietro, was one of the earliest vernacular printers. Many firms, such as that of Bonetus Locatellus, who seems to have had a University connection, and printed all kinds of learned Latin books, despised the vernacular altogether. The brothers Giovanni and Gregorio dei Gregorii were perhaps the most prolific and miscellaneous printers in both Latin and Italian. Johannes Tacuinus, a learned printer towards the end of the century, is notable for adorning his books with pictorial capitals, mostly of boys at play. Aldus Manutius will be spoken of in a later chapter.

While all this activity was displayed at Venice other cities were not idle. At Milan upwards of eight hundred incunabula were produced, mostly by its earliest printer, Antonius Zarotus, and two Germans, Leonhard Pachel and Ulrich Scinzenzeler. Ferrara seems to have been able to support only one press at a time, and at Florence it was some years before printing flourished, but in the last quarter of the century many interesting books were printed there, both learned and vernacular, as to the illustrations in which much will have to be said later on. Some of the early Treviso books from the press of Gerard Lisa are distinctly pretty. Bologna produced about three hundred incunabula. Naples probably not so many, but of much better quality. Altogether well over ten thousand Italian incunabula must still be extant, and these were produced at no fewer than seventy different places, though many of these were of no typographical importance, and only find their way into histories of printing from having sheltered a wandering printer for a few weeks as he was on his way from one large town to another.

In France also the earliest books were addressed to students of the classics, though they were produced on a much more limited scale. There the first printers, three Germans, had been invited to set up their presses at Paris in the Sorbonne by two of its professors, Guillaume Fichet and Jean Heynlin, of Stein, better known in his own day as Johannes de Lapide. Between the summer of 1470 and the autumn of 1472 eighteen works were printed at the Sorbonne, mostly of the kind which would be of use to its students. Among them was Sallust, three works of Cicero, Virgil's Bucolics and Georgics, the Satires of Juvenal and Persius, Terence, some text books, the *Speculum Humanae Vitae* of Bishop Roderic of Zamora, and the Orations of Fichet's patron, Cardinal Bessarion. In August, 1472, the Cardinal arrived in France on a fruitless mission to rouse the king to a crusade against the Turks. He was rebuffed and ordered to leave France. Fichet accompanied him, and never returned to Paris. As early as the previous March Heynlin seems to have been called away, and now the imported German printers, Michael Freiburger, Ulrich Gering, and Martin Crantz, were left wholly to their own devices. Thus abandoned they printed four books of a less special character, for which they sought princely instead of scholarly patronage, and then in April, 1473, moved from the Sorbonne and set up for themselves at the sign of the Soleil d'Or in the Rue S. Jacques. Here they printed still in Latin, but a much more popular class of books, and soon had to contend with two rival firms, that of Pieter de Keysere and Johann Stol, and the printers at the sign of the "Soufflet Vert" or Green Bellows. The finest of the subsequent printers was Jean Dupré, who used excellent capitals and issued many illustrated books, but three prolific printers, Antoine Caillaut, Gui Marchand, and Pierre Levet, along with many dull books issued some very interesting ones. Towards the end of the century an enterprising publisher, Antoine Vérard, kept many of the Paris printers busy, and Paris became noted typographically for its fine illustrated editions of the Hours of the Blessed Virgin, issued by Vérard, Dupré, Pigouchet (and his publisher, Simon Vostre), and Thielman Kerver. But these with the publications of Vérard belong to another chapter.

At Lyon printing was introduced by the enterprise of one of its citizens, Barthélemi Buyer, who engaged Guillaume Leroy (a native of Liège) to print for him, and subsequently employed other printers as well. The first Lyon book was a little volume of popular religious treatises, containing among other things the *De miseria humanae conditionis* of Pope Innocent III. It was completed 17 September, 1473. Until nearly 1490 the books printed at Lyon were mainly popular in character with a considerable proportion of French books, many of them illustrated. From 1490 onwards learned Latin books occur more frequently, and printing rapidly became as general or miscellaneous as at Paris itself, although only a single attempt was made, unsuccessfully, to rival the Paris *Horae*. The two cities between them probably produced more than three-fourths of the three thousand incunabula, which at a rough guess may be attributed to French presses, the share of Paris being about twice as great as that of Lyon. According to the stereotyped phrase, printing was introduced into no fewer than thirty-seven other French towns during the fifteenth century, but as a rule the printers were but birds of passage, and it was only at Poitiers (1479) and Rouen (1487) that it took root and flourished continuously, though on but a small scale. In other towns the struggle to maintain a press continued for several years, as at Toulouse, or was abandoned after the fulfilment of a single commission.

In Holland the first books which bear the name of their printer and date and place of imprint are those produced at Utrecht by Nicolaus Ketelaer and Gerardus Leempt, who began work in 1473. It is tolerably certain, however, that some of the so-called "Costeriana" (see Chap. II) preceded this date, and they are at least as likely to have been printed at Haarlem as at Utrecht, there being no decisive evidence in favour of either place. No namable printer appears at Haarlem until the end of 1483, when Jacob Bellaert set up a short-lived press there. For some seven years (1477–84) excellent work was done at Gouda by Gerard Leeu, who then moved to Antwerp. At Delft, where a fine Bible was printed by Jacob Jacobszoen and Mauricius Yemantszoen in 1477, printing was kept up continuously by Jacobszoen, Christian Snellaert, and Hendrik Eckert till the end of the century, though there seems to have been only work enough for one firm at a time. At Zwolle, Pieter van Os, who began work in 1479, was able to maintain himself, with a brief interval about 1482, till past the magic date 1500. Lastly, at Deventer, where Richardus Pafraet started in the same year, an output was speedily attained greater than in any other Dutch town, and for the latter years of the century a rival firm, that of Jacobus de Breda, shared Pafraet's prosperity. The great majority of the Deventer books, however, belong to the minor literature of ecclesiasticism and education, and are far from exciting.

The beginnings of printing are much more interesting in the Southern Netherlands, which correspond roughly to what we now call Belgium. Here also the first positive date is 1473, the year in which Johann of Paderborn in Westphalia, best known to English collectors as John of Westphalia, printed three books at Alost. A fourth followed in May, 1474, but by the following December John had removed to Louvain, a University town, where he remained doing excellent and abundant work till nearly the end of the century. At Louvain he had found another printer, Jan Veldener, already in the field, and seems to have hustled him away not very honourably. Veldener, however, was not ruined, but is subsequently found at Utrecht and Kuilenburg, and again for a short time at Louvain.

At Bruges the first printers were Colard Mansion and William Caxton, names well known to English booklovers, though not all the labours of Mr. William Blades and Mr. Gordon Duff have made it quite clear which of the two was the leader. Only two English books were printed, the *Recuyell of the Histories of Troy* and *The Game and Play of the Chess*, when Caxton returned to England and set up his presses in the Almonry at Westminster. Whether he had any pecuniary interest in the French *Recueil* and the *Quatre Dernières Choses*, and whether printings at Bruges began with the *Recuyell*, or, as Mr. Proctor contended, with the French Boccaccio *De la ruine des nobles hommes et femmes* of 1476, are points of controversy. From 1477 till his flight from Bruges to avoid arrest for debt in 1484, Mansion worked steadily by himself, and the total output of his press amounts to twenty-five French works and two in Latin.

At Brussels the Brothers of the Common Life, who worked also as printers in other places, published numerous popular Latin works between 1476 and 1487, about which time their press seems to have stopped. But the removal of Gerard Leeu's business from Gouda to Antwerp in 1484 soon gave that town a typographical importance which (except for a few years at the end of the century) it long maintained.

The true incunabula of the Netherlands are, of course, the "Costeriana." Whatever view we may take of their date and birthplace, they were undoubtedly home products, with a strongly marked individuality. Ketelaer and Leempt, however, at Utrecht, Veldener at Louvain and elsewhere, Caxton and Mansion at Bruges, were real pioneers. In a sense this is true also of John of Westphalia and Gerard Leeu, notably of the former, who had learnt his art in Italy and by the type which he had brought thence raised the standard of printing in his new home. It is, indeed, almost exclusively at Deventer that we get the dull commercial work which has nothing primitive or individual about it, and thus, perhaps because their grand total is so much smaller than in the case of Germany, Italy, or even France, the special interest of incunabula attaches to rather a high proportion of the early books of the Netherlands.

If this be true of the Netherlands, it is even truer of the two countries with which we have still to deal in this rapid survey, Spain and England. Of Spanish incunabula about seven hundred are now registered; of English, three hundred is a fairly liberal estimate of the grand total still extant. Within the limits of the fifteenth century neither country reached the purely mechanical stage of book production to which so many German and Italian books belong after about 1485. In England, indeed, this stage was hardly reached until the general downfall of good printing towards the end of the sixteenth century.

The first book printed in Spain was a thin volume of poems in honour of the Blessed Virgin, written by Bernardo Fenollar and others on the occasion of a congress held at Valentia in March, 1474. It offers no information itself on any bibliographical point, but it was presumably printed not long after the congress, at Valentia where the congress was held, and by Lambertus Palmart (or Palmaert), who on 18 August, 1477, completed there the third part of the *Summa* of S. Thomas Aquinas and duly described it as "impressa Valentie per magistrum Lambertum Palmart Alemanum, anno M.CCCC.LXXVII, die vero xviii. mensis Augusti." Palmart is supposed to have been a Fleming (a nationality to which the description *Alemannus* is often applied), but nothing is known of him. He printed a work called *Comprehensorium* and the *Bellum Jugurthinum* of Sallust in February and July, 1475, without putting his name to them, and these with the Fenollar and other anonymous books now attributed to him are in roman type. In 1478 he completed a Catalan Bible in conjunction with a native Spaniard, Alonzo Fernandez de Cordoba, and thereafter worked by himself until 1490, using gothic types in these later books. Seven other firms worked at Valentia during the fifteenth century, but none of these attained much importance.

Another Fleming, of the name of Matthew or Matthaeus, printed the *Manipulus Curatorum* of Guido de Monte Rotherii at Saragossa in October, 1475, and five other presses were established there before 1500, that of Paul Hurus being the most prolific. At Tortosa a single book (the *Rudimenta Grammaticae* of Perottus) was printed by Nicolaus Spindeler and Pedro Brun early in 1477, and in August of the same year Antonio Martinez, Alonso del Puerto, and Bartolome Segura completed the first fully dated book (the *Sacramental* of Sanchez de Vercial) at Seville, where printing subsequently throve as much as anywhere in Spain. The following year Spindeler and Brun, having moved from Tortosa, introduced printing into Barcelona, a date MCCCCLXVIII in a treatise by Bartholomaeus Mates, *Pro condendis orationibus*, being obviously a misprint,

75

though to what it should be corrected cannot positively be shown.[1]

At Salamanca printing was introduced as early as 1481, and continued more actively after 1492, mainly for the production of educational works. At Burgos Friedrich Biel, who had been trained under Michael Wenssler at Basel, began printing in 1485, and a native of the place, Juan de Burgos, brought out his first book in 1490, both of these firms doing excellent work. Altogether, twenty-four towns and places in Spain possessed presses during the fifteenth century, but in many cases only for a short time.

The outline of the story of printing in England during the fifteenth century may be very quickly sketched, fuller treatment being reserved for a later chapter. At Michaelmas, 1476, Caxton rented premises in the Almonry from the Abbot of Westminster, and here he stayed till his death in 1491, printing, as far as we know, about a hundred books and documents. In 1478 a press was set up at Oxford, presumably by Theodoric Rood of Cologne, whose name, however, does not appear in any book until 1481. By 1485 Rood had been joined by an English stationer, Thomas Hunte, but in 1486 or the following year the press was closed after printing, as far as we know, only seventeen books.

The few books printed at Oxford were all more or less scholastic in character, and six out of eight works printed by Caxton's second rival (apparently a friendly one), the Schoolmaster-Printer at St. Albans, belonged to the same class, his two more popular books being Caxton's *Chronicles of England*, with a new appendix, and the famous *Book of St. Albans*. Of these eight works, the earliest bearing a date was issued in 1480, the latest in 1486.

[1] In its colophon the book is said to have been "a docto viro Bertolommeo Mates conditus et per P. Johannem Matoses Christi ministrum presbiterumque castigatus et emendatus sub impensis Guillermi ros et mira arte impressa per Johannem Gherlinc alamanum." Gherlinc is only heard of again in 1494, and then not at Barcelona.

OTHER INCUNABULA

A more formidable competitor to Caxton than either the Oxford or the St. Albans printer began work in the City of London in 1480. This was John Lettou, i.e. John the Lithuanian, who, as Mr. Gordon Duff notes, used type identical save in a single letter with a fount used at Rome in 1478 by Johann Bulle of Bremen. Lettou appears to have been financed in the first instance by a Londoner, William Wilcock. In 1482 he was joined by William Machlinia (presumably a native of Malines), and after five law books had been printed in partnership, Lettou dropped out, and Machlinia continued working by himself, possibly until as late as 1490 or 1491, when his stock seems to have been taken over by Richard Pynson, a Norman, from Rouen. On Caxton's death in 1491 his business passed into the hands of his foreman, Wynkyn de Worde, a native of Lorraine. The only other press started in the fifteenth century was that of Julyan Notary, who worked at first with two partners, I.B. and I.H. Of these I.B. was certainly Jean Barbier, and I.H. probably Jean Huvin of Rouen. We have no information as to the nationality of Notary, but if, as seems probable, he was a Frenchman, printing in England for some twenty years after Caxton's death was wholly in the hands of foreigners.

Meagre and bare of details as is this sketch of the beginnings of printing in the chief countries of Europe, it should yet suffice to prove that the purely arbitrary date 1500 and the slang word *incunabula*, used to invest all fifteenth century impressions with a mystic value, are misleading nuisances. By the time that printing reached England it was beginning to pass into its commercial stage in Germany and Italy. In both of these countries, and in a less degree in France, scores and hundreds of books were printed during the last fifteen years of the century which have little more connection with the invention of printing, or the story of its diffusion, than English or Spanish books a century later. From the point of view

of the history of literature and thought there is much to
be gained from the collection in large libraries of all books
printed before 1501. From the point of view of the history of printing every decade of book-production has its
interest, and the decade 1490 to 1500 among the rest.
Incidentally it may be noted that in respect of book-illustration this particular decade in Italy is one of exceptional
interest. But books of the third generation of German
or Italian printers, men like Flach, for instance, at Strassburg, or Plannck at Rome, should not be collected under
the idea that they are in any true sense of the word incunabula.

What constitutes a true incunable cannot be defined
in a sentence. We must consider the country or city as
well as the book, the individual man as well as the art of
which he was perhaps a belated exponent. The same
piece of printing may have much more value and interest
if we can prove that it was produced in one place rather
than another. After the publication of his *Index*, Mr.
Proctor satisfied himself that some anonymous books in
roman type which he had classed as the work of an unidentified press at Naples were really among the earliest
specimens of Palmart's typography in Spain, and one
does not need to be a Spaniard to appreciate the distinction thus added to them. If sentiment is to count for
anything we must admit the interest of the first books
printed in any country which possesses an important history and literature—if only because we may legitimately
be curious to know on what books a printer, with all the
extant literature to choose from, ventured his capital as
likely in that particular country and time to bring him
the quickest and most profitable return. That the first
large book in Germany was a Bible, the first books in
Italy Latin classics, the first produced for the English
market one that we must call an historical romance, cannot
be regarded as merely insignificant. Nor are the differences
in the types and appearance of the page unimportant, for
these also help to illustrate national characteristics.

If this is true of the early books printed in any country, it is also true in only slightly less degree of those which first appeared in any great city which afterwards became a centre of printing. Strassburg, Cologne, and Nuremberg, Rome, Venice, and Florence, Paris and Lyon, Antwerp and London (if we may be permitted for once to ignore the separate existence of Westminster), each has its own individuality, and in each case it is interesting to see with what wares, and in what form, the first printers endeavoured to open its purse-strings. But when we come to towns and townlets some distinction seems needed. I may be misled by secret sympathy with that often scholarly, too often impecunious figure, the local antiquary. To him the first book printed in his native townlet, though by a printer merely stopping on his way between one great city and another, must needs be of interest, and it is hard that its price should be forced beyond his reach by the competition between dealers keen to do business with a rich collector to whom the book will have none of the fragrance it would possess for him. Typographical itinerancy, this printing by the roadside, as we may almost call it, must needs be illustrated in great collections, like any other habit of the early printers. But the ordinary private collector can surely dispense with buying books because they have been printed in places which have no associations for him, of which perhaps he has never heard.

As for the individual man, if we would keep any oases green in what may easily become a sandy desert, we must surely treasure every trace of his personality. One large element in the charm of incunabula is the human interest of difficulties overcome, and wherever a craftsman began work by cutting a distinctive type to suit the calligraphic fashion of the neighbourhood, at whatever date he started, his books will still have some interest. When he becomes articulate and tells us of his difficulties, or boasts of how they have been overcome, we may value his work still higher. As the first book printed at Florence, the Commentary of Servius on Virgil needs no added attraction, and yet how much its charm is enhanced by its printers' addresses to the reader. Here is the second of them roughly Englished:

To the Reader. Bernardino Cennini, by universal allowance a most excellent goldsmith, and Domenico his son, a youth of very good ability, have been the printers. Pietro, son of the aforesaid Bernardo, has acted as corrector, and has made a collation with many very ancient copies. His first anxiety was that nothing by another hand should be ascribed to Servius, that nothing which very old copies showed to be the work of Honoratus should be cut down or omitted. Since it pleases many readers to insert Greek words with their own hand, and in their own fashion, and these in ancient codices are very few, and the accents are very difficult to mark in printing he determined that spaces should be left for the purpose. But since nothing of man's making is perfect, it must needs be accounted enough if these books (as we earnestly hope) are found exceptionally correct. The work was finished at Florence on October 5, 1472.

It is impossible to read a colophon such as this without feeling ourselves in the very atmosphere of the printing house, with the various members of the printer's family at work around us. Blank spaces are found in many early books where Greek quotations occurred in the manuscripts from which they were printed. But it was not every printer who took so much trouble as Cennini to justify the omission.

As many as twenty-one years later, when printing in the great towns was becoming merely mechanical, we find the same personal note in a little grammar-book printed at Acqui. Here the colophon tells us:

The Doctrinale of Alexander of Villedieu (God be praised!) comes to a happy end. It has been printed amid enough inconveniences, since of several things belonging to this art the printer, in making a beginning with it, could obtain no proper supply, owing to the plague raging at Genoa, Asti and elsewhere. Now this same work has been corrected by the prior Venturinus, a distinguished grammarian, and that so diligently that whereas previously the Doctrinale in many places seemed by the fault of booksellers too little corrected, now by the application of his care and diligence it will reach men's hands in the most correct form possible. After this date books will be printed in type of another kind, and elegantly, I trow ; for both artificers and a sufficiency of other things of which hitherto the putter forth has been in need he now possesses by the gift of God, Who disposes all things according to the judgement of His will.

Late as he appeared and small as was the town at which he produced his one book—his hopes and promises as to others seem to have come to naught—this man had the true pioneer spirit, and deserves to be remembered for it.

Of a different kind, but no less, is the interest in what is perhaps my own favourite colophon, that recording the death of Gerard Leeu at Antwerp, while engaged in printing an edition of *The Chronicles of England* for the English market.

Here ben endyd the Cronycles of the Reame of Englond, with their apperteignaunces. Enprentyd in the Duchy of Braband in the towne of Andewarpe In the yere of our Lord M.cccc.xciij. By maistir Gerard de leew a man of grete wysedom in all maner of kunnyng : whych nowe is come from lyfe unto the deth, which is grete harme for many [a] poure man. On whos sowle God almyghty for hys hygh grace haue mercy. Amen.

Leeu had been killed accidentally by one of his workmen in the course of a dispute, and this testimonial to him in the colophon, which reads as if the compositor had slipped it in of his own accord, is very gracious and touching in its simplicity.

Just as the possession of a personal colophon brings a book within a circle of interest to which it otherwise would not have approached, so we may justly value a piece of printing all the more if it chances, through any accident, to throw light on the printer's methods. I have felt a peculiar affection for an edition of Valerius Maximus, printed by Schoeffer in 1471, ever since I discovered that

81

a change in the form of the punctuation at certain points of the book makes it possible to work out the number of presses on which it was being printed, the order in which the sheets were being set up, and how quickly the type of the worked pages was distributed. The slowness of the presswork in the simple form of press at first used obliged the printers to keep several presses, sometimes as many as six, occupied with different sections of the same book, and the trouble they were given to make the end of one section join neatly to the beginning of the next has left many traces. Any book which thus lets us into the secrets of the early printing offices possesses in a very high degree the charm which should attach to an incunable, if that hardly used word is to retain, as it should, any reference to the infancy of printing. But more will be said as to this aspect of early books in our next chapter.

CHAPTER VI

THE DEVELOPMENT OF PRINTING

ONE great cause of changes of fashion in book-collecting is that after any particular class of book has been hotly competed for by one genera-tion of book-lovers, all the best prizes gradually get locked up in great public or private collections, and come so seldom into the market that new collectors prefer to take up some other department rather than one in which it is impossible for them to attain any striking success. The first-fruits of printing, if reckoned strictly chrono-logically, are probably as nearly exhausted as any class of book which can be named. No matter how rich a man may be, the chances of his ever obtaining a copy of the Thirty-six Line Bible, the 1457 Psalter, or the first book printed at Venice, are infinitesimally small. Other incunabula, if not hopelessly out of reach even of the very rich, are only likely to be acquired after many years of waiting and a heavy expenditure when the moment of possible acquisition arrives. Many of the books hitherto here mentioned belong to this class. And yet, from what may be called the logical as opposed to the chronological standpoint, incunabula little, if at all, less interesting are still to be obtained at quite small prices by any one who knows for what to look. Any collector who sets himself to illustrate the evolution of the printed book from its manuscript predecessors, and the ways of the early printers, will find that he has undertaken no impossible task, though one which will need considerable pursuit and good taste and judgment in the selection of appropri-ate specimens.

Roughly speaking, it took about a century for printed

books to shake off the influence of manuscript and establish their own traditions. The earliest books had no titlepage, no head-title, no running title, no pagination, and no printed chapter-headings, also no printed initials or illustrations, blank spaces being left often for the one and occasionally for the other to be supplied by hand. At the time when printing was invented the book trade in many large cities had attained a high degree of organization, so that the work of the calligrapher or scribe was clearly distinguished from that of the luminer or illuminator, and even from that of the rubricator (rubrisher). Take, for instance, this Bury St. Edmunds bill of 1467 for a Psalter, preserved among the Paston Letters :

For viij hole vynets, prise the vynet xij^d . . .	viij^s
Item for xxj demi-vynets . . . prise the demi-vynett iiij^d	vij^s
Item for Psalmes letters xv^c and di' . . . the prise of c. iiij^d	vj^s ij^d
Item for p'ms letters lxiij^c . . . prise of c. j^d . .	v^s iij^d
Item for wrytynge of a quare and demi . . . prise the quayr xx^d	ij^s vj^d
Item for wrytenge of a calender	xij^d
Item for iij quayres of velym, prise the quayr xx^d .	v^s
Item for notynge of v quayres and ij leves, prise of the quayr viij^d	iij^s vij^d
Item for capital drawynge iij^c and di', the prise .	iiij^d
Item for floryshynge of capytallis, v^c . . .	v^d
Item for byndynge of the boke	xij^s
	li^s ij^d

It is possible that the work in this case was all done by one man, though it is equally possible that several were engaged on it, under the direction of a master-scrivener, but in either case the fact that vignettes and demi-vignettes, psalter letters (i.e. the small red letters at the beginning of each verse of a psalm, sometimes called versals), the mysterious " p'ms letters " (possibly the dabs of colour bestowed on small initials), the writing

ꝙ ꝗmaxīe ad præcepta accōmodatos curare poteris.
In imaginibus collocādis exerceri quotidie cōuenit.
non enim ſicut a cæteris ſtudiis adducimur nonnūꝙ
occupatione:ita ab hac re nos poteſt cauſa deducere
aliqua.Nunꝗ eſt enī quin aliquid memoriæ tradere
uelimus:et tum maxime cum aliquo maiore officio
detinemur.Quare cum ſiṫutile facile meminiſſe nō
te fallit:quod tantopere utile ſit:ꝗto labore ſit appe-
tendum: quod poteris exiſtimare utilitate cognita.
Pluribus uerbis ad eā te adhortari non eſt ſententia:
ne aut ſtudio difficili:aut nimis ꝗ res poſtulat dixiſſe
uideamur. De quarta parte rethoricæ deinceps dice-
mus.tu primas quaſque partes frequenta: et quod
maxime neceſſe eſt:exercitatione confirma .

VONIAM In hoc libro Heréni de
elocutione conſcripſimus:et quibus
ī rebus opus fuit exemplis uti:noſtris
exéplis uſi ſumus:et id fecimus præter cōſuetudinem græcoꝗ qui de hac
re ſcripſerūt: neceſſario faciendū eſt:ut paucis rōné
conſilii noſtri demus. Atque hoc nos neceſſitudine
facere non ſtudio ſatis erit ſigni:ꝗ in ſuperioribus
libris nihil neꝗ ante ré neꝗ præter ré locuti ſumus.
Nūc ſi pauca quæ res poſtulat dixeriūs tibi id quod
reliquū eſt artis:ita uti īſtituimus perſoluemus.Sed
facilius noſtrā rōnem ītelliges:ſi prius quid illi dicāt
cognoueris. Compluribus de cauſis putāt oportere:
cum ipſi præceperint : quo pacto oporteat ornare

of the text, the writing of the calendar, the musical notation, and the drawing and flourishing the capitals, were all charged separately, at so much a piece or so much a hundred, shows how distinct each operation was kept. Partly, no doubt, from policy, so as not to rouse the wrath of more than one industry at a time, partly to save themselves trouble and expense, the earliest printers, with few exceptions, set themselves to supplant only the calligrapher, and sold their books with all the blanks and spaces, which the most modest or perfunctory scribe could have left to be filled by his kindred craftsmen.

No better starting-point for a typographical collection could be desired than fine copies of two well-printed books in which the printer has confined himself severely to reproducing the text, leaving all headings, capitals, and ornaments to be supplied by hand. In one (as in the page from a book of Jenson's, which forms the illustration to this chapter, Plate VII) the blanks should remain blanks (as more especially in early books printed in Italy they often did remain), in the other they should have been filled in with red ink or colours by a rubricator. The owner of two such volumes is really as much at the fountain-head as the possessor of the Mainz Indulgences of 1454, or any still earlier document that may yet be found.[1] This is the logical beginning, and the logic of history is quite as interesting as the chronology.

From the starting-point of the book of which the printer printed nothing but the text the collector can advance in many different directions. There was no regular and unbroken progress in the development of the modern form of book, nor does it matter greatly that the examples of any particular improvement should be either absolutely or nearly the earliest. The main thing is that they should be good illustrations of the special feature

---

[1] It will be so much the better if the collector can add to them a copy of one of the early books printed at Rome (the German ones are too rare) in which there still survives the text of the rubrics, printed not in their appropriate places, but on a separate leaf or quire for the guidance of the rubricator.

for which they are acquired. The problem how to dispense with the aid of a rubricator had to be faced by countless printers in many different towns, for rubricating by hand must have added very considerably to the cost of a book. The obvious thing to do was to print in red all the headings, chapter-numbers, etc., which the rubricator used to add in that colour. But this was both expensive and troublesome, as it involved two printings and the placing of the paper in exactly the same position in the press in each. Caxton and one or two other early printers tried to avoid this double printing and difficulty of registration by putting on both red and black ink at the same time—very probably, where they came close together, they were rubbed on with a finger—but this so often resulted in smudges and lines half of one colour, half of another, that it was soon abandoned. Double printing was mostly soon abandoned also, except by the most expert men. It was tried and abandoned by the printer of the Forty-two Line Bible, though subsequently Fust and Schoeffer completely mastered it. Between 1472 and 1474 it was tried and abandoned by almost every printer in Strassburg. The difficulty was generally[1] overcome by substituting, for red ink used with type of the same size or face as the text, type of a larger size or heavier face, which could be printed in black ink with the text and yet stand out sufficiently clearly from it to catch the eye.

The need for this differentiation accelerated the tendency to reduce the size of types, which was doubtless in the first place dictated by a desire for economy. The earlier German text-types for ordinary books very commonly measure about 6 mm. a line. To enable small differences to be shown they are quoted in the British Museum Catalogue of Incunabula by the measurements

---

[1] By Jenson and many early printers in Italy, and by Husner and a few others in Germany, the majuscules of the founts used in the text were massed together in headings with admirable effect. But for a time the heavy heading types carried all before them.

of twenty lines, and many of the early Mainz and Strassburg types range closely round the number 120. These large text-types are often the only ones used in a book, notes or other accompaniments of the text being clumsily indicated by brackets or spaces. The better printers, however, gradually imitated Fust and Schoeffer, and along with their 120 text-types used smaller commentary types measuring about 4 to 4½ mm. a line, or from 80 to 90 mm. for twenty lines. In the great folio commentaries on the Canon and Civil Law a very fine effect is produced by two short columns of text in large type being placed two-thirds way up the page and then completely surrounded by the commentary in smaller type, also in double columns. But the economy of using the smaller type for the text of books without commentary was quickly perceived, and along with 4 to 4½ mm. small text-types, heavy and often rather fantastic types of just twice this size (8 to 9 mm. a line, 160 to 180 mm. to twenty lines) came into use for headings, and the opening words of books and chapters. The same course was followed with respect to headlines, when it was desired to add these to a book without the aid of a scribe. Eggestein printed one book with headlines in red, but the same heavy type which was used for chapter headings was soon used for headlines, and also, with very ugly effect, for numbering the leaves.

In considering what specimens of printing to collect Englishmen who have been accustomed for more than two centuries to nothing but roman types may well be bewildered, as they look through any volume of facsimiles, by the extraordinary variety of the founts. The main reasons for this variety may be sought (1) in the dependence of the first printers on the styles of writing which they found in vogue at the time, and in the countries and towns where they made their ventures ; and (2) in the different styles considered appropriate to different classes of books—Latin and vernacular, liturgical and secular, etc. Even now, when bookhands can hardly be said to exist, the varieties of handwriting are endless, and there are strongly marked differences between those of one country and another. In the fifteenth century, when there was less intercommunication between distant countries, the differences were even greater. As to this, however, it is possible to make some distinctions. The unifying effect of the Church is seen in the smaller range of variations in the books for liturgical use, and the fellowship of scholars exercised at least some influence in the same direction. In Italy, the home of ancient learning, the aristocratic bookhand was the fine round minuscules which had been evolved, by a conscious antiquarian revival, from the bookhand of the twelfth century, itself a revival of the Carlovingian bookhand of the eighth and ninth. Sweynheym and Pannartz, being Germans, failed in the first instance to realize the hopelessness of seeking scholarly favour with any other kind of character, and their Subiaco books are printed in a light and pleasing gothic much admired by William Morris, and used by Mr. St. John Hornby for his splendid Ashendene Dante. When they started afresh at Rome in 1467 they gave up their gothic fount and used instead a fine roman character noticeable for its use of the long *ſ* at the end of words, a peculiarity often found in Italian manuscripts of this period. The early printers at Venice made no false start, but all used roman characters from the outset, Venetian gothic type making its first appearance in 1472. That gothic type was used at all in Italy was due partly to the difficulty found in cutting very small roman type, so that gothic was used for economy, partly to the advantages of the heavy gothic face when a contrast was needed between text and commentary.

In Germany roman types were tried by Adolf Rusch (the R-printer) at Strassburg about 1464, and by both Günther Zainer at Augsburg and Johann Zainer at Ulm, but met with no favour until in the last years of the century they were reintroduced for the books written or

88

edited by Brant, Locher, Wimpheling, Peter Schott, and the other harbingers of the new learning. In the Netherlands John of Westphalia started with a round but rather thin roman type brought from Italy. In France the scholarly ideals of the patrons of the first Paris press were reflected in the use for the books printed at the Sorbonne of a beautiful roman type, only injured by the excessive prominence of the serifs. In Spain also the first books, those printed at Valentia by Lambert Palmart, were in roman; but in both countries gothic types long commanded the favour of the general reader, while in England their supremacy was unchallenged for a third of a century, no book entirely in roman type appearing until 1508.

As regards the æsthetic value of the different roman types in use during the fifteenth century, the superiority of the Italian is so marked that, with the exception of the first French type, the rest, from this point of view, may be neglected. Almost all the roman types used in Italy until late in the 'seventies are either beautiful or at least interesting, and it is remarkable that some of the most beautiful are found in small places like Cagli, Mondovi, Viterbo, and Aquila, or in the hands of obscure printers, such as the self-taught priest Clemente of Padua, who worked at Venice in 1471. The pre-eminence of Jenson's fount is indisputable, though he often did it injustice by his poor presswork. But those used by John and Wendelin of Speier, and at a later date by Antonio Miscomini, were also good, as also were several of the founts used at Rome and Milan. At Naples and Bologna, on the other hand, some quite early roman founts are curiously hard and heavy.

After about 1480 roman types in Italy enter on a second stage. They no longer have the appearance of being founded directly on handwriting. Doubtless the typecutters were so used to their work that they no longer needed models, but designed new types according to their own ideas. Naturally the letters are more uniform and regular than in the earlier founts, but naturally also they have less charm, and the ordinary close-set Venetian type of the end of the century is singularly dull. Even the large roman type used by Aldus to print the *Hypnerotomachia Poliphili* is no real exception, as the letters are narrow for their height. A far finer fount is the large text type used by the Silbers at Rome, on both sides of 1500. This is well proportioned and beautifully round, and it is surprising that it has not yet been imitated by any modern typecutter.

When we pass from roman to gothic types there is a bewildering field from which to choose. Here again dull commercialism gained the upper hand about 1480, and towards the end of the century an ugly upright text-type of 80 mm. to twenty lines, with a fantastic headline type of twice its size, or a little more, found its way all over Germany. But types with a twenty-line measurement ranging round 120 mm., such as those of Peter Schoeffer or the Printer of Henricus Ariminensis, are often extraordinarily handsome. Both of Schoeffer's earlier small types and the small type of Ulrich Zell at Cologne are engagingly neat, and at the opposite end there is the magnificently round gothic used by Ulrich Han at Rome.

Most of the finest gothic types were used for Latin books of law and theology, the peculiar appropriateness of roman type being considered to be confined to works appealing to classical scholars. In Germany, for some time, not much distinction was observed, but there was a tendency in classical books to use an f and long f starting from the level of the line, whereas in most vernacular books the tails of these letters came below the line, giving a strangely different appearance to the type. In the 'nineties a distinctively cursive type called Schwabacher, usually measuring 93 mm. to twenty lines, makes its appearance all over Germany. In Italy, both at Naples and by Ulrich Han at Rome, a very small text type, which is certainly cursive in its affinities, was used at the very outset, but found no favour. The typical vernacular French types are also very often on a slope. The small cursive type cut for Aldus in 1501 by Francesco da Bologna was thus not quite so great a revolution as is sometimes represented. Its clearness in proportion to its size, its extreme compactness, and the handiness of the small octavos with which it was at first specially connected, gained for it a great success, and it gradually, though only gradually, usurped the name of italic, the upright Italian bookhand being distinguished from it as roman. Few treatises on printing or the development of books give any idea of the immense popularity of italics during the sixteenth century. About 1570 they seemed to have established themselves as the fashionable vernacular type both in Italy and France, and even in England whole books were printed in them. In Switzerland also and Germany they gained some hold; but gradually the tide turned, the upright bookhand regained its predominance, and italics now survive chiefly for emphasis and quotations—in the seventeenth and eighteenth centuries they were often used for proper names—giving to the page on which they occur an unpleasantly spotty appearance. Their occasional use in prefaces and dedicatory letters is much more appropriate.

The completion of books at first by a colophon, afterwards by a titlepage, may be illustrated in the same way as that by which we have traced the evolution of the text from incompleteness to completeness and the development of different classes of types. At least one printer, Johann Mentelin of Strassburg, seems to have considered the addition of colophons as the proper business of the rubricator. While printed colophons in his books are exceptionally rare, several copies have come down to us in which full colophons have been added by hand, e.g. in a vellum copy of the *Speculum Morale* in the Bibliothèque Nationale, after praise of the book, we read :

Impressumque in inclyta vrbe Argentinensium ac nitide terse emendateque resertum per honorandum dominum Dominum

Iohannem Mentelin artis impressorie magistrum famosissimum.
Anno a partu virginis salutifero millesimo quadringentesimo
septuagesimo sexto. die mensis nouembris sexta.

Despite a few instances of this kind, however, it is
certain that the majority of printers who omitted to print
colophons to their books did so, not in the expectation
that they would be supplied by hand, but in imitation
of the manuscript books to which they were accustomed,
in which it is distinctly exceptional to find any mention
of the name of the scribe. But the men who took a
pride in their new art, and who thought that their work
was good enough to bring more custom to their press
if their name were associated with it, took the opposite
course, and so colophons from 1457 onwards are common
in the best books, and may perhaps be found in about
40 per cent of the incunables that have come down to
us. By the men who were skilful in using red ink they
were often thus printed, and whether in red or in black,
they frequently had appended to them the printer's mark
or device, which gave a very decorative finish to the
book.

Nowadays, when we have been accustomed all our
lives to the luxury of titlepages, it may well seem to us
merely perverse to hide the title of a book, the name of
the author, and information as to where, when, and by
whom it was printed in a closely set paragraph at the end
of the book. But if we think for a moment of how the
manuscript books to which the early printers were accustomed had been produced we shall see that it was the
most natural thing in the world. A scribe would take
his quire of paper or vellum, and if he were a high-class
scribe, mindful of the need of keeping his text clean, he
would leave his first leaf blank and begin at the top of
his second. But here he would begin to write straight
away, sometimes with the first words of his text, sometimes with a preliminary paragraph, which may be called
the *Incipit*, from the important word in it. In this
paragraph he would give either the name of his book

or, almost as commonly, the name of the first section of it, introducing the title only incidentally.

> Incipit Racionale diuinorum officiorum.
> Incipiunt Constitutiones Clementis pape V una cum apparatu Ioannis Andree.
> Marci Tullii Ciceronis Arpinatis consulisque Romani ac oratorum maximi Ad M. Tullium Ciceronem filium suum Officiorum liber incipit.
> Incipit epistola sancti Hieronimi ad Paulinum presbiterum de omnibus diuine historie libris.

That it did not occur to him to devote his blank page to a displayed title of the book he was copying was due to the fact that every medieval manuscript was the direct descendant, through many or few stages, of the author's own original draft, and that this was the most pretentious way and least natural in which any author could begin to write a book. So the scribes imitated the author in his normal beginning, and the early printers imitated the scribes, and because an author was more inclined to relieve his feelings at the end of a book than to express them volubly at the beginning, it was only when books multiplied so greatly that purchasers wanted to see at a glance what was the name of the book at which they were looking that titlepages superseded colophons. The proof of this explanation being the true one is that title-pages become common just about the time (1480 to 1490) that book-production was beginning to be divided up between publishers and printers, and that the publisher very quickly claimed them for his own.

The earliest titlepages, those of the Mainz *Bul zu deutsch des bapst Pius II* (1463), Rolewinck's Sermon for the Feast of the Presentation (Cologne : Arnold ther Hoernen, 1470), the *Flores Sancti Augustini* (Cologne, 1473), and the *Kalendarium* of Joannes de Monteregio and its Italian translation (Venice : Ratdolt and partners, 1476), were all more or less of the nature of " sports." When titlepages came to stay, a year or two later than the last of these precursors, they everywhere took the form of labels, a single sentence containing the short title of the book, printed sometimes in large, sometimes in small type, but with no other information. The label title, being usually printed high up on the page, left two-thirds, or thereabouts, blank beneath it, and this space was soon filled, sometimes by a pictorial woodcut, sometimes by a mark or device, which at first might be either that of the printer or publisher, but gradually came to be much more often the publisher's. The short title and device taken together filled the page sufficiently for decorative purposes, but they left room for a further paragraph of type to be added if desired, and the advantage of filling this with the name and address of the firm from whom the book might be obtained was so obvious that the " imprint," as it is rather loosely called, soon made its appearance and gradually became recognized as an essential part of the titlepage. When printers and publishers lost pride in their work and ceased to care to decorate their titlepages with pictures or devices, the title was displayed in a series of single lines and made to straggle down the page till it came nearly low enough to meet the imprint.

If we go back to the habits of the scribes it is easy to understand another point in the early history of books, their make-up into quires and the marking of these quires by signatures and catchwords. The word *quaire* or *quire* is a shortened form of the Latin *quaternio*, the name devised for four sheets of paper folded down the middle so as to form eight leaves. A gathering of five sheets making ten leaves was called a *quinternion*, and this, though it has yielded no modern word, was for generations such a popular form that *quinterniones* was sometimes used as a general expression for manuscripts. Gatherings of three sheets, making six leaves, were called *terniones;* gatherings of two sheets, making four leaves, *duerniones.* A few, but only a few, books exist—nearly all of those which I have seen are either block-books or thin folios of poetry of the reign of Charles II—which are made up in single sheets not placed one within the other, but following consecutively. But the system of gathering from two to five or more sheets together into quires was practically universal both before and after the invention of printing, and this for the excellent reason that it reduced the quantity of sewing necessary in binding a book, and reduced also the risk of the sewing cutting through the paper or vellum, as it would be very likely to do if there were only a single thickness to resist it.

When the scribe had arranged his quire or gathering he wrote first page by page on all the leaves on the left hand until he came to the middle of the quire, when he proceeded to write page by page on all the leaves on the right hand. Thus in a quire of four sheets the left half of the first sheet would be leaf 1, pages 1 and 2, and the right half would be leaf 8, pages 15 and 16, so that the same sheet formed the beginning and end of the quire. In the earliest printed books the quires were printed page by page exactly as the quires of a manuscript had been written. But early in the 'seventies (Peter Schoeffer can be proved to have adopted the practice between 1471 and September, 1474) the advantage was perceived of printing both the pages on the upper or lower side of a sheet at the same time, i.e. in a quaternion, page 16 together with page 1. As soon as a printer had learnt to print two folio pages together, it became easy to print four quarto pages, or eight octavo pages, or sixteen sextodecimo pages. In each case the amount of type to be printed at a pull would be approximately the same. It thus ceased to be disadvantageous to print small books, whereas so long as each page had to be pulled separately it was obviously wasteful to make that page a very small one.

Even when the printers had learnt how to print two folio pages at the same time the presswork remained very laborious. The earliest presses were worked with only a single screw, and when the pressman had pulled the lever one way to bring the platen down on the type, he had to push the lever back again in order to raise the platen and release the paper. Thus in order to print a large book quickly four or six sets of pressmen had to work on it at once, each at a different press. To avoid mistakes, therefore, the practice was to allot one section of the book to each press. Thus if a book were calculated to run to 288 leaves, six presses might begin simultaneously at leaves 1, 49, 97, 145, 193, and 241. What more often happened was that either to follow the natural sections of the book, or because some of the printers were engaged on other tasks and not ready to begin at once, the sections were of much less regular lengths, and we can sometimes prove that the first press was far advanced in its section before the fifth and sixth had begun. Now in all these cases, unless they were reprinting an earlier book, page for page, it is obvious that some nice calculations would be needed to make each section end with the end of a quire so as to be able to join on with the beginning of the quire containing the next section without any gap or crowding. Hence the striking irregularities in the make-up of many early books. Instead of a book being printed in a succession of quinternions or a succession of quaternions we have many a make-up which can only be expressed by a cruelly mathematical formula, such as this, which represents the quiring of the Forty-two Line Bible.

$$\text{a-i}^{10};\ \text{k}^{10+1}\ \text{lm}^{10}\ \text{n}^{6+1};\ \text{o-z}^{10}\ \text{ʒ}^{10}\ \text{ꝗ}^{10+1};\ \text{A-F}^{10}\ \text{G}^{4}:\ \text{aa-nn}^{10};$$
$$\text{oo}\ \text{pp}^{10}\ \text{qq}^{10+1};\ \text{rr-zz}\ \text{AA-CC}^{10};\ \text{DD}^{12}\ \text{EE}^{10+1};\ \text{FF}\ \text{GG}^{10}$$
$$\text{HH}^{4+1}\ \text{II}^{10}.$$

In this the index-letter shows the number of leaves in the quire, a-i¹⁰ being a short way of stating that each of the nine quires a b c d e f g h i has ten leaves in it. In the tenth quire (k) there is an extra leaf, and again in the thirteenth (n) the printer found that he had too much copy for six leaves and not enough for eight, and was therefore obliged to put in an odd one, because another press had already printed off the beginning of the next quire (o). Not infrequently it would happen that the odd amount of copy for a section was very difficult to fit exactly into a leaf even when the printer had compressed it by using as many contractions as possible, or eked it out by using no contractions at all. This accounts for the occurrence of a blank space, large or small, at the end of some sections without any break in the text, as the printer was sometimes careful to explain by the printed notice "Hic nihil deficit," or as in our page from Ulrich Zell, "Vacat."

As has been already noted, in a moment of enthusiasm Mr. Proctor once said to the present writer that it was impossible to find a fifteenth century book that was really ugly. This was certainly putting the case for his beloved incunables a peg too high, for there were plenty of bad printers before 1500, and even such a master as Jenson was by no means uniformly careful as to the quality of his presswork. But one of the legacies which the early printers received from the scribes was the art of putting their text handsomely on the page, and the difference which this makes in the appearance of a book is very marked, little as many modern printers and publishers attend to it. But in the books of the best printers of our own day, as well as in those of the best of the fifteenth century, from 65 per cent to 72 per cent of the height of the page is devoted to the text, from 28 per cent to 35 per cent being reserved for the upper and lower margins, of which at least two-thirds is for the lower and not more than one-third for the upper. As compared with the height of a page of type the breadth is usually in the proportion of about 45 to 70 (a trifle more in a quarto), and here again the outer margin is at least twice as great as the inner. Thus in a book with a page measuring 10 by $7\frac{1}{4}$ inches, the type-page should measure about 7 by $4\frac{3}{4}$ inches, with a lower margin of about 2 inches, an upper of 1 inch, an outer of $1\frac{3}{4}$ inches, and an inner of $\frac{3}{4}$ inch.

It will be greatly to the advantage of book-buyers to bear these proportions in mind, in order to measure how much a book offered to them has been cut down, and also to be able to instruct their binders as to how to reduce the absurd margins of some modern "Large Paper" copies to more artistic dimensions. Whether it is legitimate further to reduce the margins of an old book which has already been mangled by a binder in order to get the proportions better balanced is a nice question of taste. If a two-inch lower margin has been halved and a one-inch upper margin left intact, if the upper margin is reduced, the book will become a pleasant "working copy" instead of an obviously mangled large one, and the collector must settle in his own conscience whether this be a sufficient justification for snipping off a centimetre of old paper.

Exactly why the proportions here laid down, with their limits of variation, are right for books cannot easily be set forth. It is easiest to see in the case of the relation between the inner and outer margins. As William Morris was never tired of insisting, the unit in a book is, not a single page, but the two pages which can be seen at the same time. The two inner margins separate the two type-pages by a single band of white, which, if each inner margin were as large as the outer, would become insufferably conspicuous. As for the proportions between the lower and upper margins, the explanation may lie in the angle at which we habitually read books, or by the need for leaving room for the reader to hold the book in his hands. But whether it be a matter of inherent rightness or merely of long-established convention, the pleasure of handling a book with correct margins is very great, and a collector who secures an uncut copy of even a poorly printed book of the period when margins were understood, will find that it presents quite a pleasing and dignified appearance. And so in regard to other points, any book which illustrates the relations of the early printers to the scribes, the difficulties which they experienced in their work and the expedients by which they were surmounted deserves, whatever its date or present price, to be reckoned as a real incunable, and the collector who gets together a few dozen books of this kind will have far better sport for his outlay than he who is tied down too rigorously by chronology.

CHAPTER VII

EARLY GERMAN AND DUTCH ILLUSTRATED BOOKS

THE natural method of illustrating a book printed with type is by means of designs cut in relief, which can be locked up in the forme with the type, so that text and illustrations are printed together by a single impression[1] without any special preparation of the paper. So long as the design to be printed stands out clearly on the block it matters nothing whether it be cut on wood or on soft metal. Even as between the design cut by hand and the process line-block which has as its basis a photograph taken direct from a pen drawing, the difference can hardly be said to be one of better and worse. We lose the individuality of the wood-cutter or wood-engraver, but we are brought into closer touch with the individuality of the artist, and whether we gain or lose depends on the ability of the artist to dispense with a skilled interpreter. The one requisite for success is that either the artist, or an interpreter for him, should recognize the limits within which his work can be effective. The reproductions of the artist's designs will be looked at, not in isolation, but as part of an *ensemble* made up of two pages printed in a type which, perhaps with a little trouble, can be ascertained beforehand, and they will be printed not as proofs on a special press by a special workman on paper chosen solely to suit them, but with average skill

---

[1] Dr. Schreiber, in the introduction to Tome V of his *Manuel de l'amateur de la gravure sur bois au xvᵉ siècle*, dealing with German book-illustrations, shows that some little difficulty was found at first in effecting this. In Boner's *Edelstein* (Bamberg, 1461), probably the first illustrated book printed in Germany, the cuts were printed after the text. In Zainer's *Heiligenleben*, the first illustrated book printed at Augsburg, the cuts must have been printed first, as part of the text is sometimes printed over them.

rewſamlich nach ſeiner lieben můter vmbſehen vnd
gůtlich nach ir ſenftzgent gemachſam wainend/vñ
gar ſůßlich den namen ſeyner lieben můter anrůffen/
vnd ſprechen/můterlin můterlin/Des erſchrack hőzt
der blůtuerkauffer/vnd zucket bald auß ſeiner täſchē
einen ſilbzen pfennig/vnd gab den dem vnſchuldigē
Kind vnd beſchwayget es mit ſemften woz ten.

℟Nach dem aber vnd er den weg nahend haym mit
dem vnſchuldigen kind komen was/vnd ſich allent
halben ob in nyemandt mit dem kind ſahe vmſahe/
Da ſach er einen lezzer zů der lincken ſeyten arbetend
Er erſchrack ſeruaſt vñ ſtůnd mit dem villieben kind
vntz ſich der lezzer mit ſeinē geſicht abkerte/Er hůb
ſich ſchnell auf ſein fůß vnd eylte mit dem kind tzů
dem hawß des iudē Samuels/vnd ſchlappfte das
mit im hin ein in das hawß.
℟Der Samuel als er das ſchőn kind amblickte/als
ein tiger tier/begerte er des blůtes des vnſchuldigen

and care in an ordinary press and on paper the choice of which will be dictated by several considerations. Whenever relief blocks have been used for any length of time as a method of book-illustration the rivalry of artists has tended to cause these restrictions to be forgotten. In our own day line-blocks have been almost driven out of the field by "half-tones," which cannot be printed without the aid of paper specially coated, or at least rolled or "calendared." Shortly before the process line-block was perfected the extreme fineness of the American school of wood-engraving had induced a nearly similar result. The successors of Bewick worked with equal disregard of the need for clearly defined lines, and when we travel back to the first half of the sixteenth century we find the Holbeins, Burgkmair, Weiditz, and other artists producing designs far too delicate for the conditions under which they were to be reproduced. Thus the charm of the woodcuts in books of the fifteenth century is by no means confined to that "quaintness" which is usually the first thing on which the casual observer comments. The "quaintness" is usually there, but along with it is a harmony between print, paper, and woodcut which has very rarely since been attained.

The claim made in the last paragraph must be understood as applying only to books honestly illustrated with blocks specially made for them. Books decorated with a job lot of cuts, as was often the case, especially after about 1495, may accidentally be delightful and often possess some of the charm of a scrapbook. It is good sport, for instance, to take one of Vérard's later books and trace the origin of the cuts with which that cheaply liberal publisher made his wares attractive. But the incongruity is mostly manifest, and collectors might well be more fastidious than they show themselves and refuse to waste the price of a good book with homogeneous illustrations in buying half a dozen dull little volumes with an old Horae cut at the beginning and the end of each.

A second exception must be recognized in the books

illustrated by untrained wood-cutters. In Germany and the Low Countries few, if any, quite untrained wood-cutters were employed, and this is true also of Paris and Florence. But at Lyon and other provincial towns in France (the Abbeville cutters, who probably came from Paris, are strikingly good), in a few books printed at Rome and Venice, here and there in Spain, and in one or two of Caxton's and several of Wynkyn de Worde's books in England, the cutting is so bad that, though it is possible sometimes to see that excellent designs underlie it, the effect is either ludicrous or repellent. Only fanatics could admire such pictures as we find in the early Lyonnese *Quatre fils d'Aymon* (*s.n.*, but about 1480), in the *Opuscula* of Philippus de Barberiis printed by Joannes de Lignamine (Rome, 1481), in a large number of the cuts of the Malermi Bible of 1490 (Venice, G. Ragazzo for L. A. Giunta, 1490), in *Los doze trabajos de Ercules* (Zamora, 1483), in Caxton's *Aesop* or in Wynkyn de Worde's *Morte d'Arthur* (1527). Books such as these (the Malermi Bible is on a different footing from the rest owing to the wonderful excellence of the good cuts) may be bought as curiosities, or for the light they throw on the state of the book trade when such work could be put on the market, but no artistic merit can be claimed for them.

In Germany good work began early, because, to supply the demand for playing-cards and pictures of saints, schools of wood-cutters had grown up, more especially at Augsburg and at Ulm. Block-books also had come into existence in the district of the lower Rhine, and these, which in their earliest forms can hardly be later than 1460, must be divided between the Low Countries and Germany and prove the existence of competent workmen. The earliest type-printed books which possess illustrations are the little handful printed by Albrecht Pfister at Bamberg in and about 1461, described in Chapter V, but it was at Augsburg in the early seventies that book-illustration first flourished. As has been mentioned in Chapter V, trade difficulties at first stood in the way, but by the arbitration of Melchior Stanheim, abbot of the local monastery of SS. Ulrich and Afra, these were settled on the sensible basis that printers might have as many illustrations in their books as they chose to provide, but that they must be designed and cut by Augsburg craftsmen. The series seems to have begun with some tolerably good column-cuts to an edition of the Lives of the Saints in German, of which the first part was issued in October, 1471, and the second in April, 1472. In *Das guldin spiel* of a Dominican writer, Ingold, finished on 1 August of the latter year, we find for the first time real power of characterization. Lovers of woodcuts owe some gratitude to the medieval trick of attaching edifying discourses to matters of everyday interest and amusement, for whereas the edifying discourses themselves could hardly carry illustrations, hunting, chess, or, as here, seven games which could be likened to the seven deadly sins, gave opportunities for showing pictures by which the natural man would be attracted. Another important book of this year, only known to me in Bämler's plagiarism of it, was the first edition of the *Belial*, the amazing book which tells the story of Christ being summoned for the trespass committed in harrowing Hell.

In 1473 the heavy gothic type which Zainer used in these illustrated books was put at the disposal of the Abbot of SS. Ulrich and Afra and used to print a *Speculum Humanae Saluationis*, to which was added a summary in verse by Frater Johannes, an inmate of his monastery. This book was illustrated by 176 different cuts of Biblical subjects, of varying degrees of merit. In the same year, and again in 1474, Zainer printed an illustrated *Plenarium*, i.e. the Epistles and Gospels for the round of the Church's year. In or shortly after 1475 he printed and illustrated a narrative of great contemporary interest, the story, written by one Tuberinus, of a child named Simon, who was supposed to have been slain by the Jews out of hatred of the Christian faith and desire to taste Christian flesh. The tale appears to contain internal evidence of its untruth, and the unhappy Jews who were cruelly executed had much better claims to be regarded as martyrs than "das susses Kind" Simon. But some of the pictures are quite animated, especially one (see Plate VIII) of the hired kidnapper beguiling the child through the streets and then deftly hurrying him into the house of doom with a touch of his knee.

In 1475 or 1476, and again with the date 1477, Zainer produced editions of the German Bible in large folio, illustrated with great pictorial capitals at the beginning of each book. But his greatest achievement was in an undated book of this period, the *Speculum Humanae Vitae* of Rodericus Bishop of Zamora, in the German translation of Heinrich Steinhowel. If this Mirror of Man's Life had been written by a man with his eyes open instead of by a vapid rhetorician it should have been one of the most valuable documents for the social life of the fifteenth century, since it professes to contrast the advantages and evils of every rank and occupation of life, from the Pope and the Emperor down to craftsmen and labourers. There is but little joy to be gained from its text, but the Augsburg artist has atoned for many literary shortcomings by his vivid and charming pictures of scenes from the social life of his day, though it is not to be supposed that German judges took bribes quite so openly as he is pleased to represent. In addition to fifty-four woodcuts of this kind, there is a large genealogical tree of the House of Hapsburg, which is a triumph of decorative arrangement.

Two other early Augsburg printers devoted themselves to illustrated work, Johann Bämler and Anton Sorg. The former at first contented himself with prefixing a full-page frontispiece to his books, as in the *Summa* of Johannes Friburgensis and *Die vier und zwanzig goldenen Harfen*, both of 1472, and again in the picture of S. Gregory and Peter the Deacon in the Dialogues of the former printed for the monastery of SS. Ulrich and Afra, and that of the dying Empress in the *Historie von den sieben weisen Meistern* of the following year. In the *Belial* of 1473 and *Plenarium* of 1474 Bämler was content for most of the cuts to borrow or copy from the editions of Zainer, but in the *Alexander der Grosse* of the former year and *Melusine* and *Sieben Todsünden* of the latter he himself led the way with some excellent sets of woodcuts, which were copied by others. Again, in *Das Buch der Natur* of 1475 we find a dozen specially designed full-page cuts, one to each book, illustrating man, the spheres, beasts, birds, mermaids, serpents, insects, etc.; in the *Chronica von allen Kaisern and Königen* of 1476 there are four large cuts, showing Christ in glory, the dream of the Emperor Sigismund, the vision of S. Gregory at Mass, and S. Veronica holding before her the cloth with the imprint of Christ's face. It was perhaps in this same year that Bämler issued, without dating it, Jacob Sprenger's *Die Rosenkranz Bruderschaft*, with two very striking cuts, one of the offering of garlands to Our Lady, the other of Christ's scourgers looking back mockingly as they leave Him. A dated edition appeared in 1477. Another book of 1476 with a good set of cuts was the romance of Apollonius, King of Tyre. In 1477 Bämler issued a *Buch der Kunst*, which, like the *Buch der Natur*, went through several editions; it must be noted, however, that there is no such contrast between Art and Nature as the short title of this book might suggest, the full title being *Buch der Kunst geistlich zu werden*. The illustrations for the most part represent a soul in different situations, but there are also many of Biblical subjects. The last book of Bämler's which need be mentioned is the *Turken-Kreuzzüge* of Rupertus de Sancto Remigio, which has an effective frontispiece of the Pope preaching to the Crusaders and some vigorous smaller cuts.

Anton Sorg began printing in 1475 and issued his first illustrated book the next year. He was a prolific printer, and issued many close imitations of books originated by Günther Zainer and others. The most famous work specially connected with his name is Ulrich von Reichenthal's *Das Conciliumbuch geschehen zu Costencz* (1483), illustrated with forty-four larger cuts, all in the first ninety leaves, and 1158 coats of arms of the various dignitaries present at the Council. The larger cuts show the knighting of the Burgermeister of Constance, processions, a tournament, and the martyrdom of Huss (despite his safe conduct) and the scattering of his ashes over a field. The later Augsburg illustrated books, issued by the elder Schoensperger, Johann Schobsser, Peter Berger, and Hans Schauer, though they maintain a respectable level of craftsmanship, have less interest and individuality than these earlier ones. One Augsburg printer, Erhard Ratdolt, who had made himself a reputation by ten years' work at Venice (1476-86), shortly after his return issued a notable illustrated book, the *Chronica Hungarorum* of Thwrocz. His main business was the production of missals and other service books, in some of which he made experiments in colour-printing.

At the neighbouring city of Ulm, where also the woodcutters had long been at work, illustrated books began to be issued in 1473 by Johann Zainer, no doubt a kinsman of Günther Zainer of Augsburg. His chief books are (1) Latin and German editions of Boccaccio's *De claris mulieribus* (1473), with a fine borderpiece of Adam and Eve and numerous spirited little pictures which, though primitive both in conception and execution, are full of life, and (2) an *Aesop* which was reprinted at Augsburg and copied elsewhere in Germany, and also in France, the Netherlands, and England. From 1478 onwards he seems to have been in continual financial trouble. He was apparently able, however, to find funds to issue two rather notable books about 1490, the *Prognosticatio* of Lichtenberger, and a *Totentanz*. The blocks of both of these passed to Meidenbach at Mainz.

Most of the forty books of a later printer, Conrad Dinckmut (1482-96), have illustrations. His *Seelenwurzgarten* (1483) appears at first sight to be a most liberally decorated book, crowded with full-page cuts, but of its 133

illustrations only seventeen are different, one, representing
the tortures of the damned, being used as many as thirty-
seven times, a deplorable waste of good paper, which the
printer had the good sense to reduce in a later edition.
Dinckmut's most famous book is a German edition of the
Eunuchus of Terence " ain maisterliche vnd wolgesetzte
Comedia zelesen vnd zehören lüstig und kurtzwylig, die
der Hochgelert vnd gross Maister und Poet Therencius
gar subtill mit grosser Kunnst und hochem Flyss gesetzt
hat." This has twenty-eight nearly full-page cuts in which
the characters are well drawn, the setting for the most
part showing the streets of a medieval town. A *Chronik*,
by Thomas Lirer, issued about the same time, was begun
to be illustrated on a generous scale with eighteen full-page
cuts in the first twenty-eight leaves, but was hastily finished
off with only three more cuts in the remaining thirty-six.
They are less carefully executed than those of the *Eunuchus*,
but show more variety, and are on the whole very
pleasing.

Another Ulm printer, who began work in 1482,
Leonhard Holl, printed in that year a magnificent edition
of Ptolemy's *Cosmographia*, with woodcut maps (one
signed " Insculptum est per Iohannē Schnitzer de Armsz-
heim ") and fine capitals. The first of these, a pictorial N,
shows the editor, Nicolaus Germanus, presenting his book
to the Pope.

Of later Ulm books by far the most important are
two by Gulielmus Caoursin, published by Johann Reger
in 1496, and both concerned with the Knights of St. John
of Jerusalem at Rhodes. One volume gives their *Stabili-
menta* or Constitution, the other *Obsidionis urbis Rhodiae
descriptio*, an illustrated history of their defence of their
island against the Turks and their subsequent dealings
with the infidel, who at one time were so complaisant as
to present them with no less valuable a relic than the arm
of their patron, which was duly honoured with processions
and sermons. Altogether the two books contain fifty-six
full-page pictures, rather roughly cut, but full of vigour

and bringing the course of the siege and the character of the wild Turkish horsemen very vividly before the reader. William Morris was even tempted to conjecture that the designs may have been made by Erhard Reuwich, the illustrator of the Mainz *Breidenbach*, of which we shall soon have to speak.

At Nuremberg book-illustration begins with the *Ars et modus contemplatiuae vitae*, six leaves of which partake of the nature of a block-book. In or about 1474 Johann Müller of Königsberg (whose variant names, Johannes Regiomontanus, Johannes de Monteregio, have trapped more bibliographers into inconsistencies than those of any other fifteenth century author) issued calendars and other works with astronomical diagrams, and prefixed to his edition of the *Philalethes* of Maffeus Vegius a woodcut (for which Dr. Schreiber suspects an Italian origin) showing Philalethes in rags and Truth with no other clothing than a pair of very small wings. In June, 1475, Sensenschmidt and Frisner illustrated their folio edition of Justinian's *Codex*, with ten charming little column-cuts ; the following month Sensenschmidt produced a *Heiligenleben*, with more than 250 illustrations, which, according to Dr. Schreiber, are very noteworthy as they stand, and would have been more so had not the wood-cutter been hurried into omitting the backgrounds in the later cuts, those to the " Pars aestiualis." Sensenschmidt also printed an undated German Bible with pictorial capitals.

In 1477 Creussner issued the travels of Marco Polo with a woodcut of the traveller, and about the same time Latin and German editions of the tract of Tuberinus on the supposed fate suffered by "Das Kind Simon" at the hand of the Jews.

In 1481 Anton Koberger published his first illustrated book, *Postilla super Bibliam* of Nicolaus de Lyra, with forty-three woodcuts, which were imitated not only at Cologne, but at Venice, though their interest is not very great. In his German Bible of 1483 he himself was

108

content to acquire blocks previously used at Cologne. The next year he prefixed to his edition of the *Reformation der Stadt Nuremberg* a notable woodcut of S. Sebald and S. Laurence in the style of Michael Wolgemut. The 252 cuts in his *Heiligenleben* of 1488 are mainly improved rehandlings of previous versions; of his *Schatzbehalter* and Schedel's Chronicle we speak later on.

At Basel Martin Flach was the first printer of illustrated books, ornamenting his 1473 edition of the Ackermann von Böhmen with a woodcut of Death, the labourer, and the dead woman, his *Cato* with the usual picture of a master and scholar, his *Rosenkranz* with a cut of a traveller beseeching the Virgin's protection from robbers, and another of a scene in heaven, and his *Streit der Seele mit dem Korper* (these and the two preceding are undated) with eight illustrations of various moments in the dispute. More important than these are three profusely illustrated books from the press of Bernhard Richel. The first of these, his 1476 *Spiegel Menschlicher Behaltnis*, has 278 woodcuts, the work of two different hands, the earlier of the two showing less technical skill, but much more vigour and originality.[1] The other two books are undated editions of the romance of *Melusina*, with sixty-seven cuts, in which suggestions from the first Augsburg edition have been improved on by an abler workman, and a *Mandeville* with 147 cuts, most of which passed into the hands of M. Hupfuff at Strassburg, who used them in 1501. After this Richel turned his attention to liturgies, and is credited by Dr. Schreiber with being the first printer to insert in his Missals the woodcut of the Crucifixion, which thenceforth is so frequently found facing the first page of the Canon.

After the publication of these works illustration seems to have languished for some years at Basel, but was

---

[1] A set of proofs of cuts to this book, previously in the possession of the Marquis of Blandford and Mr. Perkins, was among the favourite possessions of William Morris, and is now owned by Mr. Morgan. An illustrated *Plenarium*, assigned by Dr. Copinger to Richel, appears to be a "ghost," due to some confusion with this *Spiegel*.

taken up again about 1489 by Johann von Amerbach, Lien-
hart Ysenhut, and Michael Furter, the work of the two
latter being mainly imitative. Johann Froben, who
began work about this time, was too learned a publisher
to concern himself with woodcuts, catering chiefly for
students of the University. One of the professors, however, at the University was far from sharing this indifference to pictures. Born at Strassburg, Sebastian
Brant was educated at Basel, and it was while holding
there the Professorship of Laws that he ensured the
popularity of his *Narrenschiff* (1494) by equipping it
with 115 admirable illustrations. The original edition
from the press of Johann Bergmann von Olpe was published in February, and before the end of the year Peter
Wagner at Nuremberg, Greyff at Reutlingen, Schoensperger at Augsburg had all pirated it with copies of
the Basel cuts. When the Latin translation by Brant's
friend, Jakob Locher, was published by Bergmann in
1497, the success of the book became European, and
probably no other illustrated work of the fifteenth
century is so well known.

Probably in the same year as the *Narrenschiff* was
first issued, Bergmann printed for Brant his *In laudem
gloriosae virginis Mariae*, with sixteen woodcuts by the
same hand. In 1495 Brant supplied him with two works
in honour of the Emperor Maximilian, one celebrating
the alliance with Pope Alexander VI, illustrated with
coats of arms, the other the *Origo bonorum regum*, with
two woodcuts, in which the Emperor is shown receiving
a sword from heaven. Brant was now in high favour
with Maximilian, and his appointment as a Syndic and
Imperial Chancellor at Strassburg led to his return and
a consequent notable quickening of book-illustration in
his native city.

At Strassburg Johann Mentelin had used woodcuts
for diagrams in an undated edition of the *Etymo-
logiae* of S. Isidore, printed about 1473, but the first
producer of books pictorially illustrated was Heinrich

Knoblochtzer, who worked from 1476 to 1484, and issued over thirty books with woodcuts. Most of these were copies from other men's work, e.g. his *Belial* and *Melusina* from Bämler's, his *Philalethes* from the Nuremberg edition of Johann Müller, his *Aesop* and *Historie der Sigismunda* from Johann Zainer's, his *Leben der heiligen drei Königen* probably from an anonymous edition by Johann Prüss. Early in his career in 1477 he issued two books on the great subject of the hour, the death of Charles the Bold, *Peter Hagenbach und der Burgundische Krieg* and the *Burgunderkrieg* of Erhard Tusch, in both of which he used eight woodcuts, most of them devoted to incidents of the Duke's ill-fated campaign. An anonymous edition of the *Euryalus und Lucretia* of Aeneas Sylvius (Pope Pius II) has nineteen cuts, which were apparently commissioned by Knoblochtzer, but he did not secure the services of a sufficiently skilled woodcutter. It should be said, however, that his "historiated" or pictorial capitals are apparently original and mostly good.

To Johann Prüss at Strassburg are now assigned editions in High and Low German of the Lives of the Fathers and of Antichrist, which Mr. Proctor, though he had a shrewd suspicion of their origin, left floating about among the German " adespota." The cuts to the former reach the average of early work ; those to the *Antichrist* vary greatly, that of Antichrist preaching before a queen being extraordinarily successful as a presentation of a type of coarse spiritual effrontery. The acknowledged work of Prüss includes editions of the travels of *Mandeville*, of the *Directorium Humanae Vitae*, and of the *Flores Musicae* of Hugo Reutlingensis, with a rather famous cut showing how musical notes are produced by the wind, by a water wheel, by tapping stones, and hammering on an anvil. Prüss also printed several illustrated editions of the *Hortus Sanitatis*.

Far more prolific than either of the foregoing Strassburg printers was Johann Reinhard of Grüningen, usually called Grüninger after his birthplace. Setting up his press in 1483, he began book-illustration two years later with a German Bible with woodcuts copied from those in the Low German Bibles printed at Cologne and used in 1483 at Nuremberg by Koberger. Some minor books followed, and in 1491 he issued the *Antidotarius Animae* of Nicolaus de Saliceto, with rather rude borders to each page and a woodcut of the Assumption. This, however, like some of his earlier illustrated books, appears to have been a commission, and in a reprint of 1493 the decorations disappear. It was not until 1496, under the influence of Sebastian Brant, that he undertook any important original illustrated work on his own account. In that year he produced his first illustrated classic, the comedies of Terence (*Terentius cum directorio*), with a large woodcut of a theatre and eighty-seven narrow cuts of the dramatis personae, or of scenery, used five at a time in 150 different combinations. Critically examined, the cuts are rather unpleasing, and were regarded at the time as likely to provoke mirth otherwise than by expressing the humorous intent of the playwright, but another edition and a German translation similarly decorated appeared in 1499, and Grüninger issued on the same plan a *Horace* (edited by Locher) in 1498, and the *De consolatione philosophiae* of Boethius in 1501. His full strength was reserved for the *Virgil* of the following year, which was superintended by Brant, and is crowded with wonderful pictures, in which on the very eve of the Renaissance Virgil is thoroughly medievalized. Besides these classics, Grüninger printed many other illustrated editions, minor works by Brant, medical treatises by Brunschwig, an *Evangelienbuch*, a *Legenda S. Katherinae* in Latin and also in German, editions of the *Hortulus Animae*, the romance of Hug Schapler, etc., in the fifteenth century, and in the sixteenth a sufficient number of illustrated books to bring his total up to about 150 editions. These may be said to form a school by themselves, distinguished by a certain richness of effect partly due to heavy cutting, but with less power of characterization and fewer gleams of beauty than are to be found in the best work of other towns, the figures being often unpleasing and notably lean in the legs. Martin Scott, Hupfuff, and Kistler were other Strassburg printers of the fifteenth century who also used illustrations.

At Cologne book-illustration began in 1474 with editions of the *Fasciculus Temporum* of Werner Role-winck, from the presses of ther Hoernen and Nicolaus Götz. But with the notable exception of two great Bibles issued by Heinrich Quentell, illustrated books before 1490 are neither important nor numerous. Even in 1490 the edition of the *Historia Septem Sapientum* of Johannes de Hauteselve, issued by the elder Koelhoff, was adorned with cuts obtained from Gerard Leeu at Antwerp. Quentell issued a few stock cuts in one book after another, and Johann Landen, Martin von Werden (if he be rightly identified with the printer "Retro Minores"), and Cornelis von Zierickzee all used a few cuts, some of the latter's having a curiously Italian appearance. But the only important illustrated book, other than the Bibles, is the Cologne Chronicle, issued (not to his profit, since he was imprisoned for it) by the younger Koelhoff in 1499, with armorial cuts and a few pictures of kings and queens somewhat too frequently repeated. Quentell's Bibles in High and Low German are in curious contrast to all this work. They are illustrated with 125 large oblong pictures, firmly if rather coarsely cut, and full of story-telling power, several successive incidents being sometimes brought into the same picture in true medieval fashion. The book was imitated at Nuremberg and elsewhere, and the illustrators of the Venetian Malermi Bible of 1490, and even Hans Holbein himself, did not disdain to take ideas from it.

At Lübeck a finely decorated edition of the *Rudi-mentum Noviciorum*, a universal history, was issued by

Lucas Brandis as early as 1475, with some good pictorial capitals, and pictures beginning with the Creation and coming down to the life of Christ. In 1484 we come to a *Levend S. Jeronimi*, printed by Bartholomaeus Ghotan and illustrated by an anonymous artist whose work can be traced during the next ten years in other books of Ghotan's, in several very interesting editions by the unidentified "Poppy-Printer" (so called from his mark), including a *Dodendantz* (1489 and 1496), *Imitatio Christi*, *Bergitten Openbaringe* (1496), *Reynke de Vos* (1498), *Schakspil*, etc., and in the splendid Low German Bible printed in 1494 by Stephan Arndes, with cuts which improve on those in the Cologne editions.

At Mainz, which led the way so energetically in typography, book-illustration is not represented at all until 1479, and then almost accidentally in the *Meditationes* of Cardinal Turrecremata, printed by Johann Neumeister "ciuem Moguntinensem," with thirty-four curious metal-cuts imitating on a smaller scale the woodcuts in the editions printed at Rome by Ulrich Han. Two years later these metal-cuts were used by Neumeister at Albi, and they are subsequently found at Lyon. That this book was printed at Mainz was made practically certain by the type appearing subsequently in the possession of Peter von Friedberg, but that the cuts were executed at Mainz seemed to me improbable until the publication of Dr. Schreiber's work on German illustrated books acquainted me with the existence of an *Agenda Moguntinensis* of 29 June, 1480, also attributed to Neumeister's press, with a metal-cut of S. Martin and the beggar, and the arms not only of Archbishop Diether and the province of Mainz, but of Canon Bernhard von Breidenbach, of whom we shall soon hear again. The *Agenda* and its metal-cuts are thus firmly fixed as executed at Mainz, and the metal-cuts of the *Meditationes* must therefore be regarded as Mainz work also.

In 1486 Mainz atoned for her long delay in taking up

IX. MAINZ, ERHARD REUWICH, 1486

BREIDENBACH. PEREGRINATIO IN MONTEM SYON

SARACENS AND SYRIANS

illustrated work, with the *Peregrinationes in Montem Syon* of the aforesaid Canon Bernhard von Breidenbach, printed with type of Schoeffer's, under the superintendence of Erhard Reuwich of Utrecht, the illustrator. The text of Breidenbach's book is full of interest, for he gives a vivid account of the voyage and of the hardships and extortions to which pilgrims were exposed. In his preface he states that Reuwich was expressly taken on the expedition to illustrate the narrative, and he certainly had ample skill to justify the engagement. Unfortunately, far too much of his labour was spent on great maps or views of Venice, Parenzo, Rhodes and other places passed on the way. These are certainly interesting, as they mark all the chief buildings and are very decoratively drawn. But in the text of the book there are just a few sketches from the life, Jewish moneylenders and groups of Saracens, Syrians (see Plate IX), Indians, etc., and these are so vivid and vigorous that we may well regret that the labour bestowed on the great maps left time for very few of them. They are interesting, moreover, not only as designs, but also for their cutting, as they introduce cross-hatching for the first time, and that very effectively, and are handled with equal firmness and freedom. At the end of the book is a jest, a full-page woodcut subscribed " Hec sunt animalia veraciter depicta sicut vidimus in terra sancta," among the animals thus certified as having been seen personally in the Holy Land being a unicorn and a creature (name unknown— *non constat de nomine*) with a great mane of hair and long tail, which might well serve for the missing link between a man and a gorilla. The frontispiece of the book, on the other hand, is a striking design of a woman (symbolizing the city of Mainz?) standing on a pedestal surrounded with the arms of Breidenbach and the two friends who went with him, decoratively treated, while above her is a canopy of trelliswork amid which children are joyously climbing. With the Mainz *Breidenbach* we feel that we have passed away from the naive craftsmanship of the earliest illustrated books into a region of conscious art.

Naturally craftsmanship was not extinguished by the arrival of a single artist. We find it at work again in the charming and little known cut to a Leipzig edition of the Eclogues of Theodulus, printed in 1491, which the delight of recent discovery tempts me to show here (see Plate X), and at Mainz itself in the simple cuts to the *Hortus Sanitatis*, printed by Meidenbach, also in 1491, though here again there is an advance, as instead of plants and animals drawn out of the illustrator's head merely for decorative effect we find in many of the cuts fairly careful copies made from the life.

In Conrad Botho's *Cronecken der Sassen*, printed by Schoeffer the following year, most of the armorial illustrations and pictures of the foundation of towns are merely decoratively treated, but in one cut in which a rather wild-looking Charlemagne with lean legs is shown seated in a chair of state surmounted by an eagle, an idol crushed under his feet, the designer has given free play to his imagination.

The transition to different ideals of illustration thus begun at Mainz was carried on at Nuremberg, where Michael Wolgemut illustrated two important works, the *Schatzbehalter* in 1491 and the famous *Nuremberg Chronicle* in 1493, this latter with the help of his stepson, Wilhelm Pleydenwurff, and no doubt also of several inferior designers. The *Schatzbehalter*, of which the text is ascribed to Stephanus Fridelinus, a Nuremberg Franciscan, is one of several examples of a too ambitious scheme of decoration perforce abandoned for lack either of time or of money. In the first half there are ninety-two different full-page woodcuts, mostly illustrating Scripture history, but in some cases allegorical; in the second half the number is no more than two. The pictures executed before the scheme was thus cut down vary greatly in quality, from the fine design of Christ kneeling before the throne of the Father and pointing to the emblems

X. LEIPZIG, CONRAD KACHELOFEN, 1489

THEODULUS. EGLOGA (1^b)

of the Passion, which prepares us for the work which Dürer, who was then being trained in Wolgemut's studio, was soon to execute, down to the amusing but uninspired craftsmanship of the picture of Solomon and a selection of his wives banqueting. For the *Liber Chronicarum* of Hartman Schedel plans had been much more carefully worked out than for the *Schatzbehalter*, and by studying economy a seemingly profuse system of illustration was maintained to the end. The industry of Mr. Sydney Cockerell has evolved for us the exact figures as to the illustration of this book. Real liberality is shown in the large, double-page topographical cuts of twenty-six different cities, for many of which sketches must have been specially obtained, and not one of these is used a second time ; but twenty-two other large cuts of cities and countries were made to serve for sixty-nine different subjects, and when we come to figures of emperors, kings, and popes we find ninety-six blocks used 598 times, or on an average half a dozen times apiece. Mr. Cockerell's grand totals are 1809 pictures printed from 645 different blocks, so that the repetitions number no fewer than 1164. Both in the designs and their execution there is great inequality, but no single picture can compare with that of Christ kneeling before the Father in the *Schatzbehalter*, and both books, fine as their best work is, must be regarded rather as the crown of German medieval craftsmanship in book-building than as belonging to the period of self-conscious artistic aim which is heralded by the Mainz *Breidenbach* but really begins with Dürer.

With this Nuremberg work we may perhaps class that in the one book printed at the Cistercian monastery at Zinna, near Magdeburg, the *Psalterium Beatae Mariae Virginis*, of Hermann Nitschewitz, the most richly decorated German book of the fifteenth century, executed in honour of the Emperor Frederick and his son Maximilian, who in the page here shown (Plate XI) are both represented.

Primitive Dutch and Flemish book-illustrations when

compared with German ones exhibit just the general likeness and specific differences which we might expect in the work of such near neighbours. The Low Country wood-cutters are on the whole more decorative than the Germans, they were more influenced by the work of the engravers on copper, and they were attracted by different types of the human figure, the faces and bodies of the men and women they drew being often long and thin, and often also showing a slightly fantastic touch rarely found in German work. Unfortunately, these Low Country illustrated books are even rarer than the German ones, far fewer of them have found their way to England, and no attempt has been made to reproduce a really representative selection of them in facsimile. In 1884 Sir W. M. Conway, as the result of prolonged studies on the Continent, wrote an excellent account of these illustrations and the makers of them under the title, *The Woodcutters of the Netherlands in the Fifteenth Century*, which was unhappily allowed to appear without any facsimiles to elucidate the text. Thus the study of these Low Country illustrated books is still difficult.

In the production of the early block-books (see Chapter II) the Low Countries had played a principal part, and we meet again with traces of them in later illustrated books, cuts from the *Biblia Pauperum* being used by Peter van Os at Zwolle in his *Episteln ende Evangelien* of 5 January, 1487, and one from the *Canticum Canticorum* in his edition of Mauberne's *Rosetum Exercitiorum Spiritualium* in 1494. Two cut-up pieces from the block-book *Speculum Humanae Saluationis* were used by Veldener in his *Episteln ende Evangelien* completed at Utrecht 19 April, 1481, and all the old blocks, each divided in two, in a new edition of the *Speculum* printed at Kuilenburg 27 September, 1483, with twelve new cuts added to them. Sir W. M. Conway has also shown that a set of sixty-four cuts used in a *Boec van der Houte* or Legend of the Holy Cross, issued by Veldener at Kuilenburg earlier in 1483 (on 6 March), must have

Dic imperialibus vt diligāt vginem mariam iūsticiā & iudicium quia ꝓpter
iniusticias et i nurias er ꝓtumelias regnū de gente in gentē tāsfert Ecci x.
Hec imperator fridericus tercius.

XI. ZINNA, MONASTERIUM CISTERCIENSE, c. 1493

NITSCHEWITZ. PSALTERIUM BEATAE MARIAE VIRGINIS

FREDERICK AND MAXIMILIAN

been obtained by dividing in a similar manner the double cuts of a block-book now entirely lost.

The first printer in the Low Countries who commissioned a woodcut for a book printed with movable type was Johann of Paderborn (John of Westphalia) at Louvain, the cut being a curious little representation of his own head, shown in white on a black oval. This he used in his *Institutiones* of Justinian of 21 November, 1475, and a few other books, and a similar but even better likeness of his kinsman, Conrad, appeared the next year in the *Formulae Epistularum* of Maneken (1 December, 1476). Although Johann of Paderborn thus led the way in the use of cuts, he only resorted to them subsequently for a few diagrams, and towards the end of his career for some half-dozen miscellaneous blocks for devotional books.

The portrait of Johann of Paderborn being used only as a device, book-illustration begins, though on a very small scale, with Veldener's edition of the *Fasciculus Temporum* (29 December, 1475), with its handful of poor little cuts modelled on those of the Cologne editions. Five years later Veldener reprinted the *Fasciculus* with a few new cuts, the originals of which have been found in the Lübeck *Rudimentum Noviciorum*. The only picture which seems to have been specially designed for him was a folio cut in his *Passionael* (Utrecht, 12 September, 1480), where in delicate simple outline a variety of martyrdoms are shown as taking place in the hollows of a series of hills. Mention has already been made of his two Kuilenburg reprints of block-books. In the same place he issued Dutch and Latin Herbals with cuts copied from Schoeffer's Mainz *Herbarius*, and this completes the story of his illustrated ventures.

We come now to Gerard Leeu, who on 3 June, 1480, issued at Gouda the first completely illustrated book from a Dutch press, the *Dialogus creaturarum moralisatus*, a glorified version of the old bestiaries, full of wonderful stories of animals. This was illustrated with 121 specially designed cuts (mostly about four inches by two), and Leeu's liberality was rewarded by the book passing through nine editions, six in Latin and three in Dutch, in eleven years. The first page is decorated with a picture of the Sun and Moon, a large capital, and an ornamental border of foliage, but the merit of the book lies in the simple skill with which the craftsman, working entirely in outline, has reproduced the humour of the text. To the same hand are attributed ten cuts for Leeu's vernacular *Gesta Romanorum* (30 April, 1481), four for an undated *Historia Septem Sapientum*, and four others, of the Four Last Things, which, to our puzzlement, appear first in a French edition printed by Arend de Keysere at Audenarde, and then (23 August, 1482) in a Dutch one of Leeu's. In the previous month he had brought out a *Liden ende passie ons Heeren* with thirty-two quarto cuts, part of a set of sixty-eight made for editions of the *Devote Ghetiden* or Dutch version of the *Horae*, the first of which (unless a Gouda one has perished) appeared after his removal to Antwerp. During the following nine years he made good use of his old blocks. For his Dutch *Aesop* of October, 1485, and Latin edition of September, 1486, he used cuts copied from the original Ulm and Augsburg set. These he bought from Knoblochtzer of Strassburg and sold to Koelhoff of Cologne. In 1487 he issued an illustrated *Reynard the Fox*, of which only a fragment survives, and the pleasant romance of *Paris and Vienne*, with twenty-five fairly successful cuts, with the help of which five editions were sold, the first in French, the next three in Dutch, and the last (23 June, 1492) in English. According to Sir W. M. Conway these *Paris and Vienne* cuts were the work of a Haarlem craftsman, who from 1483 to 1486 had worked for Jacob Bellaert, whose press was intimately connected with Leeu's, type and cuts passing freely from one to the other. Bellaert had begun by using some of Leeu's Passion cuts for a *Liden ons Heeren*, but seems soon to have discovered his Haarlem wood-cutter, with whose aid

willich wt nijt vandē iuedē is pijlato den president geuangē doer valsche
lijffelicke getuijgenisse gecrupst handē eñ voete doer nagelt vptē vijfthiē
stē dach in maerte veroerdelt eñ indē cruce gehangē voir ons sondarē mit
luijder stemmē help help sijnē geest geuēde eñ achterliet sijn doode lichaē
der aerden te begrauen ghelijc hij in sijn leuen voirseit hadde ende als de
waerheijt der ewangelien dat volcomelic tuijghen

Nde is mit groter gloriē als bwinder der tijttelicker doot mit dē
vaē der victoriē iu sijn hant houdēde ter stont neb gedaelt ter hel
lē die hij mit sijnre godlicker schijnsel omschenē heeft roupēde tot dē prin
cē der hellē mit sijnre soeter stēme seggēde o ghi princē ondoet v poertē eñ
daer sal ingaē de coninc der gloriē Tot welcke roepige de princē der hellē
mit bwonderige bwaert sijnēde antwoirdē wt dē hellē seggende wie is dese
conic der gloriē. hij antwoirde conic heer starc eñ mogēde idē strijde waer
bij dese princē der hellē onderlinge sprakē wie dese conic der gloriē wesen
mocht dus starc eñ machtich. eñ bwonderdē hē seer wāt sij nije soe starckē
dode eñ vreselic mit soe groter cracht eñ mogentheit ter hellē gecomē en
was eñ slotē de poertē mnerē eñ torrē vaster dā sij gewoē warē. dit deheer
siende seijde anderwerf tot dē princē der hellen ondoet v poertē ꝯ. Eñ sij
dat weijgerēde mair meer haer poertē slotē. seidē wie is dese coninck der

a iiij

he produced (15 February, 1484) *Der Sonderen troest*, The Sinners' Trust, a Dutch version of that remarkable work the *Belial* or *Consolatio peccatorum* of Jacobus de Theramo, of which the Augsburg edition has already been mentioned. This begins with a full folio-page cut combining in one panorama the Fall of Angels and of Adam and Eve, the Flood, the Egyptians overtaken in the Red Sea, and the Baptism of Christ. Six of the other cuts fill half-pages and show the Harrowing of Hell (here reproduced, Plate XII), Devils in consultation, Satan kneeling before the Lord, the Last Judgment, Ascension and Descent of the Holy Spirit. The remaining half-page pictures are all composite, made up of different combinations of eight centre-pieces and seventeen side-pieces. The centre-pieces for the most part represent the different judges before whom the trials are heard, the side-pieces the messengers and parties to the suit. The combinations are occasionally a little clumsy, but far less so than in the Strassburg books printed by Grüninger in which the same labour-saving device was adopted, and in excellence of design and delicacy of cutting this Dutch *Belial* ranks high among illustrated incunabula.

Later in 1484 (25 October) Bellaert issued a *Boeck des Golden Throens* with four-column cuts, often repeated, of an Elder instructing a maiden ; in May, 1485, Le Fèvre's *Jason*, and a little earlier than this an undated edition of the same author's *Recueil des histoires de Troie*, both in Dutch and both profusely illustrated ; on Christmas Eve in the same year a Dutch *De proprietatibus rerum*, and in 1486 versions of Pierre Michault's *Doctrinal*, in which a dreamer is shown the schools of virtue and of vice, and of Guillaume de Deguilleville's *Pélérinage de la vie humaine*, the medieval prototype of Bunyan's *Pilgrim's Progress*. The *De proprietatibus* is the only one of these books of 1485-6 that I have seen, and its full-page cuts are notable both for their own sake and as having been widely copied, although they illustrate only eleven of the nineteen books.

No other Low Country printer showed anything like the enterprise of Leeu and Bellaert in commissioning long sets of original woodcuts from competent craftsmen, but several fine illustrated books were produced by other firms. Beginning in 1484 Peter van Os printed numerous illustrated books at Zwolle, few of which attain excellence. Yet one of the earliest of them, the Sermons of S. Bernard, has a frontispiece of the Virgin and Child and the Saint gazing at them which is unequalled by any other single cut in the Low Country book in its large pictorial effect. At Gouda, in 1486, Gottfried van Os issued the *Chevalier Délibéré* of Olivier de la Marche, with sixteen large cuts, in which the author's minute instructions for each picture are faithfully carried out with extraordinary freedom and spirit, though the ambitious designs are more suitable to frescoes than to book-illustrations. About the end of the century the book was reprinted at Schiedam with the same cuts, from which facsimiles were made in 1898 by Dr. Lippmann and published by the Bibliographical Society.

At Louvain in 1487 Egidius van der Heerstraten issued the *De praeclaris mulieribus* of Boccaccio with copies of the cuts of the Ulm edition of great interest for the differences in handling revealed when the two are compared. A little later than this another Louvain printer, Ludovicus de Ravescot, published the *De anno die et feria Dominicae Passionis* of Petrus de Rivo, with a title-cut of the author kneeling before the Virgin and Child, and three large cuts of the Last Supper, Crucifixion, and Resurrection, somewhat in the temper of the illustrations in the Cologne Bibles, but with characteristic Low Country touches. Lastly, mention must be made of the clumsy outline cuts in the Bruges edition of Ovid's *Metamorphoses*, issued in 1484 by Caxton's partner Colard Mansion. Mansion certainly, and possibly Caxton also, were among the early experimenters with copperplate illustration, but the story of these will be told in Chapter XV.

122

CHAPTER VIII

EARLY ITALIAN ILLUSTRATED BOOKS

AS a frontispiece to this chapter (Plate XIII) we give a page from the 1487 edition of the *Devote medita-tione sopra la Passione del Nostro Signore*, printed at Venice by " Jeronimo di Sancti e Cornelio suo Compagno," the woodcuts in which, as already mentioned, are cut down from those in a block-book of some twenty or five-and-twenty years earlier, and must thus rank as the earliest Italian illustrations. The illustration of books printed in movable type began in Italy as early as 1468, Ulrich Han issuing that year at Rome an edition of Cardinal Turrecremata's *Meditationes*, decorated with thirty-one rude cuts chiefly from the life of Christ. A few of these have a coarse vigour, but in the greater number any merit in the original designs (professedly taken from the frescoes with which the Cardinal had decorated the cloisters of the Church of Santa Maria sopra Minerva) is lost in bad cutting. Notwithstanding this the work went through at least three editions (three new pictures being added to the second and one omitted), and served as a model for the metal-cuts of Neumeister's editions at Mainz and elsewhere, and for the small neat woodcuts of one by Plannck. But though Han's venture was thus successful beyond its deserts, it took Italy nearly twenty years to make up its mind to welcome printed illustrations. During this time nothing approaching a style of book-illustration emerges, though individual books of import-ance appeared at several towns. Thus at Verona the *De re militari* of Robertus Valturius (written not later than 1468) was printed in 1472 by a certain Joannes of that city, with over eighty woodcuts of weapons and implements of war, including a galley which looks more picturesque than seaworthy, chariots, and mangonels, all well drawn and well cut, but a little spoilt by paper and presswork much less good than was usual at this time. Eleven years later Latin and Italian editions with practically the same cuts were printed, also at Verona, by Boninus de Boninis. The only other early Veronese book with illustrations is an Italian version of one of the medieval collections of fables which sought shelter under the name of Aesop. This, which has some spirited cuts, was printed by Giovanni Alvise in 1479.

At Naples, Sixtus Riessinger printed Boccaccio's *Libro di Florio et di Bianzefiore chiamato Filicolo* in 1478, and also (without date) an Italian version of Ovid's *Heroides*, both with numerous cuts, some of them by no means devoid of charm. In 1485 an illustrated *Aesop* was produced at the expense of a book-loving jurist, Francesco Tuppo, probably from the press of certain "fidelissimi Germani." The cuts in this, which are hard and heavy but of considerable merit (see Plate XIV), may possibly be due to a mixture of Italian and German influences, but are more probably the work of a Spanish wood-cutter. A picture of an astronomer engaged on his calculations found in the *Arte di Astrologia* of Granollachs, probably also printed in 1485, may be from the same hand. In the *Aesop* each picture is placed in an architectural frame, in the upper sections of which there are representations sometimes of Hercules and a lion, sometimes of his wrestle with Antaeus, sometimes of a battle of mounted pygmies. The first page of text also has a fine decorative border, the design being in white on a black ground.

At Florence an ornamental capital in a *Psalter* printed in 1489 is the earliest woodcut in any extant dated book. But engravings on copper had been employed as early as 1477 for three pictures in Bettini's *Monte Santo di Dio*, and in 1481 for nineteen in a *Divina*

XIII. VENICE, GERONIMO DI SANCTI, 1487

BONAVENTURA. MEDITATIONE (14^b REDUCED)

THE BETRAYAL

Commedia; as to these something will be said in Chapter XV.

Two books printed at Milan in 1479 contain illustrations, the *Summula di pacifica conscientia* of Fra Pacifico di Novara, being ornamented with three engravings; two of the degrees of consanguinity and the third of a crown bearing the names of the virtues of the Madonna, while the *Breuiarium totius juris canonici* of Paolo Attavanti printed by Pachel and Scinzenzeler has a little woodcut, which purports to be a portrait of the author.

In Venice book-illustration appears to have begun in the office not of a printer, but of an illuminator. Quite a number of books printed by various firms during the years 1470 to 1472 have a woodcut groundwork to their illuminated borders, and in the Spencer copy of the Italian Bible (Malermi's translation), printed in 1471 by Adam of Ammergau, the six miniatures of the Creation, with which the blanks left on leaves 11 and 12 are filled, have in the same way rough woodcuts beneath their colouring.[1] The workshop in which these decorated borders and miniatures were supplied seems to have closed or given up the practice in 1473, and until Erhard Ratdolt and his partners Löslein and Maler began publishing in 1476, no more woodcuts were produced at Venice. The work of the new firm was decorative rather than pictorial, consisting mainly of the fine borders and capital letters with which they ornamented their Calendars (1476, 1477, and 1482), their *Appian, Gesta Petri Mocenici* of Coriolanus Cepio and *De situ orbis* of Dionysius Periegetes, all in 1477, *Arte di ben morire* of the following year, and *Euclid* of 1482. With the exception of the earlier Calendars, where the borders to the titlepage (the first so decorated) are of flower-vases, these consist of highly conventionalized foliage (jasmine? vine, oak, etc.) or

---

[1] In the masterly work of the Prince d'Essling on *Les livres à figures Vénitiens*, the discovery of this interesting fact is inadvertently ascribed to Mr. Guppy, the present librarian of the John Rylands Library. It was made by his predecessor, Mr. Gordon Duff, a note by whom on the subject was quoted in my *Italian Book-Illustrations* (p. 18), published in 1894.

strapwork, some of them unequalled in their own kind until William Morris combined the same skill with a much bolder and richer treatment of his material. Illustration properly so called begins with Georg Walch's edition (1479) of the *Fasciculus Temporum*, a chronological epitome by Werner Rolewinck of Cologne. This has a quaint little view of the Piazza of San Marco and other pictures, which Ratdolt, not at all handsomely, proceeded to copy the next year. In 1481 Ratdolt adorned the *Tractatus de Actionibus* of Baptista de Sancto Blasio with rather a graceful little figure of a woman holding the stem of a tree. In 1482 he produced an edition of the *Poeticon Astronomicon* of Hyginus with some figures of the planets which, rude as they were, served as models for many subsequent editions. In the same year the *Oratoriae artis epitomata* of Jacobus Publicius was ornamented with some figures including a chessboard, cut in white on black, designed to assist the memory.

In the later years of his stay at Venice, Ratdolt seems to have lost interest in book-decoration, but the popularity of woodcuts steadily increased throughout the 'eighties, and by the end of the decade was in full tide. In 1484 Bernardinus Benalius gave some rough illustrations to the *Fioretti* of Saint Francis; in 1486 Pietro Cremonese bestowed a formal but quite interesting decorated title-page on the *Doctrinale* of Alexander Gallus, with the title inscribed in a cartouche, above which rise an urn and lamps. In the same year we have in the *Supplementum Chronicarum* printed by Bernardinus Benalius a few cuts of some size "translated" into an Italian style from those on the same subject in Quentell's Cologne Bible (*c.* 1480), also a little view of Venice copied in reverse from the *Fasciculus Temporum*. The *Supplementum Chronicarum* was re-issued several times (the author, Jacobus Philippus Bergomensis, bringing the statement of his age up to date in each edition which he revised), and changes were constantly made in the cuts. In 1486 also

126

APOLOGVS.

Inge la fabula presente la uita & le costume qual camino se a de sequire
& quale se a de fugire. Li homini de A&ene che erano in liberta & loro
da per se se faceano le legi desiderosi de hauere Re dispiacendole la loro

p

came an edition of the *Libro de la divina lege* of Marco del Monte S. Maria, with cuts of Mount Sinai and its desert, notable as having been copied by a much more skilful wood-cutter at Florence eight years later ; 1487 produced the first of the Venetian illustrated *Aesops*, the cuts having borders of white scroll-work on a black ground and being influenced by the Naples edition of 1485. With this must be mentioned a *Fior di virtu*, with a title cut of a Friar plucking blossoms from a tree, which was thought good enough to be copied at Milan, but was replaced at Venice three years later by a delightful picture of a walled garden. It was in 1487 also that there appeared the edition of the *Devote Meditatione sopra la Passione*, with cuts taken from the old blockbook (see p. 123). In subsequent editions (of 1489, etc.) these were replaced by new woodcuts of varying merit. A later edition still (1500) has a fine picture of the Entry into Jerusalem which Prince d'Essling connects with the *Hypnerotomachia* of 1499. In 1488 we come to the first illustrated edition of the *Trionfi* of Petrarch, printed by Bernardino de Novara. This has six large cuts, showing respectively the triumphs of Love, of Chastity, Death, Fame, Time, and the Divinity. All are well designed, but spoilt by weak cutting. In the same year appeared two other illustrated books, a *Sphaera Mundi*, with a few cuts not in themselves of great importance, and the *De Essent et Essenta* of S. Thomas Aquinas, with a striking little picture of a child lighting a fire by means of a burning-glass. By studying these books in conjunction Prince d'Essling has shown that they were designed by one of their printers, Johann Santritter, and executed by the other, Hieronymus de Sanctis, and that to the latter may thus be attributed the illustrations (one at least of them of unusual beauty) in an *Officium Beatae Virginis* which issued from his press 26 April, 1494.

The information on the last two pages is all epitomized from the Prince d'Essling's great work *Les livres à figures Vénitiens* (1907, etc.), and is quoted here in some detail as showing that from the time of Erhard Ratdolt onwards book-illustrations are found with some frequency at Venice, a fact for which, until the Prince published the results of his unwearying researches, there was very little evidence available.

The event of 1490 was the publication by Lucantonio Giunta of an edition of Niccolo Malermi's Italian version of the Bible, illustrated with 384 cuts, many of them charming, measuring about three inches by two. The success of this set a fashion, and several important folio books in double columns similarly illustrated appeared during the next few years, a *Vite di Sancti Padre* in 1491, Boccaccio's *Decamerone*, Masuccio's *Novellino*, and a *Legendario* translated from the Latin of Jacobus de Voragine in 1492, a rival Italian Bible and an Italian Livy in 1493, a *Morgante Maggiore* in 1494, and an Italian *Terence* in 1497, while in quarto we have a *Miracoli de la Madonna* (1491), *Vita de la Vergine* and *Trabisonda Istoriata* (1492), *Guerrino Meschino* (1493), and several others. In some of these books cuts are found signed with F, in others with N, in others with i or ia; in the Malermi Bible and some other books we sometimes find the signature b or .b. Such signatures, which at one time aroused keen controversy, are now believed to have belonged not to the designer, but to the workshop of the wood-cutters by whom the blocks were cut. In the case of the Malermi Bible of 1490 workmen of very varying skill were employed, some of the illustrations to the Gospels being emptied of all delight by the rudeness of their cutting. Where the designer and the cutter are both at their best the result is nearly perfect of its kind, and it is curious to think that some of these dainty little blocks were imitated from the large, heavy woodcuts in the Cologne Bibles printed by Quentell some ten years earlier. In the rival Bible of 1493 the best cuts are not so good, nor the worst so bad as in the original edition of 1490. In the other books (I have not seen the Masuccio) the cutting is again more even, but the designs, though often charming and sometimes amusing, are seldom as good as the best in the Bible. Most of these books have one or more larger cuts used at the beginning of the text or of sections of it, and these are always good.

Two editions of Dante's *Divina Commedia*, both published in 1491, one by Bernardinus Benalius and Matheo Codeca in March, the other by Pietro Cremonese in November, must be grouped with the books just mentioned, as they are also illustrated with small cuts (though those in the November edition are a good deal larger than the usual column-cuts), and these are signed in some cases with the letter .b. which appears in the Malermi Bible of 1490. Neither designer has triumphed over the monotonous effect produced by the continual reappearance of the figures of Dante and his guide, and the little cuts in the March edition are far from impressive. On the other hand it has a good frontispiece, in which, after the medieval habit, the successive incidents of the first canto of the *Inferno* are all crowded into the same picture.

Popular as were the little vignettes, they were far from exhausting the energies of the Venetian illustrators of this decade. At the opposite pole from them are the four full-page pictures in the 1493 and later editions of the *Fascicolo de Medicina* of Joannes Ketham. These represent a physician lecturing, a consultation, a dissection, and a visit of a doctor to an infectious patient, whom he views by the light of two flambeaux held by pages, while he smells his pouncet-box. This picture (in the foreground of which sits a cat, afterwards cut out to reduce the size of the block) is perhaps the finest of the four, but that of the Dissection has the interest of being printed in several colours. Erhard Ratdolt had made some experiments in colour-printing in the astronomical books which he printed at Venice, and at Augsburg completed the crucifixion cut in some of his missals partly by printed colours, partly by hand. In 1490 a Venetian printer, Johann Herzog, had illustrated the

De Heredibus of Johannes Crispus de Montibus with a genealogical tree growing out of a recumbent human figure, and had printed this in brown, green, and red. But the dissection in the *Fascicolo di Medicina* was the most elaborate of the Venetian experiments in colour-printing and apparently also the last.

With the illustrations to the Ketham may be mentioned for its large pictorial effect, though it comes in a quarto, the fine cut of the author in the *Doctrina della vita monastica* of San Lorenzo Giustiniano, first patriarch of Venice. The figure of San Lorenzo as he walks with a book under his arm and a hand held up in benediction is imitated from that in a picture by Gentile Bellini, but he is here shown (Plate XV) preceded by a charming little crucifer, whose childish face enhances by contrast the austerer benignity of the saint.

However good the large illustrations in Venetian books, the merits of them are rather those of single prints than of really appropriate bookwork. The little column-cuts, on the other hand, are almost playful in their minuteness, and even when most successful produce the effect of a delightful border or tailpiece without quite attaining to the full possibilities of book-illustration. The feverish production of these column-cuts began to slacken, though it did not cease, in 1493, and about that date a few charming full-page pictures are found at the beginning and end of various small quartos. From the treatment of the man's hair and beard it is clear that the delightful frontispiece to the *Fioretti della Biblia* of 1493 (Prince d'Essling, I, 161) was the work of the illustrator of the second Malermi Bible from which the small cuts in the text are taken. The three cuts to the *Fioretti* of S. Francis, completed 11 June in the same year, that of the *Chome l'angelo amaestra l'anima* of Pietro Damiani, dated in the following November, of an undated *Monte de la Oratione*, and again of the *De la confessione* of S. Bernardino of Siena, all in the same style, form a group of singular beauty (see Prince d'Essling, I, 284

XV. VENICE, ANONYMOUS PRESS, 1494

LORENZO GIUSTINIANO. DELLA VITA RELIGIOSA

PORTRAIT OF THE AUTHOR

sqq.; II, 191, 194, 195). Those of S. Catherine's *Dialogo de la divina providentia*, 17 May, 1494 (D'Essling, II, 199 *sqq.*), were probably no less happily designed, but have lost more in their cutting, and with these must be grouped the picture of a Venetian school in the *Regulae Sypontinae* of Nicolaus Perottus, 29 March, 1492 (D'Essling, II, 86), used also in the *De Structura Compositionis* of Nicolaus Ferettus, printed three years later at Forlì. The style is continued in the *Specchio della fede* of Robertus Caracciolus, 11 April, 1495 (D'Essling, II, 260), in the headpiece of the *Commentaria in libros Aristotelis* of S. Thomas Aquinas, 28 Sept., 1496, and in the two admirable pictures of Terence lecturing to his commentators, and of a theatre as seen from the back of the stage, found in the *Terentius cum tribus commentariis* of July, 1497 (D'Essling, II, 295, and 277 *sqq.*). Still in the same style, but carelessly designed and poorly cut, are the illustrations to the well-known Ovid of April, 1497 (D'Essling, III, 220 *sqq.*), and this leads us on to the still more famous *Hypnerotomachia Poliphili* of Francesco Colonna, printed by Aldus for Leonardo Crassus, a jurisconsult, in December, 1499, and finally to the cut of Christ entering Jerusalem in the *Devote Meditatione* of the following April (D'Essling, I, 372), where the hand of the artist of the *Hypnerotomachia* is clearly visible, though he has surrounded his picture with a frame in the Florentine manner, which was then beginning to make its influence felt at Venice.

The primacy usually given to the *Hypnerotomachia* among all these books is probably in part due to considerations which have little to do with its artistic merit. The story is a kind of archaeological romance which appealed greatly to the dilettante, for whose benefit Leonardo Crassus commissioned Aldus to print it, but which was far from exciting the popular interest which shows its appreciation for a book by thumbing it out of existence. The *Hypnerotomachia* is probably almost as common a book as the *Nuremberg Chronicle* or the

First Folio Shakespeare, and thus its merits have become known to all lovers of old books. It is impressive, moreover, from its size and the profusion of its 168 illustrations of various sizes, while the extraordinary variety of these and the excellence of their cutting are further points in its favour. The initial letters of the successive chapters form the sentence POLIAM FRATER FRANCISCUS COLVMNA PERAMAVIT, and this with the colophon assigning the completion of the book to May-Day, 1467, at Treviso, reveals the author as Francesco Colonna, a Dominican, who had taught rhetoric at Treviso and Padua, and in 1499, when his book was printed, was still alive and an inmate of the convent of SS. Giovanni and Paolo at Venice. The Polia whom he so greatly loved has been identified with Lucretia Lelio, daughter of a jurisconsult at Treviso.

The story of the *Hypnerotomachia*, or " Strife of Love in a Dream," as its English translator called it, is greatly influenced by the Renaissance interest in antique architecture and art which is evident in so many of its illustrations. Polifilo's dreams are full, as the preface-writer says, of " molte cose antiquarie digne di memoria, & tutto quello lui dice hauere visto di puncto in puncto & per proprii uocabuli ello descriue cum elegante stilo, pyramidi, obelisce, ruine maxime di edificii, la differentia di columne, la sua mensura, gli capitelli, base, epistyli," etc. etc. But he is brought also to the palace of Queen Eleuterylida, and while there witnesses the triumphs or festivals of Europa, Leda, Danae, Bacchus, Vertumnus, and Pomona, which provide several attractive subjects for the illustrator. The second part of the book is somewhat less purely antiquarian. Lucrezia Lelio had entered a convent after being attacked by the plague which visited Treviso from 1464 to 1466, and so here also Polia is made to take refuge in the temple of Diana, whence, however, she is driven on account of the visits of Polifilo, with whom, by the aid of Venus, she is ultimately united.

132

One other point to be mentioned is that many of the full-page Venetian illustrations, both in quartos and folios, have quasi-architectural borders to them, the foot-piece being sometimes filled with children riding griffins or other grotesques, while school-books were often made more attractive to young readers by a border in which a master is flogging a boy duly horsed for the purpose on the back of a schoolfellow. In two of the most graceful of Venetian borders, those to the *Herodotus* of 1494 (and also in the 1497 edition of S. Jerome's Epistles) and Johann Müller's epitome of Ptolemy's *Almagest* (of 1496), the design is picked out in white on a black ground.

A few Florentine woodcut illustrations have borders of the kind just mentioned in which the design stands out in white on a black ground. In one of these borders there are rather ugly candelabra at the sides, at the top two lovers facing each other in a circle supported by Cupids, at the foot a shield supported by boys standing on the backs of couchant stags. Another has mermen at the top, a shield within a wreath supported by eagles at the foot, and floral ornaments and armour at the sides. In a third on either side of the shield in the footpiece boys are tilting at each other mounted on boars. In a fourth are shown saints and some of the emblems of the Passion, supported by angels. But as a rule, while nearly all Florentine woodcuts have borders these are only from an eighth to three-sixteenths of an inch in depth, and the pattern on them is a leaf or flower or some conventional design of the simplest possible kind. A very few cuts have only a rule round them, one of the largest a triple rule. A rude cut of the Crucifixion is found in Francesco di Dino's 1490 edition of Cavalca's *Specchio di Croce* surrounded by a rope-work border two-fifths of an inch deep, and this border, partly broken away, also surrounds a really beautiful Pietà (Christ standing in a tomb, His cross behind Him, His hands upheld by angels) in Miscomini's 1492 edition of

Savonarola's *Trattato dell' Umiltà*. When the same publisher used Dino's Crucifixion cut, also in 1492, for Savonarola's *Tractato dell' Amore di Gesù*, he left it without either border or rule round it, the only instance of a Florentine cut so treated in the fifteenth century. Dr. Paul Kristeller, whose richly illustrated monograph on *Early Florentine Woodcuts* (Kegan Paul, 1897) is the standard work on the subject, suggests with much plausibility that these two cuts, of the Crucifixion and the Pietà, were originally made for earlier books now lost, and belong to an older school of wood-cutting, more akin to that which produced the few extant Florentine single prints.

The earliest work of the new school of illustration is the magnificent cut of the Virgin in a mandorla appearing to S. Jacopone da Todi as he kneels in prayer. This, surrounded by the triple rule already mentioned, is prefixed to an edition of Jacopone's *Laude* printed by Francesco Buonacorsi and dated 28 September, 1490. Apparently the earliest dated cut with a typical Florentine border is that to the *Lunare* of Granollachs printed by Lor. Morgiani and Giovanni da Magonza in September, 1491. It measures more than 6 inches by 4, and is copied, and transfigured in the process, from the heavy cut in a Naples edition of 1485. Two months later the same firm issued the *Soliloquii* of S. Augustine with an extraordinarily fine title-cut of the saint (the same picture did duty in 1493 for S. Antonino) writing at a desk in his cell. This has a border, but with a white ground instead of a black. On 1 January, 1491-2, still from the same firm, we have surely the prettiest Arithmetic ever printed, that of Filippo Calandri, with delightful little pictures and border pieces, cut in simple outline, in the Venetian rather than the Florentine manner. On 20 March, Morgiani and his partner produced a new edition of Bettini's *Monte Santo di Dio* with the three copperplates of 1481 (see Chapter XV) skilfully translated into duly bordered woodcuts, the first two filling a folio page, the third somewhat shorter. A *Mandeville* with a single cut followed in June, and in December the *Trattati* of Ugo Pantiera, also with a single cut, perhaps by the designer of the Calandri, since it employs the same trick of representing a master on a much larger scale than a disciple as is found in the picture of Pythagoras in the earlier book.[1] One of the earliest (and also most delightful) of the title-cuts of another prolific publisher, the picture of a lecturer and his pupils in Antonio Miscomini's 1492 edition of Landini's *Formulario*,[2] measures about 6 inches by 4. But after this the period of experiment was at an end, and with very few exceptions the woodcuts in Florentine books for the rest of the century all measure either a little over or a little under 3 inches by 4, and are all surrounded by a narrow border with some simple design in white upon a black ground.

Some pains have been taken to make clear both the experiments as to style, size, and borders in the Florentine book-illustrations of 1490-2, and the external uniformity in size and borders in the great bulk of the work of the next few years, because in the first number of the *Burlington Magazine* and subsequently in his fine book on Florentine Drawings, Mr. Bernhard Berenson put forward with considerable confidence the theory that nine-tenths of the Florentine book-illustrations of this period were made from designs supplied by a single artist whom he identifies with a certain Bartolommeo di Giovanni. This Bartolommeo contracted in July, 1488, with the Prior of the Innocents to paint before the end of October seven predelle (Innocenti Museum, Nos. 63-70) for an altarpiece of the Adoration of the Magi, the commission for which had been given to Domenico Ghirlandajo. Mr. Berenson believes that in addition to these predelle (the only works with which Bartolommeo is connected by any evidence other than that of style) he

---

[1] The same trick is used in the *Rudimenta astronomica* of Alfraganus, printed at Ferrara by Andreas Bellfortis in 1493.

[2] Also used in an undated edition of the *Flores Poetarum*.

painted the Massacre of the Innocents, as an episode in Ghirlandajo's altarpiece at the Innocenti, that he must have been one of the more famous painter's apprentices in the years 1481-5, and subsequently helped him with altarpieces at Lucca and at the Accademia at Florence, and painted a fresco for the church of S. Frediano at Lucca and numerous fronts to the cassonì or ornamental chests, which were at this period the most decorative articles of Florentine furniture. As a minor painter Bartolommeo di Giovanni[1] is pronounced by Mr. Berenson to have been "incapable of producing on the scale of life a figure that can support inspection": in predelle and cassone-fronts he is "feeble, if vivacious, and scarcely more than pleasant," yet with no authenticated work to build on except the predelle in the Innocenti, Mr. Berenson does not hesitate to assert that "in Florence between 1490 and 1500 few apparently, if any, illustrated books were published without woodcuts for which Alunno di Domenico[1] furnished the designs," and on the strength of this assumption bestows on him the praise, amply deserved by the Florentine school as a whole, that he was "a book-illustrator, charming as few in vision and interpretation, with scarcely a rival for daintiness and refinement of arrangement, spacing and distribution of black and white." Mr. Berenson's theories oblige him to credit Bartolommeo with having copied at least from Filippo Lippi, Botticelli, and Piero di Cosimo, as well as from Ghirlandajo, and push the licence accorded to "connoisseurship" to its extreme limit. As I have already acknowledged elsewhere,[2] if any one man is to be credited with the whole, or nearly the whole of the Florentine book-illustrations of this decade, a minor artist used to painting predelle and cassone-fronts would be the right kind of man for the task, but on the very

---

[1] Mr. Berenson prefers to call him "Alunno di Domenico," Ghirlandajo's pupil.

[2] Introduction to the Roxburghe Club edition (presented by Mr. Dyson Perrins) of the *Epistole et Evangelii* of 1495.

136

scanty evidence at present available I am personally more inclined to attribute such unity as can be traced in these Florentine cuts to their having all come from one large wood-cutter's shop, without attempting to trace them back to a single designer.

In the year 1492, when the form of the Florentine woodcuts had become fairly fixed, Savonarola was called to the death-bed of Lorenzo the Magnificent, only to refuse him absolution. His *Amore di Gesù* and *Trattato dell' Umiltà* were printed in June of that year by Miscomini, each decorated with a single cut. During the six years ending with his execution in May, 1498, some twenty-three different tracts from his pen, illustrated with one or more woodcuts, were printed at Florence, most of them in several different editions. In the *De Simplicitate Christianae vitae* (1496) a friar is shown writing in his cell; in other cuts we see a friar preaching, or visiting the convent of the "Murate" or Recluses of Florence, or talking with seven Florentines under a tree, but in no case has any attempt been made at portraiture. This is true also of the *Compendio di Revelatione* (1495), in which there are some charming cuts showing Savonarola escorted by four holy women representing Simplicity, Prayer, Patience, and Faith, on an embassy to the Blessed Virgin. In the first of these they meet the devil attired as a hermit; in the second they arrive at the gate of the celestial city of which the wall is crowded with saints and angels; in the third they are ushered forth by S. Peter. A tract by Domenico Benivieni in defence of Savonarola, besides a cut of the usual size representing Benivieni arguing with his opponents, has a full-page one of the river of blood flowing from Christ's wounds and sinners cleansing themselves in it and marking their foreheads with the sign of the cross. One of the finest cuts in the Savonarola series represents a citizen of Florence in prayer before a crucifix. But almost all of them are good.

Besides the Savonarola tracts the miscellaneous religious treatises illustrated with one or more woodcuts are very numerous. In some cases outside models were still sought. One of the most important of these books is the *Meditatione sopra la Passione* attributed to S. Bonaventura, of which two undated editions were issued, one with eight cuts, the other with twelve, three of the additional cuts in the second edition—the Entry into Jerusalem, Christ before Pilate, and Procession to Calvary (see Plate XVI)—being exceptionally fine. The earlier designer probably had the Venetian edition of 1489 before him, but used it quite freely. Two of the three cuts in the 1494 Florentine edition of the *Libro delli commandamenti di Dio* of Marco del Monte S. Maria are improved copies of those in the Venetian edition of 1486. The third cut, which appears also in the same author's *Tabula della Salute* (also of 1494), representing the Monte della Pietà, is copied on a reduced scale from a large copper engraving attributed to Baccio Baldini, of which an example is in the Print Room of the British Museum. Of the thirty-four cuts in Cardinal Capranica's *Arte del benmorire*, eleven are imitated from the well-known series in the German block-books.

For the *Rappresentazioni* or miracle-plays in honour of various saints originality was more imperative, and numerous cuts were designed, only a few of which have come down to us in editions of the fifteenth century, most being known as they survive in reprints of the second half of the sixteenth. Our example (Plate XVII) is from an undated edition of *La Festa di San Giovanni*, in which, as on many other titlepages, an angel is shown above the title-cut as the speaker of the Prologue. Purely secular literature in the shape of *Novelle* was no doubt plentiful, despite the influence of Savonarola, but most of it has perished, thumbed to pieces by too eager readers. A volume of *Novelle* at the University Library, Erlangen, is illustrated with delightful cuts, and others survive here and there in different libraries. Of more pretentious quartos Angelo Politiano's *La Giostra di*

138

¶ Meditatioñe come el noſtro ſignore porto lacroce & come
fu condocto almonte caluario p eſſer poſto ſullegno del
lacroce & di quelle coſe che accaderono perla uia.

Apoi che lhebbono tãto dileggiato iluestirono
delleproprie ueſtimente : & apparecchiata lacro
ce alta ſecondo ilmaeſtro delle ſentẽtie tre ſtatu
re dhuomo cõ quello trauerſo molto põderoſo
& importabile : & quelli indiauolati non eſſendo moſſi ad al
chuña pietade uedendolo lacerato & inclinato inſino aterra
& che nõ ſipoteua mouere cõ grã furia ghelagittorono i col
lo appoggiata alle ſacratiſſine ſpalle. Et lomanſueto agnello
inchinando loinſpinato capo elquale mai non pote leuare da
quella hora che gliſu meſſa lacorõa di ſpine humilmẽte lapre
ſe dicendo : Vieni a me o croce diuina/ gia mille anni paſſati
dalmio padre ſe a me ordinata. Vieni a me õ croce amabile/
da me trentatre anni in queſto mõdo cõ grande faticha & ſu
dore dellamorte cerchata : Vieni ame uictoria dello inferno.

Giuliano di Medici (first edition undated, second 1513) is very finely illustrated, and Petrarch's *Trionfi* (1499) has good versions of the usual six subjects.

Many of the best of the quartos and all the illustrated folios were financed by a publisher, Ser Piero Pacini of Pescia, who was succeeded early in the sixteenth century by his son Bernardo. Pacini in 1495 began his career with a very ambitious venture, a folio edition of the *Epistole et Evangelii et Lectioni* as they were read in the Mass throughout the year. This has a decorative frontispiece, in the centre of which stand SS. Peter and Paul, while small cuts of the four evangelists are placed in the corners. The text is illustrated with 144 different woodcuts, besides numerous fancy portraits of evangelists, prophets, etc. A few of the cuts are taken from the *Meditationes* of S. Bonaventura, and one or two, perhaps, from other books already published; but the enormous majority are new, and from the consistency of the portrait-types of Christ, S. Peter, S. John, etc., appear all to have been designed by the same man. Some are less successful than others, but the average is exceptionally high, and the best cuts are full of movement and life. An *Aesop* followed in 1496, Pulci's *Morgante Maggiore* in 1500, and the *Quatriregio*, a dull poem in imitation of Dante by Bishop Frezzi, in 1508. It has been conjectured, however, that an earlier edition of the *Quatriregio* may have been printed in the fifteenth century with the same illustrations, and there is considerable reason to doubt whether any fresh cuts in the old style were made at Florence after the temporary cessation of publishing brought about by the political troubles of 1501. On the other hand, the old cuts went on being used, sometimes in the originals, sometimes in copies, throughout the greater part of the sixteenth century, and it is only in these reprints that many of them are known to survive.

At no other Italian town was there any outburst of book-illustration at all comparable to those at Venice and

Florence in the last decade of the fifteenth century. At Ferrara, after a fine cut of S. George and a much ruder one of S. Maurelius in a *Legenda* of the latter saint printed in 1489,[1] no illustration appeared until 1493, when the *Compilatio* of Alfraganus was adorned with a picture of the astronomer instructing a diminutive hermit. After this, in 1496 we have a fine cut of the Virgin and Child in the *De ingenuis adolescentium moribus*, and in 1497 two important folio books, both from the press of Lorenzo Rossi, the *De claris mulieribus* of Jacobus Philippus Bergomensis (29 April) and the Epistles of S. Jerome (12 October). The former of these is distinctly native work, with the exception of an architectural border, decorated chiefly with *putti* and griffins, etc., which is thoroughly Venetian in style, and was used again in the S. Jerome. There are two large illustrations, one show-ing the author presenting his book to the Queen of Hungary and Bohemia, the other containing eight scenes from the life of the Blessed Virgin. Fifty-six cuts in the text are made to serve as portraits of 172 different women, and under the strain of such repetition in-dividuality perforce disappears. But at the end of the book are seven cuts of Italian ladies of the fifteenth century: Bona of Lombardy, Bianca Maria of Milan, Catherine Countess of Fréjus and Imola, Leonora Duchess of Ferrara, Bianca Mirandula, Genebria Sforza, and Damisella Trivulzia, and these, some of them fair, some rather forbidding, appear all to be genuine portraits. The cutting is mostly rather stiff and heavy (Damisella Trivulzia is exceptionally tenderly treated), and much use is made of black grounds.

In contrast to those in the *De claris mulieribus*, the cuts in the *Epistulae* of S. Jerome are distinctly Venetian in style. As one of the two architectural borders is dated 1493, it is possible that the book was at first intended to be issued at Venice, but was transferred to Ferrara

---

[1] There were two issues or editions of this book in 1489, one of which is said to have only the cut of S. Maurelius.

La festa di san giouanni quando fu uisitato da christo nel diserto.

XVII. FLORENCE, BART. DI LIBRI, c. 1495

LA FESTA DI SAN GIOVANNI. (TITLE)

when Venetian interest in small column-cuts was found to be on the wane. It possesses in all over 160 of these, those illustrating conventual life in the second part of the book being much the most interesting.

At Milan the *Theorica Musicae* of Franchino Gafori, printed in 1492 by Philippus Mantegatius, has a title-cut of a man playing the organ, and four coarsely cut pictures, together occupying a page, showing primitive musical experiments. Four years later the same author's *Practica Musicae* was issued by another printer, Guillaume Le Signerre, with a title-cut illustrating the different measures and the Muses and signs of the Zodiac to which they belong, and with two fine woodcut borders surrounding the opening pages of Books I and III, and II and IV. In 1498 Le Signerre produced two much more profusely illustrated books, the *Specchio dell' Anima* of Ludovicus Besalii and an *Aesop*, some of the cuts of the former being used again in 1499 in the *Tesoro Spirituale* of Johannes Petrus de Ferrariis. After this he migrated to Saluzzo, and in 1503 produced there a fine edition of the *De Veritate Contritionis* of Vivaldus, with a frontispiece of S. Jerome in the desert. At Modena in 1490 Dominicus Rocociola printed a *Legenda Sanctorum Trium Regum*, with a rather pleasing cut of their Adoration of the Holy Child; and two years later, at the same place, the *Prognosticatio* of Johann Lichtenberger, printed by Pierre Maufer, was illustrated with three full-page quarto cuts and forty-two half-page ones, careful directions for each picture being supplied in the text, but the cuts being modelled on those in the German editions at Ulm and Mainz. At Aquila in 1493 an *Aesop* was produced, copied from the Naples edition of 1485. At Pavia in 1505 the *Sanctuarium* of Jacobus Gualla was illustrated with seventy woodcuts and some excellent initials. At Saluzzo in 1508 another work by Vivaldus, printed by Jacobus de Circis and Sixtus de Somachis, was decorated with three large woodcuts of very exceptional merit: a portrait of the Marquis Ludovico II (almost too striking for a book-illustration), a picture of S. Thomas Aquinas in his cell, and another of S. Louis of France. The treatise of Paulus de Middelburgo on the date of Easter, printed by Petruzzi at Fossombrone in 1513, contains some very fine borders, and the *Decachordum Christianum* of Marcus Vigerius, printed at Fano in 1507 by Hieronymus Soncinus, has ten cuts by Florio Vavassore, surrounded with good arabesque borders. To multiply isolated examples such as these would turn our text into a catalogue. Here and there special care was taken over the decoration of a book, and worthy results produced. But throughout Italy the best period of illustration had come to an end when the sixteenth century was only a few years old.

CHAPTER IX

EARLY FRENCH AND SPANISH ILLUSTRATED BOOKS

ALTHOUGH interrupted by the death of its veteran author, Claudin's magnificent *Histoire de l'imprimerie en France*, in the three volumes which he lived to complete, made it for the first time possible for students to trace the early history of book-illustration at Paris and Lyon, the two great centres of printing in France. No illustrated books were printed at the Sorbonne, nor by its German printers when they set up in the rue S. Jacques, nor by their rivals there, Keysere and Stoll, and the French printers at the sign of the Soufflet vert. In January, 1476-7, in the first French book printed at Paris, the *Chroniques de France* or *de S. Denis*, Pasquier Bonhomme so far recognized the possibility of illustration as to leave a space for a miniature on the first page of text,[1] but he used no woodcuts himself, and his son Jean suffered himself to be anticipated in introducing them by Jean Du Pré. Although he worked on rather narrow lines, Du Pré was the finest of the early Parisian printers, and possessed far better taste than the prolific publisher, Antoine Vérard, of whom so much more has been written. His first book, a Paris Missal issued in partnership with Didier Huym, 22 September, 1481, has a large picture of the Père Éternel and the Crucifixion. Although this is fairly well cut, it is baldly handled, and was far surpassed two months later (28 November) in a similar missal for the diocese of Verdun, by a really fine metal-cut of a priest and other worshippers at prayer at an altar. From the priest's uplifted hands a little figure

[1] Similar spaces were left in the typographically anonymous French version of Valerius Maximus, printed about the same date.

of a man is rising up to a vision of the Père Éternel, seen with His angels against the background of a sky full of stars. The little figure is the priest's soul, and the cut (often confused with pictures of the Mass of S. Gregory, in which the Host is seen as a figure of Christ) illustrates the opening words of the introit : " Ad te levavi animam meam." In the same Missal are a number of smaller cuts which look as if they had been prepared for a Horae, and may indeed have been used for one now entirely lost. The " Ad te levavi" cut reappears in many of the later Missals of Du Pré, and subsequently of Wolfgang Hopyl. Du Pré's first secular book to be illustrated was an edition of Boccaccio's *De la ruine des nobles hommes*, completed 26 February, 1483-4, and of peculiar interest to English bookmen because the woodcuts were acquired by Richard Pynson, and used in his edition of Lydgate's *Falles of Princes*, an English verse-rendering of the same work. They are well designed and clearly cut, if rather hard, and till their French origin was discovered were justly praised as " some of the very best" English woodcuts of the fifteenth century. Only a few weeks later Jean Bonhomme (12 May, 1484) issued Maistre Jacques Millet's *L'Histoire de la destruction de Troye la Grant*, illustrated with a number of cuts rather neater and firmer, but of much the same kind, and possibly from the same workshop. They passed almost at once into the possession of Vérard, and cuts from the series illustrating battles, landings, councils, audiences, and other romantic commonplaces are found in his *Végèce* of 1488 and *Les Commentaires Iules César* of about the same date (see Macfarlane's *Antoine Vérard*, cuts vi–ix). A new edition of Millet's book was printed by Jean Driard for Vérard 8 May, 1498. Two of the best of the cuts are those of the lamentation over the dead body of Hector and the sacrifice of Polyxena on the tomb of Achilles. The only other illustrated book published by Jean Bonhomme was his edition of the *Livre des ruraulx prouffitz*

Vado mori prefut: baculum: fandalia: mittrá
Nolens fiue Volens defero: Vado mori.

Vado mori miles: belli certamine Victor.
Mortem non didiá Vincere: Vado mori

Dcurrút animo pereundi mile figure. Mors qz minus pene q̃ mora mortis habet

La mort

Que vous tires la tefte arriere
Arceuefque: tires vous pres
Auez vo° paour quon ne vo°fiere
Ne doubtez: vous védres apres
Neft pas toufiours la mort epres
Tout hôme fuiuant cofte a cofte
Rendre côuient debtes: et preft.
Vnefoys fault compter a lofte.

Larceuefque

Las: ie ne fay ou regarder
Tât fuis par mort a grát deftroit
Ou fuiray ie pour moy aider
Certes qui bien la cõgnoiftroit
Hors de raifon iamais niftroit
Plus ne gerray en châbre painte
Mourir me conuient ceft le droit
Quât faire fault ceft grát côtraite

La mort

Vous qui entre les grãs barons
Auez eu renom cheualier:
Oubliez trompetes: clarons
Et me fuiues fans fommeiller
Les dames foulies reueiller:
En faifant danfer longue piece
A autre danfe fault veiller
Ce que lun fait lautre depiece

Le cheualier

Or ay ie efte auctorife
En plufeurs faitz: et bien fame
Des grans et des petis prife
Auec ce des dames ame.
Ne onques ne fus diffame
A la court de feigneur notable
Mais a ce cop fuis tout pafme.
Deffoubz le ciel na riens eftable.

XVIII. PARIS, MARCHAND, 1491

DANSE MACABRE (5ª). DEATH AND THE ARCHBISHOP. (REDUCED)

du labeur des champs, a French version of Crescentius, with a frontispiece of the translator presenting his book to Charles VII (15 October, 1486). Meanwhile, a new publisher of illustrated books had arisen, Guyot Marchant, who in September, 1485, issued a *Danse macabre* which went through several editions. Its grim fantastic pictures (executed with unusual skill and delicacy, see Plate XVIII) of Death as a grinning skeleton claiming his prey from every class of society seem to have become quickly popular, and additional cuts were made for later editions, including one in Latin (15 October, 1490), in which the Dance is called *Chorea ab eximio macabro versibus ale-manicis edita*. A *Danse macabre des femmes* followed (2 May, 1491), but the figures in this are mostly less good, as are those of a third part (the Debate between Soul and Body, and other pieces), despite the vivacity with which they represent the tortures of the damned. Akin to the *Danse Macabre* is the *Compost et Kalendrier des Bergers* (also of 1491), a medley of weather-lore, rules for health, and moral and religious instruction, liberally illustrated with cuts of shepherds, of Moses, Christ and the Apostles, and of the tortures of the damned. This in its turn was followed, in 1496, by a similar book for the Shepherdesses, of which a new edition appeared in 1499, with added pastoral cuts, some of which have unusual charm. Besides Guyot Marchant, Pierre Levet began book-illustration in 1485, but most of his work was done for Vérard. His earliest venture, an *Exposition de la salutation angélique*, has a cut of the Annunciation, the shading in which suggests that he may have imported a cutter from Lyon.

In 1486 Jean Du Pré was very busy. At Paris he completed in June a *Vie des anciens Saintz Pères*, with a large cut of S. Jerome writing in a stall and the holy fathers passing before him, also numerous very neat column-cuts and capital letters. Meanwhile, at Abbe-ville Du Pré was helping Pierre Gérard to produce one of the finest French books of the fifteenth century, the magnificent edition of S. Augustine's *Cité de Dieu*. Early in 1486 Gérard had already printed there an edition of *La somme rurale*, but this had only a single woodcut, and it was probably mainly in connection with the illustrations that he now enlisted the help of Du Pré. In the first volume of the *Cité de Dieu* (finished 24 November, 1486) there are eleven woodcuts, in the second (finished 12 April, 1486–7) twelve, i.e. a woodcut at the beginning of each of the twenty-two books and a frontispiece of S. Augustine writing, and the translator, Raoul de Preules, presenting his book to the King of France. The subjects and general design of the cuts correspond with greater or less closeness to those in Royal MS. 14 D. 1 at the British Museum (Books I–XI only), so that the same original was probably followed by both. One of the most effective pictures is that to Book XIV, which shows a man seated in a tree, offered a crown by an angel and a money-chest by a devil, while Death is sawing the tree asunder, and two dragons wait at its foot. Another shows S. Augustine writing, while five devils play with his books, and an angel protects his mitre. The cutting throughout is excellent, and the pictures, though sometimes fantastic, are very effectively drawn. There can be little doubt that they were the work of Paris craftsmen. As for Pierre Gérard, in 1487 he printed by himself, still at Abbeville, an edition of *Le Triomphe des Neuf Preux*, with rather childishly conventional cuts of the legendary heroes, but for Bertrand Du Guesclin a portrait which at least faithfully reproduces his bullet head. We find Du Pré forming a similar alliance two years later with Jean Le Bourgeois of Rouen, for whom he completed at Paris the second volume of a *Roman des Chevaliers de la Table ronde*, 16 September, 1488, while Le Bourgeois was still struggling at Rouen with Vol. I, which ultimately got finished 24 November. This has some large cuts of the Feast at the Round Table, etc. In 1489 Du Pré produced a *Legende dorée*, a companion volume to his *Vie des Saintz Pères* of 1486. But by this time he was already producing Horae, which will be spoken of later on, and Horae and Missals were his main occupations for the rest of his career, though he produced a fine edition of the allegorical romance *Le Chevalier Délibéré* by Olivier de la Marche, Bonnor's *Arbre des Batailles* (in which he used some of the same cuts), 1493, *Les vigilles du roi Charles VII* and some other secular books.

The great Paris publisher Antoine Vérard started on his busy career in 1485, and the history of book-illustration at Paris is soon immensely complicated by his doings. Many of the printers at Paris printed for him ; illustrations originally made for other men gravitated into his possession and were used occasionally for new editions of the book for which they had been made, much more often as stock cuts in books with which they had nothing to do ; while if another firm brought out a successful picture-book, Vérard imitated the cuts in it with unscrupulous and unblushing closeness. The monograph of my late friend and colleague John Macfarlane[1] describes some 280 books published by Vérard between 1485 and 1512, and like most bibliographical work done at first hand by personal examination of the books themselves gets at the root of the matter, although the absence of information as to Vérard's predecessors and contemporaries, such as has since been supplied by M. Claudin, prevented the author from pressing home some of his points. Thus in his estimate that sets of blocks had been "expressly cut to adorn some thirty editions," Macfarlane did not make sufficient allowance for the cases in which these apparent sets were themselves not original, having been acquired by Vérard from earlier owners. Nevertheless, he had no difficulty in finding support for his contention that "the illustrations in Vérard's books, when closely examined, hardly bear out their reputation." Thus he showed that "besides being repeatedly used in book after book, it not

---

[1] *Antoine Vérard.* By John Macfarlane. Illustrated monographs published by the Bibliographical Society. No. VII. Printed at the Chiswick Press, September, 1900.

uncommonly happens that the same cut is used again and again in the same book," and gave as an extreme instance of this the repetition no fewer than twenty times of the same cut in the *Merlin* of 1498.[1] He pointed out, moreover, that some far-fetched plea is nearly always needed to justify the presence of a cut in any but the work it was designed for. "For instance, in the *Josephus* of 1492 the spoliation of a country is represented by the burial of a woman, the death of Samson by a picture of the Temple, and the Sacrifice of Isaac helps the reader to conceive the execution of a malefactor, while a mention of the sea brings out a cut of Noah's Ark." However crowded a book may be with cuts, if the cuts are mostly irrelevant it cannot truly be said to be illustrated, and the number of Vérard's books which a rigorous application of this principle would condemn is very large. An explanation of at least some of these incongruities may be found in Vérard's early training as an illuminator, and his habit of preparing special copies on vellum for Charles VIII of France, Henry VII of England, the Comte d'Angoulême, and other royal and noble patrons. A woodcut in itself quite inappropriate to the text might save an illuminator some trouble by suggesting the grouping of the figures in a picture, and a cut of Saturn devouring his children was actually used in this way in one of the Henry VII books in the British Museum as a ground plan for an illumination of a Holy Family. If King Henry ever held that illumination up to the light he would have had no difficulty in seeing the scythe of Chronos and the limbs of a child protruding from Saturn's mouth, but I have never seen a paper copy of this book, and can only wonder whether the same cut was allowed to appear in it.

Vérard's earliest book was the translation of Boccaccio's *Decamerone* by Laurent du Premierfait, completed 22 November, 1485, and illustrated with a single

---

[1] So in the *Lucain Suetonne et Saluste* of 1490, five cuts of battle-scenes, all borrowed from the *Mer des Histoires*, printed by Lerouge in 1488, are made to do duty sixty-four times.

cut of the author writing in an alcove looking out on a garden where the storytellers are seen seated. An edition of *Les dits moraux des philosophes* of Guillaume de Tignonville (Caxton's *Dicts and Sayings of the Philosophers*) followed in April, 1486, and the *Livre des ruraulx prouffitz*, translated from Crescentius, with a few small cuts, not so good as those in the edition just issued by Jean Bonhomme, in the following July. His first important illustrated book was the *Cent nouvelles nouvelles* of Christmas Eve, 1486, with two large cuts, very alike in style, of an author presenting his book to a king, and forty column-cuts, most of them used several times, occasionally with mutilations intended to erase features unsuitable to the later stories. The next important book was a *Chevalier Délibéré* of 8 August, 1488, with some excellent cuts which reappear frequently in later books. Passing over many inferior books, we come in 1492 to a really fine one, containing four separate treatises : (1) *Art de bien mourir*, illustrated with copies of the old German blockbook ; (2) *Traité des peines d'enfer* (otherwise known as *L'Aiguillon de crainte divine*), with grotesque but striking cuts of the tortures of the damned ; (3) *Advenement de antichrist* and fifteen Tokens of Judgment, very poorly illustrated compared with the other parts of the book ; and (4) *L'Art de bien vivre*, copiously decorated with scenes from Bible history, an oblong set, illustrating the Adoration of the Virgin and Child, the Lord's Prayer, Commandments, Apostles, etc. ; (5) a very fine set of cuts illustrating the Sacraments.

In June, 1493, Vérard published in three large folio volumes, printed for him by Jean Morand, *Les Croniques de France*, with pictures of a coronation, royal entry into a town, a king sitting in judgment, etc. etc., the cutting being only of average delicacy, but good enough to do justice to the vigour of some of the designs. From this point onwards his interest seems more and more to have centred in his illuminated copies, and almost all the later Vérard illustrations in M. Claudin's great work are taken from these. Along, however, with many old cuts in his undated *Bible historiée* there are two very fine ones specially made for the work, one of Adam and Eve in Eden, a round cut placed, below the roots of a tree, in a square of black, from which it stands out with extraordinary vividness (see Plate XIX), and a picture of the Trinity and the four evangelists. In an undated *Terence en francois*, printed about 1500, Vérard availed himself of an idea already exploited by Grüninger and some of the Low Country illustrators, the use of blocks made up of five or six pieces used in different combinations, so as to give an effect of great variety at very small expense. Many of the individual blocks, though the figures are not at all Terentian, are very charming, and a few of them were freely copied for the English market, where they may be traced for over a century. About the same time as this Vérard published a *Livre des Ordonnances de la Prevosté des Marchans et Eschevinage de la Ville de Paris*, with numerous small illustrations of different crafts and a most interesting picture of the court of the Prevosté with its judges and officials. After the first few years of the sixteenth century Vérard seems to have relied more than ever on his stock of old cuts, and does not seem to have produced any notable new books.

A few books printed or published by less prolific firms remain to be noticed before we speak of the Horae which form so important a section among Paris illustrated books as to require separate treatment. One of Vérard's printers was Pierre Le Rouge, a member of a family which worked also at Chablis and at Troyes. In July, 1488, and February, 1488-9, Le Rouge printed " pour Vincent Commin Marchand libraire" *La mer des histoires* in two great folios with large cuts of the kind Vérard subsequently used in his *Chroniques de France*, and on the titlepage a particularly fine capital L. Philippe Pigouchet, mainly a printer of Horae, produced in 1499 for his usual publisher, Simon Vostre, a charmingly illustrated edition of a dull poem, *Le Chasteau de Labeur*, attributed to the play-

¶Comment le ciel ꜯ la terre furent creez ꜯ tous les
auttes eſemens   ¶Chapitre.i.

A D commencement crea dieu ſe ciel ꜯ la terre
La terre eſtoit ʙaine ꜯ ʙuide ꜯ tenebres eſ
toient ſur la face de ſabiſme ꜯ ſes eſptis de
noſtre ſeigneur eſtoient poztees ſur les
eaues.

¶Chiſtoire ſur ceſte partie de geneſis.

A D commencemēt fut le filz. Et ſe filz eſtoit
ſe commencement par ſeꜯl et en quel ſe pere
crea ſe monde. Ie monde eſt dit en trois ma
nieres. Aucuneﬀois eſt ſe monde appeſſe ſe
ciel empire pour ſa nectete. Aucuneﬀois eſt il appeſſe
ſentable. Aucuneﬀois eſt il appeſſe ſa hauſte region.
De ſaꜯlſe il eſt eſcript. ¶Princeps mundi eiicietur
foras. Ie prince du mōde ceſt ſe diaſſe q̄ en ſera gecte
                                                                    a ij

wright of Victor Hugo's *Notre Dame de Paris*, Pierre Gringore. Wolfgang Hopyl printed some fine Missals, mostly after 1500; Le Petit Laurens, besides working for Vérard, printed for G. Marnef *La nef des folles*, with a few cuts by one of the most skilled of Paris craftsmen, and these were rivalled by Jean Treperel in an undated *Paris et Vienne;* Gillet Couteau and Jean Ménard printed a *Danse Macabre* in 1492 (not so good as Gui Marchant's) and a new version of the *Biblia Pauperum* entitled *Les figures du vieil testament et du nouveau;* Jean Lambert, in 1497, produced *La nef des folz du monde*, with cuts imitating those in the Basel editions. It would be easy to mention other books, but not without turning our pages into a catalogue.

We must turn now to the Paris Horae. As already noted, among the pictures in Jean Du Pré's Verdun Missal of November, 1481, there are a set of cuts which seem to have been designed for a Horae, though if they were even put to this use no copy of the edition in which they appeared has been recorded. The earliest illustrated Horae of which copies exist are three editions published by Vérard, in February 1485-6, August 1486, and July 1487, all of them small and with insignificant cuts, and all known only from single copies, of which that of the earliest edition (in private hands) is imperfect, while the woodcuts in the other two, both at the Bibliothèque Nationale, are heavily coloured.

Vérard's Horae of 1486 and 1487 are said to have been printed for him by Jean Du Pré, and in the next group of editions Du Pré on his own account seems to have played the chief part, with Levet and Caillaut as subordinate actors. It is probable that the group may have been started by a Psalter printed by Levet 23 September, 1486, and reprinted 19 February, 1488-9, the cuts of these appearing in an undated *Horae ad usum Romanum*, printed by Du Pré, now in the British Museum. This measures about $4\frac{5}{8} \times 3\frac{1}{4}$ inches, and of the same size, but with different woodcuts, are another undated Horae by Du Pré in the Bodleian, and a third, with Caillaut's mark at the end, in the Bibliothèque Nationale. The cuts in all three are delightfully simple and naive, and those in the Bodleian Du Pré edition show really delicate work. The group, which comprised other editions only known from fragments, seems to be continued by two dated respectively 10 May, 1488, and 4 February, 1488–9, each measuring about $5\frac{5}{8} \times 3\frac{5}{8}$ inches, the illustrations in which are distinctly stated to have been cut on copper (*les vignettes de ces presentes heures imprimees en cuyvre*). The illustrations especially referred to are the borderpieces, which are of great importance as containing the earliest examples of a series of small Horae cuts continued from page to page, in this case depicting incidents in the life of Christ and their prefigurements, on the plan of the old block-book *Biblia Pauperum*. Lastly, in 1490, we have a Du Pré Horae, with very fine cuts and with some of the miscellaneous borderpieces of the editions just mentioned, which is of exceptional interest in the history of French book-illustration and printing, since the cuts and borders in it are printed in different colours, faint red, blue and green, two colours (laid on the same block and printed at the same time) usually appearing together. The British Museum possesses one of two known copies of this Horae, and the late Prince d'Essling bought the other.

In the Horae of the group we have been describing the subjects of the larger cuts became fairly well settled, in accordance with the normal contents of the prayer book. For the Kalendar there is the figure of a man with an indication of the parts of his body presided over by the different planets: for the sequence of the Gospels of the Passion, sometimes a Crucifixion, sometimes a picture of S. John; for the Hours of the Blessed Virgin, the Annunciation, Visitation, Nativity, Shepherds, Magi, Circumcision, Massacre of the Innocents or Flight into Egypt, and Assumption of the Blessed Virgin; for the Hours of the Cross, a Crucifixion; for the Hours of the

XX. PARIS, VÉRARD, 1490

GRANDES HEURES (SIG. C 6 VERSO). MASSACRE OF THE INNOCENTS

Holy Spirit, His Descent at Pentecost; for the Penitential Psalms, David's fall (Bathsheba bathing or the death of Uriah) or repentance; for the Office of the Dead, either a Funeral, Dives and Lazarus, or the three Gallants and three Skeletons (*les trois vifs et trois morts*); for the Suffrages, small pictures of various saints. Any edition might have one or more additional cuts with less usual subjects, but those named occur in almost all.

Passing on, we come now to Vérard's countermove to Du Pré's group, Horae measuring 6 inches or a little under by about 3½. Editions of these were issued in April, 1488-9, and in January, February, and April of the following year. The last of these, completed 10 April, 1489-90, I wrongly described, in an article in Vol. III of *Bibliographica*, as having a titlepage bearing the words *Les figures de la Bible*. It has such a titlepage in the copy in the British Museum, but I have now woke up to the fact that it is a modern fabrication, added either by an artful bookseller or an artless owner. In these Horae the borders are made up of four pieces, one of which extends along most of the outer and lower margins, and shows children wrestling with each other, or playing with hobbies or go-carts. On 10 July, 1493, these are found in a Horae issued by Laurens Philippe. Vérard could the better afford to part with them, since in August, 1490, perhaps earlier, he had substituted much larger borders, the subjects in which seem imitated from those of Du Pré's metal-cuts, the printed page now measuring about 8×5 inches, and thus winning for them the title Grandes Heures, by which they are generally known (see Plate XX). The large cuts, of which, though not all appear in every edition, there seems to have been seventeen, illustrate the following subjects:—

1. Prayer to the Virgin; 2. Anatomical Man; 3. A chalice the circumference of which represents the measurement of Christ's wound; 4. Fall of Angels; 5. Creation of Eve and Fall; 6. Controversy in heaven between Mercy, Justice, Peace, and Reason, and Annunciation; 7. Reconciliation of Joseph and

Mary, and Visitation ; 8. Nativity and Adoration by the Shepherds ; 9. Angels and Shepherds, Shepherds dancing ; 10. Magi ; 11. Circumcision ; 12. Massacre of Innocents ; 13. Coronation of the Virgin ; 14. David's choice of punishments ; 15. Hearse in a Chancel ; 16. Invention of the Cross ; 17. Pentecost.

The cutting is good and the pictures are both quaint and decorative, their larger size enabling them to avoid the overcrowding which had damaged the effect of the earlier sets. These cuts continued in use till 1498, successive editions in May, July, and October of that year, from the press of Jean Poitevin, showing their gradual replacement by copies of Philippe Pigouchet's second set.

This famous printer-illustrator was certainly printing as early as 1488, though Mr. Proctor in his "Index" makes the Horae for the use of Paris, finished 1 December, 1491, his earliest book. Although not his earliest book, I still believe that this was Pigouchet's earliest Book of Hours, and regret that M. Claudin, while rejecting supposed editions of 1486 and 1487, should have accepted as authentic one of 16 September, 1488, said to have very rude and archaic cuts, while owning that he could not trace a copy. Until the book can be produced I shall continue to believe that this edition of 16 September, 1488, is a ghost begotten of a double crime, a bookseller's manipulation of the date of one of Pigouchet's best-known editions, that of " le xvi iour de Septembre Lan Mil cccc.iiii.xx et xviii," by omitting the x in xviii, and a bibliographer's endeavour to make this imaginary edition of 16 September, 1488, more credible by assuming—and asserting—that its cuts were rude and archaic because over three years earlier than any authenticated Horae from Pigouchet's press. His edition of 1 December, 1491, was printed partly for sale by himself, partly for de Marnef, who subsequently owned the blocks. Besides the usual illustrations for the Hours, it has pictures of S. John writing and of the Betrayal for the Gospels of the Passion, of David's choice of punishments for the Penitential Psalms, and of Les trois vifs et trois morts, and Dives and Lazarus for the Office for the Dead; also a small cut, with a criblé background of the Vision of S. Gregory, and numerous small cuts of saints. The sidepieces, which are marked with letters to indicate their sequence, illustrate the Creation, the prophecies of the Sibyls, and the subjects of the *Biblia Pauperum*. During the years 1491 and 1495 at least eight or ten Horae for various uses were printed by Pigouchet, mostly for Simon Vostre. Of most of these a good many copies have survived printed on vellum and often illuminated for wealthy purchasers. The paper copies, which presumably formed the bulk of each edition, are now far rarer, and to students of book-illustration much preferable to the coloured vellum copies. Good vellum copies with the pictures and borders uncoloured, but with their pages brightened by illuminated capitals and coloured paragraph marks, are the pleasantest to possess.

At the end of 1495 or early in 1496 Pigouchet began replacing the woodcuts of this series of editions with a new set much more graceful and less stiff, a few changes being made in the subjects. At the same time he substituted new borderpieces for the old, among the new blocks being a fine series of the Dance of Death, which were brought into use as they were completed, so that we can trace the increase of them from month to month, so frequent now were the editions. In 1497 and 1498 further additions were made to the large pictures by the addition of new metal cuts with criblé backgrounds for the Anatomical Man, chalice, Stem of Jesse, Adoration by the Shepherds, Descent from the Cross, Death of Uriah, and the Church Militant and Triumphant. By the end of 1499 new criblé borderpieces had been added, illustrating the life of Joseph, history of the Prodigal Son, history of Susanna, Fifteen Tokens of Judgment, Christ Seated in Judgment, the Cardinal Virtues, and woodland and hunting scenes. From August, 1498, to the end of 1502 Pigouchet's editions were at their finest. Meanwhile the cuts of his second set were slavishly copied in editions printed for Vérard. From 1497, moreover, he had to face serious competition from Thielman Kerver, who issued closely similar editions with pictures and borders by cutters little, if at all, inferior either in technical skill or charm. On 5 April, 1503, Jean Pychore and Remy de Laistre completed an edition, in which Pigouchet probably had a hand, with three very large cuts of the Annunciation, Nativity, and Adoration by the Magi, and eight smaller ones surrounded by architectural framework, representing S. John before the Latin Gate, the Crucifixion, the Emperor Octavian and the Sibyl, the Massacre of the Innocents, Descent of the Holy Spirit, Death of the Virgin, and Raising of Lazarus, some of them showing strong traces of the influence of Dürer. From this point onwards the Renaissance spirit became increasingly powerful in these prayer books, and while in almost all their advances to meet it the work of Pigouchet himself, and of Thielman Kerver, continues interesting (though the mixture of old and new styles in their editions is often confusing), in the numerous editions poured forth by Germain and Gillet Hardouyn, many of them printed for them by Guillaume Anabat, and again in those printed by Nicolas Higman for Guillaume Eustace, the cuts are very inferior, so that they look best when most heavily illuminated. In a few editions published by the Hardouyns spaces appear to have been left for the illuminator to work unaided. In most of these late editions only the pages with cuts have borders, and these of the nature of picture frames, as contrasted with the old historiated borders.

In 1525 Geoffroi Tory, a native of Bourges (born about 1480), who at this period of his life was at once a skilled designer, a scholar, and a printer, completed a Horae which, though somewhat thin and unsatisfying compared with the richer and more pictorial work of Pigouchet at his best, far surpassed any edition produced at Paris for the previous twenty years. Part of the edition was taken up by the great publisher of the day,

Simon Colines, and while the body of the book was only printed once, differences in the titlepages and colophons and in the arrangement of the almanac and privilege constitute altogether three different issues. Whereas the best earlier editions had been printed in gothic letter this is in roman, and both the borders and the twelve illustrations aim at the lightness and grace necessary to match the lighter type. The vase-like designs of the borders are meaningless, but the pictures, despite the long faces and somewhat angular figures, have a peculiar charm. They were used again, with some additions, in a Horae completed 20 October, 1531. An edition of 1 October, 1527, described by Tory's chief biographer, Auguste Bernard, as printed, "chez Simon de Colines en caractères romains avec des vignettes de même genre, mais beaucoup plus petites," I have never seen. Three weeks later Tory printed in gothic letter a Paris Horae with borders of birds and fruits and flowers rather in the style of some of the Flemish manuscripts. In February, 1529, he produced a much smaller Horae in roman type without borders, but with some very delicate little cuts, used again by Olivier Mallard, who married his widow, in 1542. Tory appears to have died in 1533, and attributions of later work to him on the ground of its being marked with a "cross of Lorraine" (i.e. a cross with two transverse strokes) should be received with caution, unless the cuts are found in books by Tory's widow or her second husband. It is not quite clear that the cross is not the mark of a wood-cutter rather than a designer, and if it really marks the designer we must believe that it was used by others beside Tory, so various is the work on which it is found.

Illustrated books were published at Lyon somewhat earlier than at Paris, and in point of numbers, if the comparison be confined to secular books with sets of cuts especially appropriated to them, the provincial city probably equalled, if it did not surpass, the metropolis. But if it must be reckoned to the credit of Lyon that it had no Antoine Vérard, reckless in his use of unsuitable stock cuts, it must be noted, on the other hand, that strikingly good illustrations are rare and bad ones numerous. Inasmuch as Lyon, before it welcomed the art of printing, had established some reputation for the manufacture of playing-cards, the number of rude and badly cut illustrations is indeed surprisingly large. The first Lyonnese printer to use pictorial woodcuts in a dated book was Martin Huss, who issued a *Miroir de la Rédemption*, 27 August, 1478, with the aid of blocks previously used (1476) by Bernard Richel at Basel; cuts of surgical instruments appeared in the following March, 1478-9, in the *Chirurgia* of Guido de Cauliaco printed for Barth. Buyer by Nicolaus Philippi and Marcus Reinhart, and the same printers' undated *Legende dorée* with very rude pictures is probably contemporaneous with this. The earliest woodcut of any artistic interest and of Lyonnese origin is a picture, occupying a folio-page, of the Blessed Virgin, with the Holy Child in her arms, standing in front of a curtain. This is found in the *Histoire du Chevalier Oben qui vouloist acuplir le voiage de S. Patrix*, printed by Leroy about 1480, of which the only known copy is at the British Museum.

After 1480 all the firms we have named continued to issue illustrated books of varying merit. On 30 September, 1483, Leroy completed a *Livre des Eneydes* with cuts which are often grotesque, though sometimes neat and sometimes giving evidence of a vigour of design too great for the wood-cutter's skill. In 1485 he found a Lyonnese cutter able to copy for him the Paris cuts of Jean Bonhomme's edition of the *Destruction de Troye la Grant* quite competently, though in a much heavier style. In May, 1486, he printed a *Livre des Sainctz Anges* with a figure of Christ in a mandorla (perhaps suggested by the engraving of the same subject in Bettini's *Monte Santo di Dio*), and this, despite a certain clumsiness in the face, is quite good. In the same year, in an edition of *Fierabras*, Leroy went back to cuts of incredible rudeness, while about 1490 in *Les Mysteres de la Saincte Messe*, we find him employing for a cut of the Annunciation a skilled craftsman, signing himself I. D. (Jean Dalles?), whose work, though lacking in charm, is neatness itself. Some shaded cuts in his romance of Bertrand Du Guesclin (undated, but *c.* 1487) are among the best work in any book by Leroy. Among his other undated illustrated books are editions of *Pierre de Provence*, *Melusine*, and the *Roman de la Rose*.

Nicolaus Philippi and Marcus Reinhart in 1482 illustrated a *Mirouer de la vie humaine* (from the Latin of Rodericus Zamorensis) with Augsburg cuts purchased from the stock of Günther Zainer,[1] and copied a Paris edition in their *Vie des Saintz pères hermites* and German originals in their *Mandeville* and *Aesop*. Their edition of the *Postilla Guillermi* (*c.* 1482) has rather a fine Crucifixion and some primitive but vigorous illustrations of the gospels.

Martin Huss issued an undated *Exposition de la Bible* with rude cuts and a French *Belial* (version of Pierre Ferget), first printed in November, 1481, and at least five times subsequently. After his death in 1482 his business was carried on by a kinsman, Mathieu Huss, who became a prolific publisher of illustrated books, with cuts of very varying merit. Two of his earliest ventures were the *Proprietaire des Choses* (2 November, 1482), a French version of the *De proprietatibus rerum* of Bartholomaeus Anglicus, and a *Fasciculus temporum* (1483), both with very rude cuts. During a partnership with Johann Schabeler he issued (about 1484) a French version of Boccaccio's *De casibus illustrium virorum*, the pictures in which are hard, stiff, and a little grotesque, but not without character. Of his later books several are illustrated with cuts borrowed or copied from other editions; but beyond a *Legende dorée* with shaded column-cuts, frequently reprinted, he does not seem to have commissioned any important illustrated book.

[1] In 1491 these are found at Saragossa in an edition printed by Hurus.

While the pictorial work of the Lyonnese presses was thus largely imitative, at least two very important books were first illustrated there. The earlier of these was the *Roman de la Rose*, of which the first printed edition, decorated with eighty-six cuts mostly small and rudely executed, but which at least have the merit of intelligently following the text, is now attributed to the press of Ortuin and Schenck at Lyon about 1481.[1] These primitive pictures were quickly copied by a cutter of somewhat greater skill but much less intelligence, who "improved" the original designs without troubling to understand them. This new set of cuts was used twice at Lyon, by Jean Syber (about 1485) and by Leroy (about 1487), and was then acquired (less one of the two larger cuts) by Jean Du Pré of Paris, who issued an edition about 1494. About 1497, and again a few years later, new editions were issued in which most of the same cuts reappear, Jean Petit having a share in both editions and Vérard in the first, despite the fact that he had issued a rival edition about 1495.[2]

The other famous Lyonnese illustrated book was an annotated edition of *Terence* "with pictures prefixed to every scene" printed in 1493 by Johann Trechsel. This has a curious full-page picture at the beginning, giving the artist's idea of a Roman theatre, with a box for the aediles at the side and a ground floor labelled "Fornices." The text is illustrated by 150 half-page cuts, a little hard, but with abundance of life (see Plate XXI). These certainly influenced the Strassburg edition of Grüninger (1496), and through Grüninger's that published at Paris

[1] It has also been attributed to Jean Croquet at Geneva, but there is only a typographical argument for this ascription, whereas on the side of Lyon, in addition to (rather weaker) typographical arguments, we have to reckon with Lyonnese paper, the similarity of the illustrations to those of a cutter employed by Martin Huss, and the fact that the book was copied in two editions undoubtedly Lyonnese. See F. W. Bourdillon's *The Early Editions of the Roman de la Rose* (1906).

[2] Only a few of the cuts in this were specially designed for it, all the later ones being taken from stock in Vérard's most haphazard fashion.

Sostrata.   Chremes.

Rofecto &c. Hic
exprimit̃ q̃ ima
go diffidii int̃ ui
rũ & uxorẽ qui natura
morofi funt ac diffici/
les. Sostrata. o hõ p cõ
téptũ & cũ ftomacho ẽ
pnunciandũ nõ eft di/
gnata dicere. o uir uel
coniunx. profecto nifi
tu caues.i. ,puides. con

Rofecto nifi caues: tu homo aliquid gna
to conficies mali. idq̃ adeo miror quomo
do tam ineptum quicq̃ tibi uenite in mé
tem mi uir potuerit. Chre. Oh. pergin mulier ef
fe: nullam ne ego rem ũnquã in uita mea uolui:
quin tu in ea re mihi aduerfatrix fueris Sostrata.

ficies.i. ,pcurabis.cõparabis aliquid mali. gnato.i.filio.f.Clitiphoni. & adeo.i.ual/
de miror quo mõ o mi uir.i.mi coniúx.núc redit ad lenitatẽ difcedẽte paulatim in
dignatiõe.quicq̃.i.aliquid.tã ineptũ.i.ab oïbus i̇probatũ potuerit uenire in men
tem tibi.i. occurrere tuæ uoluntati faciendũ. Chre. oh interiectio indignantis & rí
dentis.pergin.i.perfequeris ne.effe mulier.1.mulieris partes exercere & officium
quæ femp uult loqui & marito repugnare. ne.i.certe. nullã rem uolui unq̃ in uita
mea.qn.i.q̃ nõ.tu Sostrata fueris aduerfatrix.i.cõtraria mihi in ea re quã uolebã.

by Vérard about 1500, and to an even greater extent the illustrated editions issued at Venice.

How eagerly Lyonnese publishers looked out for books to imitate may be seen from the rival Lyonnese renderings of Breidenbach's *Peregrinationes* and Brant's *Narrenschiff*. Of the Breidenbach, Michel Topie and Jac. de Herrnberg issued in November, 1480, an adaptation by Nicolas Le Huen with copies on copperplate of the maps and on wood of the smaller pictures, both very well executed. Rather over a year later, in February, 1490, a translation by "frere iehan de Hersin" was published by Jacques Maillet with the original Mainz blocks. As for the Ship of Fools, Jacques Sacon, the leading publisher at the end of the century, issued an edition of Locher's Latin version with close copies of the Basel cuts in June, 1498, and in the following August a French edition was published by Guillaume Balsarin with cuts so hastily executed that in many cases all the background has been omitted.

A few illustrated incunabula were issued at Chambéry, and isolated books elsewhere, but with the exception of Lyon and Abbeville no French provincial town produced any notable work. In Spain the fine gothic types and frequent use of woodcut capitals give a very decorative appearance to most of the incunabula, but pictorial illustrations are rare, and of the few sets of cuts known to us several are borrowed or copied from French or German editions. The earliest Spanish illustrated book known to me is a *Fasciculus Temporum*, printed by Bart. Segura and Alfonsus de Portu at Seville in 1480, with a dozen metal-cuts of the usual stock subjects; the earliest with original illustrations, the Marquis of Villena's *Trabajos de Hercules*, printed by Antonio de Centenera at Zamora, 15 January, 1483, with eleven extraordinarily rude cuts of the hero's adventures. In 1484 and 1485 an unidentified printer at Huete produced editions of the *Copilacion de Leyes* of Diaz de Montalvo, with some striking metal-cut pictorial capitals, illustrating the subjects of the successive books. In one copy of the 1484 edition I have seen a very fine full-page cut, but could not satisfy myself as to whether this belonged to the book, or was an insertion. An edition of Martorell's romance, entitled *Tirant lo blanch*, printed at Valentia in 1490 by Nic. Spindeler, has a decorative metal-cut border to the first page of text, and during the following decade illustrated books become fairly numerous. At Saragossa Paul Hurus issued in 1491 a Spanish version of the *Speculum humanae vitae* of Rodericus Zamorensis, with cuts copied from the Augsburg edition, another in 1494 of Boccaccio's *De claris Mulieribus*, with seventy-two cuts, copied from the editions printed by Johann Zainer at Ulm, and four from some other source, another in 1498 of Breidenbach's *Peregrinatio*, and other books, not known to me personally, but which from their titles almost certainly contain copies of foreign cuts. In 1500, when his press had been taken over by three partners, Coci, Hutz, and Appentegger, there issued from it an *Officia quotidiana*, ornamented with some fifty pictures and many hundreds of fine capitals.

At Barcelona several illustrated books were printed by Juan Rosenbach, one of the earliest of them, the *Carcel d'Amor* of Diego de San Pedro (1493), having sixteen original cuts, characteristically Spanish in tone and showing good craftsmanship. In or about the same year Friedrich Biel of Basel (usually quoted as Fadrique de Basilea, or Fadrique Aleman) headed an edition of the *Passion de Christo* with a striking metal-cut of Christ standing upright in the tomb, watched by the B. Virgin and S. John. For his Spanish *Aesop* of 1496 he presumably copied the German cuts, and he certainly did so for his *Exemplario contra engaños* of 1498, the 116 cuts of which are all careless copies of those in Prüss's edition of the *Directorium humanae vitae*. Even when in (or about) the next year he was issuing the first edition of the *Celestina* or *Tragicomedia de Calisto y Melibea*, he could not do so without German models,

Jmpbatío. alcorarí

XXII. SEVILLE, STANISLAUS POLONUS, 1500

RICOLDUS. IMPROBATIO ALCÖRANI, (TITLE)

and based his sixteen little pictures on some of those in Grüninger's *Terence*, while for his *Stultiferae naues* of Badius Ascensius he went, of course, to the charming French cuts of De Marnef.

As a rule, these Spanish versions of foreign cuts have the interest which always attaches to a free rehandling by a craftsman with a characteristic touch and style of his own. None the less it is refreshing to turn to more original work, and at least a little of this (though some one with wider knowledge than myself may further minimize the statement) is to be found at Seville. Here in 1494 Ungut and Stanislaus Polonus issued a *Regimiento de los principes*, translated from the Latin of Aegidius Columna, with a fine title-cut of a young prince (his hair is long) seated in a chair of state, holding a sword and royal orb. The same partners were responsible for another striking titlepage in 1495, that of the *Lilio de Medicina*, Bernardus de Gordonio, where two angels are seen upholding seven lilies in a pot; they also issued in the same year the *Contemplaciones sobre el Rosario de Nuestra Señora*, a fine and typically Spanish book, printed in red and black, with good capitals, two large cuts and fifteen smaller ones, enclosed in borders of white tracery on a black ground. In the last year of the century they issued an *Improbatio Alcorani* with a swart picture of a disputation on the titlepage, not easily forgotten (see Plate XXII). It was at Seville also that in 1498 Pedro Brun printed in quarto the romance of the Emperor Vespasian, illustrated with fourteen excellent cuts, some of them full of life and movement; but for these a foreign model is quite likely some day to be discovered. On the other hand, at Valentia also there was at least a little work indisputably of native origin, as in the case of the title-cut to the *De regimine domus* of S. Bernard, printed by Nic. Spindeler about 1498, and (less certainly) another to the *Obra allaors de S. Christofol*, issued by Peter Trincher in the same year. Pictorial title-cuts are not so common in Spanish books as in those of other countries, because of the Spanish fondness for filling the titlepage with an elaborate coat of arms. But nearly all their early bookwork is strong and effective, and the printer who placed a cut on a titlepage nearly always secured a good one. Is it too much to hope that Dr. Conrad Haebler, who has already done such admirable work in recording Spanish incunabula and printing facsimiles of their types, will some day complete his task by publishing a similar volume of facsimiles of Spanish cuts?

CHAPTER X

LATER FOREIGN BOOKS

ONE of the chief charms of the books of the fifteenth century is that they are so unlike those of our own day. In the first year of its successor a great step was taken towards their modernization by the production of the first of the Aldine octavos, and the process went on very rapidly. In the early days of printing all the standard works of the previous three centuries that could by any possibility be considered alive were put on the press. By 1500 men were thinking of new things. New editions of many of the old religious and didactic treatises, the old poems and romances, continued to be printed, though mostly in a form which suggests that they were now intended for a lower class of readers, but the new publishers would have little to do with them. Scholarship, which till now had been almost confined to Italy, spread rapidly to all the chief countries of Europe, and amid the devastation which constant war soon brought upon Italy, was lucky in being able to find new homes. With the new literary ideals came new forms for books, and new methods of housing them. Before 1500 several publishers had found it worth their while to print editions in five huge volumes of the *Speculum* of Vincent de Beauvais, each volume measuring eighteen inches by thirteen and weighing perhaps a dozen pounds, though paper in those days was not yet made of clay. These great volumes had been cased in thick wooden boards, covered with stout leather and protected with bosses or centre-pieces and corner-pieces of metal. They were not intended to stand on shelves like modern books, but were laid on their sides, singly, on shelves and desks, and from

pictures which have come down to us we can see that
the library furniture of the day included a variety of
reading-stands with the most wonderful of screws. The
men for whom Aldus catered wanted books which they
could put in their pockets and their saddlebags, and it
was not long before the publishers of Paris and Lyon
outdid Aldus in the smallness and neatness of their
editions. Of course large books continued to be issued.
The *Complutensian Polyglott* will not easily be got either
into a pocket or a saddlebag, but it is a good deal smaller
than the *Speculum* of Vincent de Beauvais, and, speaking
generally, small folios took the place of large folios,
and octavos the place of quartos, and in a little time the
octavos themselves were threatened by the still smaller
sextodecimos. There is, indeed, no stop till in the
seventeenth century we come to the tiny Elzevirs, which
remained the last word in book-production until the
diamond editions of Didot and Pickering.

Aldus Manutius, who led the revolution, has often
been wrongly praised. He can hardly be called a great
printer. He burdened Greek scholarship for three centuries with a thoroughly bad style in Greek types, and the
cursive substitute which he provided for the fine roman
founts for which Italy had been famous almost drove
them from the field. Both the Greek type and the
italics were the outcome of confused thinking. They
were based upon styles of handwriting which Aldus and
his scholarly friends doubtless found more expeditious
than the formal book-hands which had previously been
in use. Quickness in writing is an excellent thing. But
a sloping type takes just as long to set up as an upright
one, and absolutely nothing is gained by the substitution
of an imitation of a quicker hand for the imitation of a
slower one.

Aldus had begun publishing at Venice early in 1495[1]
with an edition of the Greek grammar of Lascaris, an
earlier edition of which, issued at Milan in 1476, had

---

[1] He was born at Bassiano in the Papal States in 1450.

been the first book wholly in Greek to obtain the honour of print. The Idylls of Theocritus and the poem of Hesiod called *Works and Days* had been printed at the same place in 1479 and a Greek Psalter in 1487. At Florence the famous first edition of Homer was printed (by Bartolommeo Libri) in 1488, and was followed in the years 1494–6 (i.e. about the time that Aldus began work) by five books printed entirely in majuscules on the model of the letters used in inscriptions. Among these books were the Greek Anthology, four plays of Euripides, and an Apollonius Rhodius. The printing of the Greek classics had thus made a start, although a slow one. Aldus now greatly quickened the pace, producing his great Aristotle in four (or, as it is sometimes reckoned, five) volumes, between the years 1495 and 1498, and following it up with nine comedies of Aristophanes in 1498, Thucydides, Sophocles, and Herodotus in 1502, Xenophon's *Hellenics*, and the plays of Euripides in 1503 and Demosthenes in 1504. The service which he thus rendered to Greek scholarship was incalculable, but it was accompanied by a very serious drawback, the evil effects of which lasted for nearly three centuries. The Greek quotations in many books printed in Italy before this time had been printed in types imitating the writing in fairly old Greek manuscripts, handsome in appearance and fairly free from contractions; Aldus is said to have taken as his model the handwriting of his friend Marcus Musurus, with all its crabbed and often fantastic ligatures, and the simplicity of the Greek alphabet was thus intolerably complicated.

As we have seen, the introduction of the Aldine italics, though in themselves a better fount than the Greek type, was almost as mischievous in its effects. On the other hand, the service which Aldus rendered to scholarship by his cheap and handy series of the Latin and Italian classics was very great. The first book which he printed in his new type was a Virgil, and this was quickly followed by works by Petrarch and Dante and a whole series of similar editions. Aldus had powerful supporters in these ventures, among them being Jean Grolier, the famous bibliophile, who for many years was resident in Italy as Treasurer of the Duchy of Milan. Despite this encouragement he did not find printing very profitable, partly, no doubt, on account of the wars in which Venice was at this time engaged.

On the death of Aldus in 1515 his business was for some time carried on by his father-in-law, Andrea de Torresani, an excellent printer, but with little of Aldus's scholarship. In 1533, at the age of twenty-one, Paulus Manutius, the youngest son of Aldus, took over the management of the firm, and proved himself an even finer scholar than his father. Financially he was no more successful, and when he was made printer to the Pope the anxiety of carrying on business at Rome as well as at Venice only added to his difficulties. On his death in 1574 his son, Aldus Manutius the younger, succeeded him and worked till 1597, but without adding anything to the reputation of the firm, perhaps because he had been pushed on prematurely in his boyhood, as is witnessed by his compilation of a volume of elegant extracts at the age of nine.

The family of printers and publishers which came nearest to rivalling the fame of the Aldi in Italy during the sixteenth century was that of the Giunta. Springing originally from Florence, members of it worked for some time simultaneously at Florence and Venice, and Lucantonio Giunta, the earliest member of it to rise into note, was already one of the foremost publishers at Venice in the closing years of the fifteenth century, and subsequently printed for himself instead of always employing other men to print for him. The speciality of this Venetian firm was at first illustrated books of all kinds, afterwards the production of large and magnificent missals and other service books of the Roman Church, and these they continued to publish until nearly the end of the sixteenth century.

At Florence, Filippo Giunta competed with Aldus of Venice in printing pretty little editions of the classics, his competition sometimes taking the form of unscrupulous imitation.

At Rome, Eucharius Silber and his successor Marcellus were the chief printers from 1500 to 1516. A little later the Bladi took their place, and under the auspices of the Council of the Propaganda of the Faith a press was set up for printing in Syriac, Armenian, and other Oriental languages. The output also of the presses in other Italian cities was still considerable. Nevertheless, from the same causes which produced her political decay Italy rapidly ceased to be the head-quarters of European printing, yielding this honour to France about the end of the first quarter of the century, and by some thirty or forty years later becoming quite uninfluential.

To the German printing trade, also, the sixteenth century brought a notable decline of reputation. In its first two decades Johann Schoeffer (son of Peter) produced some fine books at Mainz; at Strassburg Grüninger poured forth illustrated books, and Johann Knoblouch and Matthias Schürer were both prolific. The importance of Cologne diminished, though the sons of Heinrich Quentell had a good business. Augsburg, on the other hand, came to the front, the elder and younger Schoensperger, Johann and Silvanus Otmar, Erhard Oglin, Johann Miller, and the firm of Sigismund Grim and Marcus Wirsung all doing important work. At Nuremberg the chief printing houses were those of Hieronymus Hölzel, Johann Weissenburger, and Friedrich Peypus. Leipzig and Hagenau both greatly increased their output, and with the advent of Luther, Wittenberg soon became an important publishing centre. Luther's activity alone would have sufficed to make the fortunes of any publisher had it not been for the fact that as each pamphlet from his pen was produced at Wittenberg by Hans Lufft, or some other authorized printer, it was promptly pirated in

other cities, often with the retention of the original imprint. Many of these Luther tracts had ornamental
borders, and, as will be narrated in another chapter, the
German book-illustrations of this period were often very
finely designed, but the paper used, even in important
books, was poor compared to that found in German
incunabula, and the presswork too often careless. These
defects are found intensified in almost all the German
books published after this date, and German printing
soon lost all its technical excellence, though the output of
its presses continued to be large, and the great annual
fair at Frankfort during the course of the sixteenth
century became the most important event in the book-
trade of Northern Europe.

A little before Germany gave herself up to theological
strife, the conjunction at Basel of the great printer Johann
Froben and the great scholar Erasmus temporarily raised
that city to importance as an intellectual centre. Froben
had begun printing at Basel in 1491, but until he formed
his friendship with Erasmus in 1513 published only a
few editions of the Bible, some of the papal Decretals,
the works of S. Ambrose, and a few other books of no
special interest. From 1513 onwards his output increased rapidly both in quantity and importance, so that
by the time of his death in 1527 he had printed over three
hundred books, including almost all the works of Erasmus
and many books in Greek. During this period, also,
border-pieces and initials were designed for him by the
two Holbeins (Hans and Ambrosius) and other skilful
artists, and he was entitled to rank as the greatest
printer-publisher in Europe in succession to Aldus.
After his death in 1527 the supremacy of European
printing rested for the next generation indisputably with
France.

During the fifteenth century printing in France had
developed almost entirely on its own lines. Vernacular
books of every description had poured from the presses
of Paris and Lyon, and many of them had been charm-

170

ingly illustrated in a style worthy of the great French school of illustrators of manuscripts. In the first half of the sixteenth century the publication of these popular books—romances, poetry, and works of devotion—still continued, though with some loss of quality, the print and paper being less good and the illustrations often consisting of a medley of old blocks, or where new ones were made being executed in a coarser and heavier style. But to the vernacular literature there was now added a learned and scholarly literature which soon rose to great importance. As early as 1492 Johann Trechsel, a printer of Lyon, had possessed himself of sufficient Greek type to print quotations in that language, and in the following year he issued the profusely illustrated edition of *Terence*, the cuts in which were imitated by Grüninger at Strassburg. Trechsel's press corrector and general editor was a young scholar named Josse Bade, of Asch, near Ghent, better known by the Latin form of his name as Jodocus Badius Ascensius, or Ascensianus. In 1503, after Trechsel's death, Ascensius started business for himself in Paris, and his editions of the classics, well known from the device of a printing-press found on many of their titlepages, obtained a considerable reputation. Almost simultaneously, in 1502, Henri Estienne, the first of a famous family of scholar-printers, had started in business by an expedient of which we hear a great deal in the annals of English printing, that of marrying a printer's widow. Of Henri Estienne's three sons the eldest, François, became a bookseller, Robert a scholar-printer, and Charles, in the first instance, a physician. In the technical side of his business Henri had been helped by Simon de Colines, who, on his employer's death, in 1520, became his widow's third husband, and carried on the business until 1526, when he handed it over to Robert Estienne, and started on his own account in another house in the same street. Thus, just as the co-operation of Erasmus with Froben, which began shortly before the death of Aldus, brought the Basel press into prominence,

so this duplication, just before the death of Froben, of
the business of Henri Estienne with the two firms of
Robert Estienne and Simon de Colines materially aided
the rivalry of Paris. Greek printing, which by this time
had become essential to a printer's reputation for scholarship, had at last begun there with the publication of a
Greek Grammar in 1507, and had increased somewhat,
though not very rapidly. In 1539 François I appointed
Robert Estienne royal printer for Latin and Hebrew,
and Conrad Neobar, a German from the diocese of
Cologne, his printer for Greek. It was soon after this
that plans were formed for the printing of Greek texts
from manuscripts in the royal library, and the preparation for this purpose of a special fount of Greek type.
Neobar died from overwork the following year, and the
office of royal printer in Greek was added to Robert
Estienne's other honours, and with it the supervision of
the new Greek type. For this Angelus Vergetius, a
celebrated Greek calligrapher, had probably already made
the drawings, and the cutting of the punches was
entrusted to Claude Garamond. By 1544 a fount of
great primer had been completed and a book printed in
it, the *Praeparatio Euangelica* of Eusebius. A smaller
type, of the size known as pica, was next put in hand,
and a pocket Greek Testament in sextodecimo printed
with it in 1546. Lastly, a third fount, larger than either
of the others, was produced and used for the text of a
folio Greek Testament in 1550, the other two founts
appearing in the prefatory matter and notes. These
royal Greek types became very famous and served as a
model to all designers of Greek characters for nearly two
centuries. Technically, indeed, they are as good as they
could be, showing a great advance in clearness and
dignity upon those of Aldus, from which nevertheless they inherited the fatal defect of being based on
the handwriting of contemporary Greek scholars, instead of on the book-hand of a nobler period of Greek
writing.

172

While the name of Robert Estienne is thus connected with these royal Greek types he was himself distinctly a Latinist, and his own personal contribution to scholarship was a Latin Dictionary (*Thesaurus Linguae Latinae*) published in 1532, which remained a standard work for two centuries. He published, too, as did also Simon de Colines, many very pretty little editions of Latin classics in sextodecimo, some in italics, others in roman type, thus carrying a step further the triumphant march of the small book, which Aldus had only taken as far as octavos. Simon de Colines, while sharing in work of this kind, did not neglect other classes of literature, and, as has already been noted, joined with Geoffroi Tory, another scholar-printer, who was also a scholar-artist, in producing some remarkable editions of the Hours of the Blessed Virgin.

This scholar-artist, Geoffroi Tory, was a native of Bourges, who had been a professor at several of the Paris colleges and was at one time proof-reader to Henri Estienne. His career as a printer began in 1522 and ended with his death in 1533, after which his business was carried on by Olivier Mallard, who married his widow. Tory printed a few scholarly books and wrote and published a curious work, to which he gave the name *Champfleury*, on the right forms and proportions of the letters of the alphabet. It is, however, by his Books of Hours that he is now chiefly remembered.

While all this good work was going on in Paris the printers at Lyon were no less busy. At the beginning of the century Aldus had been justly annoyed at the clever counterfeits of his italic octavos which were put on the market at Lyon. But in Sebastian Gryphius (a German, born in 1491 at Reutlingen) Lyon became possessed of a printer who had no need to imitate even Aldus. After printing one or two works in the four preceding years his press got into full swing in 1528 and, by the time of his death in 1556 he had issued very nearly a thousand different editions, mostly in Latin, and many of them in the dainty format in sextodecimo which Estienne and de Colines were using in Paris. In 1534 the luckless Etienne Dolet, soon to be burnt as a heretic, arrived at Lyon, and with some friendly help from Gryphius printed between 1538 and 1544 some seventy editions. In 1546 Jean de Tournes, who had been a journeyman in the office of Gryphius, started business for himself, and soon proved a worthy rival to his master. Meanwhile excellent popular work was being done by other printers, such as François Juste, Claude Nourry, Macé Bonhomme, and Guillaume Roville. From the old Lyonnese firm of Trechsel proceeded in 1538 two books illustrated by Holbein (the *Dance of Death* and *Historiarum Veteris Testamenti Icones*, see p. 192), and numerous other Lyonnese books were charmingly illustrated and also, it may be added, charmingly bound, a very pretty style of trade bindings being just then in vogue.

Against the pretty bindings and vignettes and the popular books to which they were applied little or no opposition was raised, and they continued to be issued till the taste for them died out about 1580. But against all the scholarly work of the French presses the leaders of the Church took up an attitude of unrelenting hostility. Foremost in this opposition, regretful that their predecessors had introduced printing into France, were the theologians of the Sorbonne, who forbade the study of Hebrew as dangerous and likely to lead to heresy, and looked with eyes almost as unfriendly on that of Greek. In 1546 (just after the iniquitous campaign against the Vaudois) Etienne Dolet was hanged on a charge of atheism, and his body cut down and burnt amid a pile of his books. In 1550, despite his position as a royal printer, Robert Estienne, who had just completed his fine folio edition of the Greek Testament, was obliged to seek safety by flying to Geneva, and a generation later Jean de Tournes the younger, of Lyon, was obliged to follow his example. The kings of France and their advisers at this period were determined to be rid of both Huguenots and Freethinkers at all costs, and French scholarship and French printing were both the recipients of blows from which it took them some generations to recover.

When Robert Estienne fled to Geneva, his brother, the physician, Charles, was allowed to succeed to his office at Paris, and he in turn was followed by a younger Robert, who died in 1571. Meanwhile Robert I had taken with him a set of matrices of the royal Greek types, and with these and other founts printed at Geneva until his death in 1559. His son, Henri Estienne II, then took over the business, but was of too restless and roving a disposition to conduct it with success. As a scholar he was even greater than his father, excelling in Greek as Robert had in Latin, and producing in 1572 a Greek dictionary (*Thesaurus Graecae Linguae*) which became as famous as the Latin one which Robert had published forty years earlier. Henri Estienne the younger died in 1598, but the Estienne tradition was kept up by his son Paul (1566–1627) and grandson Antoine (1592–1674), the latter bringing back into the family the office of royal printer at Paris, and printing an edition of the Septuagint.

Under the discouraging conditions of the middle of the sixteenth century French printers gradually ceased to be scholars and enthusiasts, but Christopher Plantin, a Frenchman, born in the neighbourhood of Tours in 1514, built up by his energy and industry a great business at Antwerp, the memory of which is preserved in the famous Plantin Museum. He had started at Antwerp in 1549 as a binder, but about six years later turned his attention to printing, in consequence (it is said) of an accident which disabled him for binding-work. The most famous of his books is the great Antwerp Polyglott edition of the Bible in eight volumes, published between the years 1569 and 1573. Over this he came so near to ruining himself that the Spanish Government granted him special privileges for the production of service-books by way of compensation. The sack of Antwerp by the Spaniards in 1576 was another heavy financial blow, and for a time Plantin removed to Leyden, and also for a time kept a branch business at Paris. But he ultimately returned to Antwerp, and his premises remained in the possession of the descendants of one of his sons-in-law, Joannes Moretus, until they were purchased in 1877 for £48,000 as the Musée Plantin.

After Plantin's death the branch business which he had left at Leyden was carried on by another of his sons-in-law, Franciscus Raphelengius, who printed some pretty little editions of the classics and other good books. Plantin's own work as a printer was costly and pretentious rather than beautiful, and the bad style of his ornaments and initials exercised a powerful influence for evil on the printers of the ensuing century.

The mention of Plantin's Antwerp Polyglott may remind us that the first Polyglott edition of the Bible had been printed between 1514 and 1518 at Alcalà, in Spain, under the auspices of Cardinal Ximenes. The Latin name of Alcalà being Complutum, this edition is generally quoted as the Complutensian Polyglott. Among the notable features in it is the use of a singularly fine Greek type in the New Testament. Absolutely different from the Aldine and all the other Greek types imitating the rapid handwriting of the Greek scholars of the sixteenth century, this was based on the book-hand used in some early manuscript, possibly the one which the Pope had lent from the Vatican to aid Cardinal Ximenes in forming his text. It was on this Greek type that Mr. Robert Proctor, shortly before his death, based his own fount of Greek, supplying the majuscules which (with a single exception) are wanting in the original and making other improvements, but keeping closely to his model and thus producing by far the finest Greek type ever cast. This has been used to print notable editions of the *Oresteia* and *Odyssey*, the former at the Chiswick, the latter at the Clarendon Press.

Save for the Complutensian Polyglott there is nothing striking to record of the Spanish printing of the sixteenth century, which retained its massive and archaic character for some decades, and then became as dull and undistinguished as the printing of all the rest of Europe tended to be towards the end of the century. The enthusiasm with which the new art had at first been received had died out. Printers were no longer lodged in palaces, monasteries, and colleges ; Church and State, which had at first fostered and protected them, were now jealous and suspicious, even actively hostile. Thriving members of other occupations and professions had at one time taken to the craft. A little later great scholars had been willing to give their help and advice, and at least a few printers had themselves been men of learning. All this had passed or was passing. Printing had sunk to the level of a mere craft, and a craft in which the hours appear to have been cruelly long and work uncertain and badly paid. In the eighteenth century the Dutch journeymen were certainly better paid than our own, and it may be that it was through better pay that they did better work in the seventeenth century also. It seems certain, moreover, that the improvements in the construction of printing presses which were introduced in that century originated in Holland. The primacy of the Dutch is proved by the large amount of Dutch type imported into England, and indeed the Dutch books of the seventeenth century are neater and in better taste than those of other countries. It was in Holland also that there worked the only firm of printers of this period who made themselves any abiding reputation. The founder of this firm, Louis Elzevir, was a bookseller and bookbinder at Leyden, where, in 1583, he began printing on his own account, and issued between that year and his death in 1617 over a hundred different books of no very special note. No fewer than five of his seven sons carried on his business, and the different combinations of these and of their successors in different towns are not a little bewildering. Bonaventura Elzevir with his nephew Abraham issued pretty little editions of the classics in very small type in 12mo and 16mo, of which the most famous are the Greek Testament of 1624 and 1633, the Virgil, Terence, Livy, Tacitus, Pliny, and Caesar of 1634-6, and a similar series of French historical and political works and French and Italian classics. After the deaths of Abraham and Bonaventura in 1652 the business was carried on by their respective sons Jean and Daniel, who issued famous editions of the *Imitatio Christi* and the Psalter. Meanwhile Louis Elzevir (another grandson of the founder) had been working at Amsterdam, and in 1654 was joined there by Daniel, the new partnership producing some fine folio editions. Other members of the family went on working at Utrecht and Leyden until as late as 1712, so that its whole typographical career extended over a hundred and thirty years. But it is only the little classical editions, and a French cookery book called *Le Pastissier François*, that are at all famous, and the fame of these (the little classics being troublesome to read and having more than a fair share of misprints, though edited by David Heinsius) probably rests on a misconception. These small classical editions were the last word for two centuries in that development of the Small Book which we have already traced in the Aldine editions at Venice, those of De Colines and Robert Estienne of Paris, of Sebastian Gryphius at Lyons, and of the successors of Plantin at Antwerp. Now the small books of the Elzevirs were produced at a very important period in the history of bookbinding, and when we hear of large sums having been paid for an Elzevir it will mostly turn out that the excellence of its binding has had a good deal to do with the price. The cookery book is an exception, the value of this, though often enhanced by a fine binding, being yet considerable, even in a shabby jacket. But the interest in this case is due to the antiquarian instincts of book-loving gourmets, and not in any way to the printing. The little classics, even when of the right date and with all the right little headpieces and all the right misprints, have never been worth on their own merits more than a few pounds, while shabby, cropped copies have no selling value whatever.

CHAPTER XI

FOREIGN ILLUSTRATED BOOKS OF THE SIXTEENTH CENTURY

AS we have already said, the charm of the woodcut pictures in incunabula lies in their simplicity, in their rude story-telling power, often very forcible and direct, in the valiant effort, sometimes curiously successful in cuts otherwise contemptibly poor, to give character and expression to the human face, and as regards form in the harmony between the woodcuts and the paper and type of the books in which they appear. In the book-illustrations of the sixteenth century the artist is more learned, more self-conscious, and his design is interpreted with far greater skill by the better trained wood-cutters of his day. More pains are taken with accessories, and often perhaps for this reason the cut does not tell its story so quickly as of old. It is now a work of art which demands study, no longer a signpost explaining itself however rapidly the leaf is turned. Lastly, the artist seems seldom to have thought of the form of the book in which his work was to appear, of the type with which the text was to be printed, or even of how the wood-cutter was to interpret his design. Book-illustration, which had offered to the humble makers of playing-cards and pictures of saints new scope for their skill, became to the artists of the sixteenth century a lightly valued method of earning a little money from the booksellers, their better work being reserved for single designs, or in some cases for the copperplates which at first they executed, as well as drew, themselves. Thus the book-collector is conscious, on the one hand, that less pains have been taken to please him, and on the other that he is separating by his hobby

180

XXIII. NUREMBERG, SODALITAS CELTICA, 1501

HROSWITHA. OPERA (4^b). HROSWITHA AND THE EMPEROR OTHO

(ATTRIBUTED TO DÜRER)

one section of an artist's work from the rest, in connection
with which it ought to be studied. He may even be in
some doubt as to where his province ends, since many of
the illustrated books of the sixteenth century, although
they possess a titlepage and are made up in quires, are
essentially not books at all, the letterpress being confined
to explanations of the woodcuts printed either below them
or facing them on the opposite pages. The bibliographer
himself, it may be added, feels somewhat of an intruder in
this field, which properly belongs to the student of art,
although in so far as art is enshrined in books and thus
brought within the province of the book-collector, bibliography cannot refuse to deal with it.

Although we have taken off our caps in passing to
Erhard Reuwich and Michael Wolgemut for their
admirable work, the one in the Mainz *Breidenbach*, the
other in the *Schatzbehalter* and *Nuremberg Chronicle*, it
is Albrecht Dürer who must be regarded as the inaugu-
rator of the second period of German book-illustrations.
During his Wanderjahre Dürer had produced at Basel
for an edition of S. Jerome's Epistles, printed by
Nicolaus Kesler in 1492 (reprinted 1497), a rude woodcut
of the saint extracting a thorn from his lion's foot.
Dürer's important bookwork begins in 1498, when his
fifteen magnificent woodcuts illustrating the Apocalypse
(which influenced all later treatments of this theme) were
issued twice over at Nuremberg, in one edition with
German title and text, in the other with Latin. Stated in
their colophons to have been " printed by Albrecht Dürer,
painter," neither edition bears the name of a professional
printer. The types used in each case were those of
Anton Koberger, Dürer's godfather, and the effect of the
artist's personal superintendence, which the colophons
attest, is seen in the excellence of the presswork. The
following year Koberger published an illustrated edition
of the *Reuelationes Sanctae Birgittae* (German reprint in
1502), and Dürer has been supposed to have helped in
this, but the theory is now discredited. In 1501 he

probably contributed two woodcuts to an edition of the comedies of Hroswitha, a tenth century nun of the Benedictine Abbey at Gandersheim. Conrad Celtes had unearthed these comedies some years previously in a Ratisbon library, and they were now printed under his editorship for the *Sodalitas Celtica* at Nuremberg. The illustrations to the comedies themselves, which vie in heaviness with their subjects, are attributed by Mr. Campbell Dodgson to Wolfgang Traut.[1] One of the cuts assigned to Dürer represents Celtes offering the book to Frederick III, Elector of Saxony; the other shows Hroswitha herself presenting her plays to the Emperor Otto I (see Plate XXIII). In 1502 Dürer designed another cut of a presentation and an illustration of Philosophy (both very feebly rendered by the cutter) for the *Quatuor libri Amorum* of Celtes. In 1511 the Latin Apocalypse was reprinted, and three other sets of woodcuts by Dürer appeared in book form, in each case with Latin text by Benedictus Chelidonius. One of these commemorated in twenty designs the life of the Blessed Virgin (*Epitome in Diuae Parthenices Marie Historiam ab Alberto Durero Norico per Figuras digestam cum versibus annexis Chelidonii*), the other two the Passion of Christ, the Great Passion (*Passio domini nostri Jesu ex hieronymo Paduano, Dominico Mancino, Sedulio et Baptista Mantuano per fratrem Chelidonium collecta cum figuris Alberti Dureri Norici Pictoris*, in folio) in twelve large woodcuts, the Little Passion (*Passio Christi ab Alberto Durer Norembergensi effigiata cū varij generis carminibus Fratris Benedicti Chelidonij Musophili*, in quarto) in thirty-seven smaller ones. After this Dürer was caught up by the Emperor Maximilian and set to work on some of the various ambitious projects for illustrating his reign, as to which more will be said later. His later bookwork includes a Crucifixion and S. Willi-

---

[1] Mr. Dodgson also ascribes to Traut the illustrations in the *Legend des heyligen vatters Francisci* (Nuremberg, 1512), and some of the cuts in the *Theuerdank* (1517).

bald for an Eichstätt Missal (Nuremberg, H. Hölzel, 1517), some large designs for the *Etliche vnderricht zu befestigung der Stett Schloss vnd flecken* (Nuremberg, 1527), and his own book on the Proportion of the Human Body, which was issued both in German and in a Latin translation by Camerarius.

Several borders and illustrations formerly ascribed to Dürer are now attributed to one of his pupils, Hans Springinklee, who lived in Dürer's house at Nuremberg, where he worked from about 1513 to 1522. Most of Springinklee's bookwork was done for Anton Koberger, who published some of it at Nuremberg, while some was sent to the Lyon printers, Clein, Sacon, and Marion, who were in Koberger's employment. A border of his design bearing the arms of Bilibaldus Pirckheimer is found in several works which Pirckheimer edited (1513–17). In a *Hortulus Animae*, printed by J. Clein for Koberger at Lyon, 1516, fifty cuts are by Springinklee. The *Hortulus Animae* was as popular in Germany as the illustrated *Horae* in France and England. In 1517 another edition appeared with Erhard Schön as its chief illustrator, and only a few of Springinklee's cuts. The next year Springinklee produced a new set of cuts, and Schön's work was less used. Springinklee and Schön were also associated in Bible illustrations printed for Koberger by Sacon at Lyon, and to Springinklee are now assigned two full-page woodcuts in an Eichstätt Missal (H. Hölzel, Nuremberg, 1517), and a border to the *Reuelationes Birgittae* (F. Peypus, Nuremberg, 1517), formerly ascribed to Dürer. A woodcut of Johann Tritheim presenting his *Polygraphia* to Maximilian, formerly attributed to Holbein as having been printed at Basel (Adam Petri, 1518), is now also placed to the credit of Springinklee, who, moreover, worked for the *Weisskunig* and probably for other of the artistic commemorations of himself which Maximilian commissioned.

Hans Sebald Beham is best known as a book-illustrator from his work for Christian Egenolph at

183

Frankfurt am Main, which began in 1533. But he belonged to the Nuremberg school, had worked for ten or twelve years for Merckel, Peypus, Petreius and other Nuremberg firms, and has had the honour of having some of his single cuts attributed to Dürer. His most important books for Egenolph were the *Biblische Historien*, a series of small illustrations to the Bible, first printed in 1533, which went through many editions in German and Latin, and another series illustrating the Apocalypse, of which the first edition appeared in 1539, the texts of the Latin *Historiae* and also to the Apocalypse cuts being supplied by Georgius Aemilius. A set of medallion portraits of Roman emperors by him also appeared in several German and Latin chronicles published by Egenolph.

Between the Nuremberg book-illustrators and those of Augsburg, to whom we must now turn, a connecting link may be found in the person of Hans Leonhard Schäufelein, born about 1480, soon after his father, a Nordlingen wool merchant, had settled at Nuremberg. He worked under Dürer, and his earliest book-illustrations were made for Dr. Ulrich Pinder, the owner of a private press at Nuremberg. Several unsigned cuts in *Der beschlossen gart des rosenkrantz Marie* (Pinder, 1505), and thirty out of thirty-four large cuts in a *Speculum Passionis* (Pinder, 1507), are ascribed to Schäufelein, his associate in each book being Hans Baldung. About 1510 Schäufelein removed to Augsburg, and, despite his return to his paternal home at Nordlingen where he took up his citizenship in 1515, he worked for the chief Augsburg publishers for the rest of his life, though between 1523 and 1531 nothing is known as to what he was doing.

Among the earlier Augsburg books with illustrations attributed to Schäufelein are Tengler's *Der neu Layenspiegel* (1511), Henricus Suso's *Der Seusse* (1512), *Heiligenleben* (1513), Geiler's *Schiff der Penitentz* (1514), and the *Hystori und wunderbarlich legend Katharine von*

Senis (1515), all published by J. Otmar. In 1514 he had illustrated for Adam Petri of Basel a *Plenarium* or *Evangelienbuch*, which went through several editions. Another *Evangelienbuch*, printed by Thomas Anshelm at Hagenau in 1516, contains several cuts with Schäufelein's signature, but in a different style, probably partly due to a different wood-cutter; these were used again in other books.

In the *Theuerdank* of 1517 about twenty cuts are assigned to Schäufelein, some of them bearing his signature. The following year he illustrated Leonrodt's *Himmelwagen* for Otmar with twenty cuts, mostly signed, some of which were used afterwards on the titlepages of early Luther tracts. After an interval Schäufelein is found in 1533 working for Heinrich Steyner of Augsburg, who employed him to illustrate his German editions of the classics, Thucydides (1533), Plutarch (1534), Cicero (1534), Apuleius (1538), etc. The blocks for some of his cuts subsequently passed into the possession of Christian Egenolph of Frankfort.

The first native Augsburg artist whom we have to notice is Hans Burgkmair, who was born in 1473, and began bookwork in 1499 by illustrating missals for Erhard Ratdolt with pictures of patron saints and of the Crucifixion. The chief Augsburg publisher for whom he worked in his early days was Johann Otmar, for whom he illustrated several books by the popular preacher, Johann Geiler von Kaisersberg (*Predigen teutsch*, 1508 and 1510, *Das Buch Granatapfel*, 1510, *Nauicula Poenitentiae*, 1511), and other devotional and moral works. In 1515 Hans Schoensperger the younger employed him to supply a dedication cut and seven designs of the Passion for a *Leiden Christi*, and to the *Theuerdank* published by Schoensperger the elder at Nuremberg in 1517 he contributed thirteen illustrations (only one signed). He had already been employed (1510) on a few of the cuts in the Genealogy of the Emperor Maximilian, which a wholesome fear lest its accuracy should be doubted caused that self-celebrating monarch to withhold from publication, and much more largely (1514-16) on the *Weisskunig*, which was first printed, from the original blocks, at Vienna in 1775; and he was the chief worker (1516-18) on the woodcuts for the Triumphal Procession of Maximilian printed by order of the Archduke Ferdinand in 1526. While these imperial commissions were in progress Burgkmair designed a few title-cuts for Johann Miller, notably the very fine one (see Plate XXIV) to the *De rebus Gothorum* of Jornandes (1515), showing kings Alewinus and Athanaricus in conversation, and subsequently worked for Grimm and Wirsung and for H. Steiner, although not nearly to the extent which was at one time supposed, as most of the illustrations supplied to these firms with which he used to be credited are now assigned to Hans Weiditz.

Jörg Breu, who was born and died (1537) some half-dozen years later than Burgkmair, like him illustrated Missals for Ratdolt and contributed Passion-cuts to Mann's *Leiden Christi*. His most important piece of bookwork was the redrawing of the cuts in Anton Sorg's edition of Reichenthal's *Conciliumbuch* for a reprint by Steiner in 1536. Illustrations by him also occur in a *Melusina* (1538), and German versions of Boccaccio's *De claris mulieribus* and *De Casibus Illustrium virorum* issued after his death by the same firm. Leonhard Beck contributed largely to the illustration of Maximilian's literary ventures, especially the *Theuerdank, Weisskunig*, and Saints of the House of Austria (published at some date between 1522 and 1551).

We come now to Hans Weiditz, the immense extension of whose work by the attributions of recent years can only be compared to Mr. Proctor's raising of Bartolommeo de' Libri from one of the smallest to one of the most prolific of Florentine printers. Only two or three Augsburg woodcuts bearing his initials are known, while scores and even hundreds are now assigned to him, most of which had previously been credited to Burgkmair.

IORNAN
DES DE REBVS
GOTHORVM, PAV
LVS DIACONVS
FOROIVLIEN·
SIS DE GESTIS
LANGOBARDO·
RVM

ALBVVINVS·
·REX·

ATHANARICVS
·REX·

XXIV. AUGSBURG, J. MILLER, 1515

JORNANDES. DE REBUS GOTHORUM. (TITLE). ATTRIBUTED TO
BURGKMAIR

Weiditz began bookwork in or before 1518, in which year he contributed a title-cut to the *Nemo* of Ulrich von Hutten, while in 1519 he made twelve illustrations to the same author's account of Maximilian's quarrel with the Venetians. In 1518 he had begun working for the firm of Grimm and Wirsung, and this, with a few commissions from other Augsburg publishers, kept him busy till about 1523, when he himself moved to Strassburg, whence his family had come, while in the same year Grimm and Wirsung gave up business and sold their blocks to Steiner. These included not only many title-borders by Weiditz, twenty illustrations to two comedies of Plautus and a set of cuts to the *Deuotissime meditationes de vita et passione Christi*, and another to a German *Celestina*, all published in 1520, but a series of some 260 masterly illustrations to a German version of Petrarch's *De remediis utriusque fortunae*. Steiner used some of these cuts in a Cicero *De Officiis* of 1531, which has in addition sixty-seven important cuts by Weiditz, presumably of the same period, and also in a *Justinus* of the same year, but the work for which they were specially designed did not appear until a year later. Needless to say, selections from both the Petrarch and the Cicero sets appear in later work.

After removing to Strassburg, Weiditz copied some Wittenberg Bible cuts and also Holbein's Apocalypse set for Knoblauch in 1524. In 1530 he illustrated for J. Schott the *Herbarium* of Brunfels, which went through several editions both in Latin and German, and for this comparatively humble work was praised by name in both editions, so that until 1904 it was only as the illustrator of the Herbal that he was known. Many of his Augsburg woodcuts subsequently passed to that persistent purchaser of old blocks, Christian Egenolph of Frankfort.

Before passing away from the Nuremberg and Augsburg book-illustrators, it seems necessary to describe briefly, but in a more connected form, the literary and artistic enterprises of the Emperor Maximilian, to which

187

so many incidental allusions have been made. The
Emperor's first attempt to glorify himself and his lineage
took the form of a Genealogy for which several antiquaries
—Mennel, Sunthaim, Tritheim, and Stabius—made researches. Burgkmair made designs of some ninety
ancestors and their heraldic coats in 1509-11, and the
wood-blocks were cut. It was apparently intended to
print them in 1512, but the whole project was abandoned,
and the work is now only known from a few sets of
proofs, no one of which is quite complete.

After this failure Maximilian planned a Triumphal
Arch and Procession, the programme for the Arch being
drawn up by Stabius, that of the Procession by Treitzsaurwein. The plan of the Arch was largely worked out
by Dürer, with help from Springinklee, Traut, and
Altdorfer, whose designs were carried out in 192 wood-
blocks cut by Hieronymus Andrea and his assistants.
When the impressions from these are put together they
make a design measuring nearly twelve feet by ten. In
the centre is the Gate of Honour, to the left and right the
gates of Praise and Nobility. Above the main gate rises
a tower on which are displayed the Emperor's ancestors
and their arms, above the other gates a series of incidents
of Maximilian's life, surmounted by busts of his imperial
predecessors and of contemporary princes. This was
printed in 1517-18 at Nuremberg, and in 1526-8 and
1559 at Vienna. On the Procession or Triumph, Dürer,
Springinklee, Schäufelein, Burgkmair, and Beck were all
engaged. The 138 blocks composing it were cut by
Andrea and Jost de Negker in 1516-18, and it was
printed by order of the Archduke Ferdinand in 1526. A
Triumphal Car designed by Dürer in 1518, in connection
with the same project, was published in eight sheets in
1522.

A series of representations of Saints of the House of
Hapsburg had been planned soon after the abandonment
of the Genealogy, and assumed shape in 1514. From
drawings now attributed to Leonhard Beck, 123 wood-

blocks were made, and an edition in book form was printed some time after 1522.

The romance of *Theuerdank* was written by Melchior Pfintzing, under Maximilian's direction, to celebrate his wooing of Mary of Burgundy and other exploits. The bulk (seventy-seven) of the illustrations in it are now ascribed to Beck, seventeen to Schäufelein, thirteen to Burgkmair, and three, two, and one respectively to Schön, Traut, and Breu. It was published as a sumptuous folio, several copies being struck on vellum by the elder Schoensperger at Nuremberg in 1517, and reprinted two years later.

The *Weisskunig*, or White King, an account of Maximilian's parentage, education, and exploits, was dictated by him in fragments to Treitzsaurwein, but never fully edited. Of the 249 illustrations about half are by Burgkmair, most of the others by Beck. With the exception of thirteen the blocks were preserved at Vienna, and the book was printed there for the first time in 1775.

Lastly, the *Freydal*, which was to have given an account of Maximilian's tourneys and "Mummereien," is known to us by the preservation of the original miniatures from which the illustrations were to have been made, but only five blocks out of 256 were actually cut.

The patronage of the Emperor Maximilian gives special importance to the work done during his lifetime at Nuremberg and Augsburg, but there was no lack of book-illustrations elsewhere. At Tübingen some of the mathematical works of Johann Stöffler were curiously decorated, and the second edition of his *Ephemerides* (1533) has a fine portrait of the author in his seventy-ninth year. At Ratisbon, Albrecht Altdorfer was the most important worker for the wood-cutters, and to him are now attributed thirty-eight cuts illustrating the Fall and Redemption of Man, published at Hamburg in 1604, under the name of Dürer, as "nunc primùm è tenebris in lucem editæ." Their minute and rather niggling style renders the bad printing which they have mostly received peculiarly destructive to them. Another Ratisbon artist, Michael Ostendorfer, illustrated a few books published at Ratisbon itself, and others printed at Ingolstadt.

At Wittenberg, from a little before 1520, the influence of Martin Luther made itself as much felt as that of Maximilian at Augsburg and Nuremberg. Hither, in 1505, had come a Franconian artist, Lucas Cranach, who had already illustrated some missals for Winterburger of Vienna. Numerous pictures of saints, which he drew for the Wittenberg *Heiligthumsbuch* of 1509, are subsequently found dispersed in other works, such as the *Hortulus Animae*. A few title-cuts on tracts by Luther and others are assigned to him, but a great mass of book-work, including numerous fine borders, found in Wittenberg books of the Luther period, while showing abundant traces of the elder Cranach's influence, is yet clearly not by him. It has recently been assigned, with some probability, to his eldest son, Hans. His younger son, Lucas Cranach II, also supplied a few borders and illustrations to the Wittenberg booksellers. Georg Lemberger also produced borders for titlepages and some Bible cuts, and two other Wittenberg Bible-illustrators of this school were Erhard Altdorfer, brother of Albrecht, whose best bookwork is found in a fine Danish Bible printed at Copenhagen in 1550, and Hans Brosamer, Bibles, or parts of the Bible, with whose cuts appeared both at Wittenberg and at Frankfort.

At Strassburg, Hans Baldung Grien, whose work shows the influence of Dürer, illustrated the *Granatapfel* (1510) and other works by Geiler of Kaisersberg, the *Hortulus Animae* printed by Flach (1510), etc. Johann Wächtlin, who had contributed a Resurrection to a set of Passion cuts published by Knoblauch in 1506, illustrated a *Leben Christi* for the same printer in 1508. We find his work again in the *Feldbuch der Wundarznei* of Hans von Gersdorff, printed by Schott in 1517. The work of

Hans Weiditz for Strassburg publishers has already been mentioned. It was here also that Urs Graf worked for some little time for Knoblauch, to whose Passion set of 1507 he contributed, and other publishers. In 1509 he is found at Basel, where two years later he became a citizen, supplying ninety-five little woodcuts to an edition of the *Postilla* of Guillermus, and also designing title borders. As a centre of printing Basel was now rapidly increasing in importance, and when Erasmus allied himself with the foremost Basel printer, Johann Froben, for a time the city succeeded, in point of quality though not of quantity, to the typographical supremacy which Venice was fast losing. Scholarly works such as approved themselves to Erasmus and Froben offered, of course, very little scope for book-illustration properly so called, but the desire for beauty found vent, not only with them, but with the other Basel printers of the day, Valentin Curio, Johann Bebel, Adam Petri, Andreas Cratander, etc., in elaborate borders to titlepages, headpieces and tailpieces, ornamental capitals and trade devices. The arrival of Hans Holbein (born at Augsburg in 1497) at Basel in 1516 on his Wander-jahre supplied a decorator of a skill altogether outshining that shown in the rather tasteless architectural work, varied with groups of children, produced by Urs Graf, though Holbein himself was content to begin in this style. In his most characteristic work the footpiece of the border illustrates some classical scene, Mutius Scaevola and Porsenna, the death of Cleopatra, or Quintus Curtius leaping into the abyss; less commonly a scriptural one, such as the death of John the Baptist. The most elaborate of his titlepages was that to the *Tabula* of Cebes (1521), in which little children crowd through the gate of life to meet all the varied fortunes which life brings. Delightful humour is shown in an often used headpiece and tailpiece, showing villagers chasing a fox and returning home dancing. During 1517 and the following year, when Hans Holbein was absent from Basel, his brother Ambrosius worked there on the same lines, and decorated, among other books, More's *Utopia*.

After his return to Basel in 1519, Hans Holbein remained at work there until 1526, and it was during this period that his book-illustrations, properly so called, were executed, including those to the Apocalypse and his two most famous pieces of bookwork, his *Dance of Death* and *Historiarum Veteris Testamenti Icones*, both of which were first published in 1538 at Lyon by Melchior and Gaspar Trechsel. These (with perhaps some exceptions) and many of his other designs[1] were cut in wood by Hans Lutzelburger who signed a Holbein titlepage to a German New Testament printed by Thomas Wolff in 1523, and who, if rightly identified with the Hans Formschneider with whose widow the Trechsels were in correspondence in 1526 and 1527, must have died about the time that Holbein left Basel. Pen copies, moreover, of some of the cuts of the *Dance of Death* are preserved at the Berlin Museum, and one of these is dated 1527, so that there can be no question that the originals belong to this period of Holbein's life, and the British Museum possesses a set of proofs of forty out of the original series of forty-one, printed on four sheets, ten on a sheet. It has been conjectured that the occupations of some of the great personages whom Death is depicted as seizing may have been considered as coming under the offence of *scandalum magnatum* and so have caused the long delay before the blocks were used, but as this explanation does not apply to the illustrations to the Old Testament it seems inadequate. As published in 1538 by the Trechsels the cuts are accompanied by French quatrains from the pen of Gilles Corrozet and other appropriate matter, and have prefixed to them a titlepage reading: *Les Simulachres & Historiees Faces de la Mort, autant elegammēt pourtraictes que artificiellement imaginees.*

---

[1] Including perhaps the four sets of decorative capitals attributed to Holbein, one ornamental, the others representing a Dance of Peasants, Children, and a Dance of Death.

A Lyon, soubz lescu de Coloigne, M.D.XXXVIII. A second edition with Latin instead of French verses was published by Jean and François Frellon, and others followed, in one of which, that of 1545, one, and in another, that of 1547, eleven additional cuts were printed, while in 1562, when the book was still in Frellon's hands, five woodcuts of children make their appearance, though they have no connection with the original series.

That Holbein's Old Testament designs also belong to his Basel period is shown by copies of them appearing in a Bible printed by Froschouer in 1531, though the original cuts were not published till seven years later. As printed by the Trechsels they are eighty-six in number, and while the cutting of the best is worthy of Lutzelburger, their execution is too unequal for it to be certain that the whole series was executed by him. The cuts were also used by the Trechsels in a Bible of the same year, and both the Bible and the cuts under their own title *Historiarum Veteris Testamenti Icones* were republished by the Frellons.

Considerations of space forbid more than a bare mention of the *Bambergische Halssgericht* (1508), with its all too vivid representations of the cruel punishments then in use, and the illustrated classics published at later dates by Johann Schoeffer at Mainz, or of the work of Jakob Köbel at Oppenheim with its rather clumsy imitations of Ratdolt's Italian ornaments, or of the illustrated books printed by Johann Weissenburger at Landshut, or of those from the press of Hieronymus Rodlich at Siemen, the *Thurnierbuch* of 1530, *Kunst des Messens* of the following year, and *Fierabras* of 1533. After about 1535 little original book-illustration of any importance was produced in other German cities, but in Nuremberg and Frankfurt it continued plentiful, Virgil Solis and Jobst Amman working assiduously for the booksellers in both places.

In no other country did the first thirty years of the sixteenth century produce so much interesting work as in

Germany. Interesting, moreover, as this German work is in itself, it is made yet more so by the fact that a sufficient proportion of it is signed to enable connoisseurs to pursue their pleasant task of distributing the unsigned cuts among the available artists. Less intrinsically good, and with very few facilities for playing this fascinating game, the book-illustrations of other countries have been comparatively little studied. In Italy the new century brought some evil days to the book trade. Printing itself ceased for a time at Brescia; at Florence publishers for many years relied chiefly on their old stock of cuts; at Milan, at Ferrara and Pavia a little new work was done. At Venice the thin delicate outline cuts of the last decade of the fifteenth century ceased to be produced any longer, though the old blocks sometimes reappear. More often the old designs were either simply copied or imitated in the more heavily shaded style which was now coming into vogue. The interest of some of this shaded work is increased by the occasional appearance on it of a signature. Thus in the *Missale Romanum* of 30 July, 1506, published by Stagninus, some of the cuts in this shaded style bear the same signature, "ia," as appears on the outline work in the Ovid of 1497. Work done by "ia" is also sometimes found copied by another cutter calling himself VGO, whose name is also found on some copies of French Horae cuts in a Venice Horae of 1513.

Signatures which occur with some frequency between 1515 and 1529 are the z.a., z.A., and I.A. used by Zoan Andrea, i.e. Johannes Andreas Vavassore. This Zoan Andrea was an assiduous copyist. Early in his career (1515-16) we find him imitating Dürer's large illustrations to the Apocalypse; in 1517 his title-cut for the *De modo regendi* of Antonio Cornazano imitates that of Burgkmair on the 1515 *De rebus Gothorum* of Jornandes. In 1520 he prefixed to a Livy printed by Giunta an excellent portrait modelled, as the Prince d'Essling has shown, on a sculpture set up at Padua to the memory either of the historian himself or of one of his descendants; in

194

XXV. VENICE. GREG. DE GREGORIIS, 1518

MISSALE ROMANUM (246^b). THE ASCENSION

1521 he copied Marcantonio Raimondi's engraving of Horatius Cocles, and in the same year another by Raimondi of Quintus Curtius. This was for an edition of Boiardo, and for a later edition of 1524 Zoan Andrea copied yet another engraving, that of Scipio Africanus. In 1525 he imitated Holbein's elaborate border to the *Tabula Cebetis*, applying it to a *Dictionarium Graecum*. About this time also he produced the well-known block-book (at least three editions known) *Opera noua contemplatiua*, imitating Dürer's Little Passion in some of the cuts. Because of the rarity of signed woodcuts in Italian books Zoan Andrea has attracted more attention than the quality of his work deserves. It seems probable that he was the head of a workshop, and the craftsmanship of the cuts bearing his signature is very unequal.

Turning to the general course of book-illustration in Venice as it may be studied in the great work of the Prince d'Essling, unhappily left without the promised introduction at the time of his lamented death, we find several different influences at work. As has been already noted, the shaded work which had begun to make its appearance before 1500, as in the frontispiece to the *Epitome Almagesti* of Regiomontanus (1496), rapidly became the predominant style. We find it combined with some of the charm of the earlier outline vignettes in the small pictures of a Virgil of 1507, and in some of those of another edition in 1508, though the larger ones in this are heavy and coarse. The extreme of coarseness is found in an edition of the *Legendario di Sancti* of 1518, the woodcuts being more suited to a broadside for a cottage wall than to Venetian bookwork. The style is seen at its best in the illustrations of a well-known Horae printed by Bernardinus Stagninus in 1507, and, generally speaking, it is in the Missals, Breviaries, and Horae published by L. A. Giunta, Stagninus and the De Gregoriis (see Plate XXV) that the most satisfactory bookwork of this period is found.

Another style which may be traced in many books of

the early years of the century is a rather coarse development of the characteristic Florentine manner of the fifteenth century. The cuts are as a rule considerably larger than the Florentine ones, and the ornamental borders which surround them are much deeper. As in many of the Florentine cuts, more use is made of black spaces than was usual at Venice, but the cutting as a rule is coarse, and there is none of the charm of the best Florentine work. Woodcuts in this style are found most frequently on the titlepages of popular books in small quarto, published by the Sessas, who apparently did not see their way to commissioning more than a single illustration to each book. But the influence of the style affected the pictures in a few works of larger size—for instance, the 1503 edition of the *Chronica Chronicarum* of Bergomensis, and the well-known picture of a choir in the *Practica Musices* of Gafori (1512).

Despite his connection with the *Hypnerotomachia*, which, however, was printed on commission, Aldus concerned himself little with book-illustrations, and if the miserable cuts which he put into his edition of *Hero and Leander* of Musaeus are fair specimens of what he thought sufficiently good when left to himself, he was well advised in holding aloof from them. Nevertheless, the popularity which he gained for the small octavos which he introduced in 1501 was an important factor in the development of book-illustration in the sixteenth century. Although Aldus did not illustrate them himself, it was impossible that the lightly printed handy books which he introduced should remain permanently unillustrated, and when italic type was ousting roman and small books taking the place of large, the introduction of smaller illustrations, depending for their effect on the delicacy of their cutting, became inevitable. If we take any popular book of the century, such as the *Sonetti* of Petrarch, and note the illustrations in successive editions, we shall find them getting smaller and smaller and more and more lightly cut and lightly printed, in order to match better with the thin italic types. The new style is seen at its best in the books of 1540-60, the Petrarch of 1544 printed by Gabriel Giolito, Boccaccio's *Decamerone* printed by Valgrisi in 1552, Ovid's *Metamorphoses* by Giolito in 1553. Finally, book-illustration peters out at Venice in pictorial capitals, which take as their subjects any heroes of Greek and Roman history and mythology whose names begin with the required letter, on the principle of the nursery alphabet in which "A was an Archer who shot at a frog, B was a Butcher who had a great dog." To an age which, not otherwise to its loss, neglects the study of Lemprière's Classical Dictionary, many of these puzzle initials are bafflingly obscure, relieved only by a recurring Q, which in almost all alphabets depicts Quintus Curtius leaping into the chasm at Rome. Some similar sets of Old Testament subjects are much easier. Books decorated with capitals of this kind are found as late as the end of the seventeenth century. Isolated initials designed on this plan are found also in other countries, but outside Italy it is only seldom that we come across anything approaching a set.

As to French book-illustrations of the sixteenth century, a competent historian should have much to say, but the present writer has made no detailed study of them, and in the absence of any monograph to steal from must be content with recording general impressions, only here and there made precise by references to books which he has examined. Far more than those of Germany or Venice, French publishers of the sixteenth century relied on the great stock of woodcuts which had come into existence during the decades 1481–1500. That they did so may be regarded as some compensation for the exceptional rarity of most of the more interesting French incunabula. We have spoken disrespectfully of the little devotional books printed about 1500 with an old Horae cut on the back of the titlepage or at the end, but in the popular books printed by the Lenoirs and other publishers as late as 1530, and even later, cuts will be found from Millet's *Destruction de Troie* and other incunabula now quite unobtainable, and it is even possible at times from salvage of this kind to deduce the former existence of fifteenth century editions of which no copy can now be found.

After about 1503 the French Horae decline rapidly in beauty and interest, but many fine missals were issued by Wolfgang Hopyl and other firms, some with one or more striking pictures, almost all with admirable capitals.

Among non-liturgical books it is difficult to find any class for which new illustrations were made at all freely. Several books of Chronicles by Monstrelet, Robert Gaguin, and others have one or more cuts at the beginning which may have been made for them, e.g. a folio cut of S. Denis and S. Rémy, with shields of arms found in the *Compendium super Francorum gestis* by Robert Gaguin (this, however, dates back to 1500), a double cut of S. Louis blessed by the Pope and confronting the Turks (found in Gaguin's *Sommaire Historial de France*, c. 1523, and elsewhere), another double cut of Clovis baptized and in battle (Gaguin's *Mer des Chronicques*, 1536, but much earlier), a spirited battle scene (*Victoire du Roy contre les Vénitiens*, 1510), etc. But wherever we find illustrations in the text, there we are sure to light on a medley of old cuts (e.g. in *Les grands chronicques de France*, 1514, Gaguin's *Chronicques*, 1516, and the *Rozier historial*, 1523), and it will be odds that Millet's *Destruction de Troie* will be found contributing its woodcuts of the Trojan War as illustrations of French history. When an original cut of this period can be found, it seldom has the charm of the best work of the last five years of the fifteenth century, but is usually quite good ; there is, for instance, a quite successful metal-cut with criblé background of Justinian in Council in an edition of his laws printed by Bocard for Petit in 1516, and some of the liturgical cuts are admirable. There is thus no reason to impute the falling off

198

in new cuts to lack of artists. It seems clear that the demand for illustrations had for the moment shifted to an uncritical audience who liked (small blame to them) the fifteenth century cuts which had delighted more educated people a generation earlier, and were not at all particular as to their appropriateness. Meanwhile the educated book-buyers were learning Greek and preparing themselves to appreciate the severe, unillustrated elegance of the books of the Estiennes, and new cuts were not needed.

The inception of a new style must certainly be connected with the name of Geoffroi Tory, whose best work is to be found in his Books of Hours, which have already been described in an earlier chapter. Its predominant note is a rather thin elegance of outline, in which the height of the figures is usually somewhat exaggerated. Tory is supposed to have brought home this style after his visit to Italy, but its application to bookwork appears to have been his own idea. There is, indeed, a striking resemblance between the little cuts of Tory's third Horae set, dated 8 February, 1529, and those in an Aldine Horae of October of the same year, but to the best of my belief Tory reckoned his year from 1 January, not in the old French style from Easter, and if so it was Tory who supplied the Aldine artist with a model, which indeed is a logical continuation of his editions of 1525 and 1527. It is greatly to be regretted that his own *Champfleury* of 1527 is so slightly illustrated. The little picture of Hercules Gallicus which comes in it is quite delightful.

If any guide were in existence to the illustrated French books of the thirties in the sixteenth century it would probably be possible to trace the spread of Tory's influence. In 1530 Simon Colines illustrated Jean Ruel's *Veterinaria Medicina* with a good enough cut in the old French style slightly modified. For the same author's *De Natura Stirpium* of 1536 he provided a woodcut, of an alcove scene in a garden, the tone of which is quite new.

It is evident that French publishers were waking up to new possibilities and sending their artists to foreign models, as a *Perceforest* printed for Gilles Gourmont in 1531 and a *Meliadus de Leonnoys* for Denis Janot in 1532, have both of them elaborate title borders in the style which the Holbeins had made popular at Basel. The latter is signed .F., a signature found in several later books in the new style. In 1534 we find Wechel issuing a *Valturius* with neat adaptations of the old Verona illustrations. Doubtless there were many other interesting books, with cuts original or copied of this decade, but the only one of which I have a note is the *L'amant mal traicte de sa mye* (translated from the Spanish of Diego de San Pedro), printed by Denis Janot for V. Sertenas in 1539, in which the title is enclosed in a delicately cut border, the footpiece of which shows the lovers in a garden. Not long after this Janot printed (without putting his name or a date) *La touche Naifue pour esprouver Lamy and le Flateur* of Antoine Du Saix, in which the rules enclosing the title cut into a pretty oval design of flowers and ribbons. In 1540 we find the new style fully established in the *Hecatongraphie Cest à dire les descriptions de cent figures & hystoires*, a book of emblems, by Gilles Corrozet, printed by Denis Janot, which I only know in the third edition, that of 1543. Here we find little vignettes, much smaller than those in the Malermi Bible, with a headline over them and a quatrain in italics beneath, the whole enclosed in an ornamental frame. The little cuts have the faults inevitable in emblems, and some of them are poorly cut, but the best of them are not only wonderfully delicate, but show a sense of movement and a skill in the manipulation of drapery never reached in the fifteenth century.

In 1543 appeared, again from the press of Denis Janot, "imprimeur du Roy en langue françoise," another emblem book, *Le Tableau de Cebes de Thebes, ancien philosophe & disciple de Socrate: auquel est paincte de ses couleurs, la uraye image de la vie humaine, & quelle uoye l'homme*

XXVI. PARIS, J. LOYS FOR V. SERTENAS, 1545

HOMER. L'ILIADE EN VERS FRANCOIS. (TITLE-CUT)

doit elire, pour peruenir à vertu & perfaicte science. Premieremēt escript en Grec & maintenant expose en Ryme Francoyse. The French rhymester was again the author of the *Hecatongraphie*, and the imprint, " A Paris On les uend en la grand [*sic*] salle du Palais en la boutique de Gilles Corrozet," shows that he not only wrote the verses and perhaps inspired the illustrations, but sold the books as well.

In 1545 we find this same style of design and cutting on a larger scale in *Les dix premiers livres de l'Iliade d'Homère, Prince des Poetes, traduictz en vers François, par M. Hugues Salel,* and printed by Iehan Loys for Vincent Sertenas. The cuts are in two sizes, the smaller being surrounded with Toryesque borders. It is difficult to pass any judgment other than one of praise on such delicate work. Nevertheless, just as the *fanfare* style of binding used by Nicolas Eve, with its profuse repetition of small tools, is much more effective on a small book cover than on a large, so here we may well feel that some bolder and clearer design would be better suited to the illustration of a folio. In the title-cut here shown (Plate XXVI) a rather larger style is attempted with good results.

The year after the Homer there appeared at Paris from the press of Jacques Kerver a French translation of the *Hypnerotomachia* by Jean Martin. This is one of the most interesting cases of the rehandling of woodcuts, the arrangement of the original designs being closely followed, while the tone is completely changed by the substitution of the tall rather thin figures which had become fashionable in French woodcuts for the short and rather plump ones of the Venetian edition, and by similar changes in the treatment of landscape.

In the second half of the century at Paris excellent woodcut portraits, mostly in an oval frame, are sometimes found on titlepages, and in other cases decoration is supplied by a neatly cut device. Where illustrations are needed for the explanation of works on hunting or any other subjects they are mostly well drawn and cut. But the use of woodcuts in books of imaginative literature became more and more rare.

At Lyon, as at Paris, at the beginning of the century the store of fifteenth century cuts was freely drawn on for popular editions. Considerable influence, however, was exercised at first by Italian models, afterwards by Germany, so that while in the early sixteenth century Latin Bibles the cuts are mostly copied from Giunta's *Malermi* Bible, these were gradually superseded by German cuts, which Anton Koberger supplied to the Lyonnese printers who worked for him. While in Italy the small octavos popularized by Aldus continued to hold their own, in France, from about 1530, editions in 32° came rapidly into fashion, and about the middle of the century these were especially the vogue at Lyon, the publishers often casing them in very gay little trade bindings sometimes stamped in gold, but often with painted interlacements. The publication by the Trechsels in 1538 of the two Holbein books, the *Dance of Death* and illustrations to the Old Testament, must have given an impetus to picture-making at Lyon, but this was at first chiefly visible in illustrated Bibles and New Testaments. Gilles Corrozet, who had written the verses for both the Holbein books, continued his career, as we have seen, at Paris. The most typical Lyonnese illustrated books were the rival editions of Ovid's *Metamorphoses* in French, one printed by Macé Bonhomme in 1556, with borders to every page and little cuts measuring about 1½ in. by 2, and a similar edition (reissued in Dutch and Italian) of the next year from the press of Jean de Tournes, the borders and little pictures in which are attributed to Bernard Salomon. In 1557 De Tournes issued also the *Devises Héroiques* of Claude Paradin, and he was also the publisher of a *Calendrier Historial*, a memorandum book charmingly decorated with cuts of the seasons.

Partly owing to religious troubles the book trade at Lyon soon after this rapidly declined, but the French style was carried on for a while at Antwerp by Christopher Plantin, who printed Paradin's *Devises Héroiques* in 1562 and in 1564, and the two following years three books of Emblems, those of Sambucus, Hadrianus Junius, and Alciatus himself. His earlier Horae are also illustrated with woodcuts, and in at least one edition we find the unusual combination of woodcut borders and copperplate pictures. But although Plantin never wholly gave up the use of woodcuts, for his more sumptuous editions he developed a marked preference for copperplates, and by his example helped to complete the downfall of the woodcut, which by the end of the sixteenth century had gone almost completely out of fashion.

CHAPTER XII

PRINTING IN ENGLAND (1476–1580)[1]

SOMETHING has already been written about the earliest English books on the scale to which they are entitled in a rapid survey of European incunabula. We may now consider them more in detail as befits a book written in English.

William Caxton, a Kentishman, born about 1420, had been brought up as a mercer in the city of London, and the relations between the English wooltraders and the clothmakers of Flanders being very intimate, he had, as he tells us himself, passed thirty years of his life (in round numbers the years from twenty years of age to fifty) "for the most part in Brabant, Flanders, Holland, and Zealand." During the last few years of this time he had held the important position of Governor of the English merchants at Bruges, but about 1469 he surrendered this in order to become secretary to Edward IV's sister, Margaret, wife of Charles the Bold, Duke of Burgundy. Some years before this, Raoul Lefèvre, chaplain to the Duke's predecessor, had compiled an epitome of the histories of Troy, *Le Recueil des histoires de Troye*, and in March, 1469, Caxton amused himself by beginning to translate this into English. Dissatisfied with the result he laid it on one side, but was bidden by his patroness, the Duchess, to continue his work. This he finished on 19 September, 1471, while staying at Cologne. According to a distinct statement by Wynkyn de Worde, whom (at least as early as 1480) he employed as his foreman, Caxton printed at Cologne "himself to avaunce" the first Latin edition of the *De Proprietatibus Rerum*, a kind of

---

[1] For English provincial printing after 1500 see Chapter XIII.

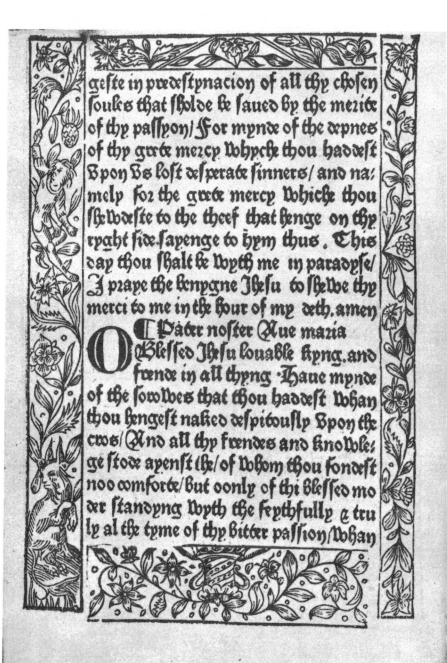

geste in predestynacion of all thy chosen
soules that sholde be saued by the merite
of thy passyon/ For mynde of the depnes
of thy grete mercy whyche thou haddest
vpon vs lost desperate sinners/ and na=
mely for the grete mercy whiche thou
shewdeste to the theef that henge on thy
ryght side.sayenge to hym thus . This
day thou shalt be wyth me in paradyse/
J praye the benygne Jhesu to shewe thy
merci to me in the hour of my deth. amen

O Pater noster Aue maria
Blessed Jhesu louable kyng. and
frende in all thyng ·Haue mynde
of the sorowes that thou haddest whan
thou hengest naked despitously vpon the
cros/ And all thy frendes and knowle=
ge stode ayenst the/ of whom thou fondest
noo comforte/ but oonly of thi blessed mo
der standyng wyth the feythfully & tru
ly al the tyme of thy bitter passion/Whan

XXVII. WESTMINSTER, CAXTON, c. 1490

THE FIFTEEN OES.

encyclopaedia "on the properties of things," by an English friar of the thirteenth century named Bartholomew. Now the first edition of this work is undoubtedly one printed at Cologne about 1471 or 1472 at an anonymous press which Bradshaw called that of the printer of the 1473 edition of the *Dialogi decem Auctorum*, and Mr. Proctor, less happily, that of the printer of the *Flores Sancti Augustini*, an undated book in the same type. The *De Proprietatibus Rerum* is certainly slightly earlier than either of these, and there are some typographical differences which suggest that between the completion of the one book and the beginning of the other two the press may have changed masters. The *De Proprietatibus* is by far the largest book of the whole group, and being by, or credited to, an English author, it is highly probable that the well-to-do ex-Governor of the English merchants became temporarily a member of the firm for its production and shared in the venture. This is the natural meaning of Wynkyn de Worde's statement that Caxton was the "first prynter of this boke," and is quite as likely to be true as the supposition that he took part in printing it as a kind of amateur journeyman to advance himself in the art. It may be noted, moreover, that the books of this anonymous press belong to the less advanced school of printing at Cologne, a school technically several years behind that of Ulrich Zell, and this takes the force out of the objection raised by William Blades, that if Caxton had learnt printing at Cologne, he must have printed better when he made his start.

Caxton does not seem to have followed up this beginning at all quickly, and it was not till printing had been brought much nearer to Bruges by the starting of presses at Alost in 1473 and at Louvain in 1474 that he was stirred to action. The first printer at Louvain was Jan Veldener, who worked there from 1474 to 1477, and Mr. Gordon Duff conjectures that Caxton may have received some help from him. There is no doubt, however, that his partner at Bruges was Colard Mansion, a skilled calligrapher, who continued printing there till 1484, when he fled from the town, leaving his rent unpaid. Caxton's own account in the *Recuyell of the Histories of Troye* of how he came to start is that

for as moche as in the wrytyng of the same my penne is worn, myn hande wery and not stedfast, myn eyen dimmed with ouermoche lokyng on the whit paper . . . and also because I haue promysid to dyuerce gentilmen and to my frendes to adresse to hem as hastily as I myght this sayd book. Therfore I haue practysed & lerned at my grete charge and dispence to ordeyne this saide book in prynte after the maner & forme as ye may here see.

There is nothing here to encourage the idea which Mr. Proctor seems to have entertained that Colard Mansion had already begun work on his own account, and that Caxton obtained his help for his English books. It seems more likely that it was Caxton who made the start, and that the first two books printed at Bruges were both in English, the first being the *Recuyell*, and the second *The Game and Pleye of the Chesse*, a translation of a moral treatise in which the functions of the chessmen were used as texts for sermonizing, written in Latin by Jacobus de Cessolis. After this a new type was cut and another didactic book, *Les Quatre Derennières Choses*, a treatise of the Four Last Things (Death, Judgment, Hell, and Heaven) printed in it in French. These three books probably appeared in 1475 and the early months of 1476. By this time Charles the Bold was picking a quarrel with the Swiss, and his disastrous defeat at Morat on 21 June, 1476, must have powerfully quickened the desire with which we may reasonably credit Caxton, of being the first printer in his native land. He made arrangements to rent a shop in the Sanctuary at Westminster from the following Michaelmas and departed for England, taking with him the newer of the two types and leaving the older one to Colard Mansion, who printed with it the original French of Lefèvre's *Recueil des histoires de Troye*, and the same author's *Les Fais et prouesses du noble et vaillant cheualier Jason*, and then abandoned it, having already cut a larger type for his own use.

The first dated book produced by Caxton in England was *The Dictes or Sayengis of the Philosophers*, a translation by Earl Rivers (the brother of Edward IV's queen) from a French version of an anonymous Latin book of the fourteenth century. Caxton was entrusted by the Earl with the oversight of the translation, and contributed to it an amusing Epilogue, in which he gives some unfavourable remarks about women attributed to Socrates, with his own comments. The Epilogue is dated 1477, and in one copy more minutely, 18 November. Though this is the first dated English book, it cannot be said that it was the first book printed in England, as it was probably preceded both by Caxton's English version of Lefèvre's *Jason*, and also by some of the thin quartos in the same type.

Among the earlier books printed by Caxton after he set up his press at Westminster was Chaucer's *Canterbury Tales*, of which later on he printed a second edition which he imagined to be from a better text, and ornamented with clumsy pictures of the pilgrims. He printed also in separate volumes most of Chaucer's other works, including his translation of Boethius, *De Consolatione Philosophiae;* also Gower's *Confessio Amantis*, some of the shorter poems of Lydgate, Malory's *Morte d'Arthur*, and several translations of French romances (*Charles the Great, Paris and Vienne*, the *Four Sons of Aymon*, etc.), translations of *Aesop* and of *Reynard the Fox*, Higden's *Polychronicon*, and the *Chronicles of England*, the *Golden Legend* (the name given to the great collection of Lives of the Saints by Jacobus de Voragine), several editions of the Hours of the Blessed Virgin, a Latin Psalter, a decorative edition of the Prayers called the *Fifteen Oes* with a border to every page (see Plate XXVII), numerous moral treatises and books of devotion, and several Indulgences. In all just one hundred books and documents issued from his press, printed in eight different types (including that left behind at Bruges). More than twenty of these books he had translated himself, and to others he contributed interesting prologues or epilogues. While many printers on the Continent easily surpassed him in typographical skill, few published more books which can still be read with pleasure, and his prefaces and epilogues show a real love of good literature (especially of Chaucer) and abundant good sense, kindliness, and humour. Caxton died in 1491 while engaged on translating into English the Latin Lives of the Fathers, and the account-books of the churchwardens of S. Margaret's, Westminster, show that he was buried in its churchyard, four torches being supplied at a cost of two shillings and sixpence, and another sixpence being charged for the bell.

During Caxton's lifetime only one other Englishman set up a press, an anonymous schoolmaster at St. Albans, who began work in 1480 (possibly in 1479) and printed till 1486, producing first six scholastic books and then two English ones. He appears to have borrowed some type from Caxton, so that it was presumably with the latter's goodwill that he reprinted his version of the *Chronicles of England*, adding thereto an appendix entitled *Fructus Temporum*, or Fruits of Time. It is from Wynkyn de Worde's reprint of this edition in 1497 that we obtain our only knowledge of the printer, for we are there told that it was "compiled in a booke and also enprynted by one sometyme scolemayster of saynt Albons, on whose soule God haue mercy." His other popular book was that famous trio of treatises *Of Haukyng and Huntyng and also of Cootarmuris*, commonly known as the *Book of St. Albans*. The second treatise, which is in metre, ends with the words "Explicit Dam Julyan Barnes in her boke of huntyng," and this is the only basis for the popular attribution of all three treatises to a hypothetical Juliana Bernes or Berners, who is supposed to have been the daughter of Sir James Berners (executed in 1388), and Prioress of the Nunnery of Sop-

208

well, a dependency of St. Albans, of which the list of prioresses has conveniently perished.[1]

Between 1478 and 1486 or '87, some seventeen books were printed at Oxford by Theodoric Rood of Cologne, who towards the end of his career was in partnership with an English bookseller named Thomas Hunte. The earliest of his books,[2] all of which are in Latin, was an Exposition on the Apostles' Creed wrongly attributed to S. Jerome. By the accidental omission of an X this is dated MCCCCLXVIII, i.e. 1468, but such misprints are common in early books, and no one now maintains that it was printed until ten years later. Among the other books printed at Oxford we may note an edition of Cicero's *Pro Milone*, the spurious Letters of Phalaris, and a very large folio, Lyndewode's *Provincial Constitutions* of the English Church. That the Oxford press came to an end so soon and that none was started at Cambridge during the fifteenth century may be attributed to a statute of Richard III's permitting the free importation of books into England. Although this measure was amply justified by the interests of learning, it made it practically impossible for any scholastic press to maintain itself in the limited English market against the competition of the fine editions which could be imported from Italy.

Caxton's press was at Westminster, which in the fifteenth century was much more sharply distinguished for business purposes from the city of London than it is

[1] A fourth treatise, that on Fishing with an Angle, is often included in the attribution with even less reason. This was first printed by Wynkyn de Worde in 1496, with the following curious explanation of its being tacked on to the *Book of St. Albans*: " And for by cause this present treatyse sholde not come to the hondys of eche ydle persone whyche wolde desire it yf it were enprynted allone by it self & put in a lytyll paunflet, therfore I haue compyled it in a greter volume of dyuerse bokys concernynge to gentyll & noble men, to the entent that the forsayd ydle persones whyche sholde haue but lytyll mesure in the sayd dysporte of fyshynge sholde not by this meane utterly destroye it."

[2] Two points may be noted about Rood: (i) he does not put his name in his earliest books, and as there is a change of type in his signed work, it is possible, though unlikely, that the books in type 1 are from another press; (ii) he is not to be identified, as was once proposed, with a certain Theodoricus of Cologne, lately proved by Dr. Voullième to be Theodoricus Molner, a stepson of ther Hoernen.

now. The first press set up within the city itself was that of John Lettou, whose surname shows him to have been a native of Lithuania, which in Caxton's time, as in Chaucer's, was known in England as Lettowe. Mr. Gordon Duff thinks that John Lettou must have learnt to print at Rome and brought his punches with him to England, as the type with which he started to print here is indistinguishable from one used by a small printer at Rome, who bore the curiously English name John Bulle, though he came from Bremen. Lettou printed an Indulgence in 1480, and also a commentary on the Metaphysics of Aristotle, a curiously learned work for a city press, but which he was commissioned to print by a certain William Wilcocks, for whom the next year he printed also a commentary on the Psalms.

After 1482 Lettou was joined by William of Mechlin, or Malines, in Belgium, usually known by the Latin name of his birthplace, Machlinia. Lettou and Machlinia printed five law books together, and then Lettou disappears and Machlinia in 1483 started working by himself, at first at a house near the bridge over the Fleet, where he printed eight books, and then in Holborn, where he printed fourteen. When working by himself he printed in addition to law books some works of a more popular character, a Book of Hours, the *Revelation to a Monk of Evesham*,[1] *Speculum Christiani* (a devotional work interspersed with English verse), the *Chronicles of England*, and several editions of "A little treatise against the Pestilence" by a certain Bishop Canutus of Aarhus. One of these editions was the first English book which has a titlepage. It is printed in two lines, and reads :—

> "A passing gode lityll boke necessarye &
> behouefull agenst the Pestilens."

The exact date at which Machlinia died, or gave up work, is not known. He was printing in 1486, but his books after that are undated. We may take 1490 or a little

---

[1] The place-name here is an early misreading for "Eynsham."

earlier as the year of his disappearance, and it is practically certain that his stock of books was taken over by Richard Pynson from Normandy, who probably began printing in 1491 or 1492 (his first dated book was finished in November of the latter year), and while he was getting his workshop ready commissioned Guillaume Le Talleur of Rouen to print two law books for him for sale in England.

Up to the death of Caxton the only native English printer besides himself was the unidentified schoolmaster-printer at St. Albans, Thomas Hunte, who joined Theodoricus Rood at Oxford, being only a stationer. After his death, for over twenty years there was no native Englishman at work as a master printer[1] at all. Two of the three presses at work were in the hands of Wynkyn de Worde of Lorraine and Richard Pynson of Normandy, and the third was worked for some time with two French partners by Julyan Notary, who was probably a Frenchman himself, since in 1498 he spells his name as Notaire.

By far the most prolific of these three firms was that of Wynkyn de Worde, who was born, as his name implies, at Worth, now in Alsace, but formerly part of the Duchy of Lorraine. He probably came to England with Caxton in 1476, since we hear of him as early as 1480 in a legal document about a house. After Caxton's death De Worde made a cautious start, only issuing five books in the first two years and not putting his own name in an imprint until 1494. By the end of the century, however, he had printed 110 books of which copies or fragments survive, and by the time of his death in 1534 the number had risen to 800, an extraordinarily high total, more especially when it is remembered that the small quarto editions of romances and popular works of devotion, of which he printed a great many, were peculiarly likely to be thumbed to pieces, so that his actual output was probably much greater. As far as his choice of books was con-

---

[1] This statement should perhaps be modified to admit of the possibility that Julian Notary was English rather than French, as is generally assumed.

cerned he showed himself a mere tradesman, seldom printing an expensive book unless Caxton's experience had shown it to be saleable. For two apparent exceptions to this lack of enterprise there were special reasons. The first, a translation of the *Lives of the Fathers*, he was almost bound in honour to take up, since Caxton had completed it on his death-bed. The second book, a really fine edition (issued about 1495) of Trevisa's version of the *De Proprietatibus Rerum*, was also, as we have seen, connected with Caxton, who, De Worde tells us, had acted as "the fyrst prynter of this boke In latin tongue at Coleyn himself to avaunce." De Worde's edition is itself notable as being the first book printed on English paper, the manufacturer being John Tate of Hertford.

In 1500 De Worde moved from Caxton's house at Westminster to the sign of the Sun in Fleet Street, perhaps for the greater protection offered by the city against attacks by anti-alien mobs. In 1508 he was appointed printer to the Countess of Richmond and Derby, mother of Henry VII, a very old lady, who died the following year. De Worde himself must have been a very old man at his death towards the end of 1534 or early in January, 1535, as he had by that time been at work in England for between fifty and sixty years. Towards the end of his life he seems to have had some of his books printed for him by John Skot, and Robert Copland was also employed in his business.

The output of Richard Pynson was only about half that of Wynkyn de Worde, and his taxable property amounted to only £60 against over £200 at which De Worde was assessed. Nevertheless the fact that for the last twenty-two years of his life (1508 30) he was the King's Printer helped to procure him a few important books, and also kept his workmanship at a considerably higher standard. As already mentioned, he probably came to England about 1490 and took over Machlinia's stock, employing Guillaume Le Talleur of Rouen to print two law books for him while his own type was being made. He probably began work with a fine edition of Chaucer's *Canterbury Tales*, but his first dated book is an ugly little edition of the *Doctrinale* of Alexander Gallus, issued in November, 1492. A copy of this was unearthed a few years ago in the library of Appleby Grammar School, and to secure the first dated book printed by Pynson the British Museum had to pay over £300 for it. In 1494 Pynson brought out Lydgate's poem on the *Falles of Princes*, translated from the Latin of Boccaccio, illustrating it with woodcuts borrowed from Jean Du Pré's French edition of the same book.[1] In 1495 he printed a *Terence*. Up to the close of the fifteenth century he had printed about eighty-eight books known to Mr. Gordon Duff, against the 110 printed by Wynkyn de Worde. In 1500 he moved from the parish of S. Clement Dane's, outside Temple Bar, to the sign of S. George, at the corner of Chancery Lane and Fleet Street, the change bringing him inside the city walls. Among the best of the books printed by him after this are Alexander Barclay's *Ship of Fools* (1509), a translation of Sebastian Brant's *Narrenschiff;* Fabyan's *Chronicle* (1516), Barclay's translation of Sallust (about 1520), Henry VIII's *Assertio Septem Sacramentorum* (1521), and Lord Berners' translation of Froissart's *Chronicles* (1522-5). He also printed some fine service-books, notably a Sarum Missal, called after Cardinal Morton who favoured it the Morton Missal (1500). Mr. Duff conjectures that in the Latin books he printed from 1518 onwards Pynson was aided by Thomas Berthelet.[2]

Julian Notary's business was on a far smaller scale than those of Wynkyn de Worde and Pynson, for less than fifty books are known to have been printed by him.

---

[1] This and the *Dives and Pauper* of 1493 (which, until the discovery of the *Doctrinale*, was reckoned Pynson's first dated book) and several other of his earliest editions were published partly at the expense of a merchant named John Rushe, who took six hundred copies of the *Dives* and the *Boccaccio* at 4s. apiece. See *Two Lawsuits of Richard Pynson*, by H. R. Plomer, in *The Library*, second series, Vol. X.

[2] See *The Library*, second series, Vol. VIII, pp. 298 *sqq.*

He began work in London about 1496 in partnership with Jean Barbier and another printer or bookseller whose initials were I. H., probably Jean Huvin of Rouen. In 1498 I. H. had left the firm and Notary and Barbier were at Westminster. In 1500, like De Worde and Pynson, he changed houses, moving to just outside Temple Bar, possibly to Pynson's old house, giving his new premises the sign of the Three Kings. At a later date he had also a bookstall in S. Paul's Churchyard, and ultimately moved his printing office into the city. Notary's books were of much the same kind as De Worde's—the Golden Legend, the Chronicles of England, the Shepherds' Calendar, Sermons, Lives of the Saints, etc. He has the distinction of having printed the smallest English incunable of which any trace has come down to us, an edition of the Hours of the Blessed Virgin, finished in April, 1500, measuring only an inch by an inch and a half. He seems to have ceased printing about 1520, but was alive in 1523.

Summing up the work of these printers who were active before 1500, we may note that Caxton printed 100 books and editions that have come down to us; De Worde 110 before 1500, about 800 altogether; Pynson 88 before 1500, nearly 400 altogether; Notary about 8 before 1500, and 48 altogether; Lettou and Machlinia about 30, Oxford 17, St. Albans 8. Thus the total number of English incunabula at present known is about 360, but Pynson and Wynkyn de Worde were both large printers in the sixteenth century.

As we have seen, Pynson became King's Printer in 1508. He had been preceded in that office by William Faques, who like himself was a Norman, and was the first to hold the title. He was worthy of the distinction, for though he only printed eight books and documents that have come down to us, his work was very good. His dated books belong to the year 1504, when he printed a proclamation against clipped money, with a fine initial H and some neat woodcuts of coins; also a beautiful little

Latin Psalter. His business was in the heart of the city, in Abchurch Lane. After his death it passed to Richard Faques, who made his name more English by spelling it first Fakes, then Fawkes. Richard worked in S. Paul's Churchyard, and among his publications were the *Salus corporis salus anime* of Gulielmus de Saliceto, a Sarum Horae, Skelton's *Goodly Ballad of the Scottish King* (1509), and *Garland of Laurell* (1523), and lastly, *The Myrroure of Our Lady* (1530).

With Robert Copland we come to the first native English printer after Caxton and the schoolmaster of St. Albans. Copland is rather an interesting person, who made translations and wrote prefaces and addresses to the reader in verse, besides printing books. His name occurs in the imprints of only twelve books, spread over twenty-two years, 1514-35, the explanation being that he was probably working for De Worde during this time, and only occasionally indulged in a private venture. After a long interval he printed two books for Andrew Borde in 1547-8, and appears to have died while the second was in progress. He was succeeded by William Copland, probably his son, who printed numerous romances and other entertaining books, and died in 1568 or 1569.

At intervals during the years 1516-28, John Rastell, an Oxford graduate, barrister of Lincoln's Inn and brother-in-law of Sir Thomas More, issued nine dated law books. In 1526 he printed two jest books, in 1529 he became involved in religious controversy on the Protestant side, and died in poverty and prison in 1536. Altogether some forty books are attributed to him, including some plays, which may perhaps rather have been printed by his son William. William Rastell was also a lawyer, and not sharing his father's Protestantism, became a Judge of the Queen's Bench under Mary, on whose death he fled to Louvain. As a printer he worked only from 1530 to 1534, printing over thirty books, including several works by his uncle, Sir Thomas More, and five plays by John Heywood.

Between 1518 and 1524 Henry Pepwell printed a few popular books at the sign of the Trinity in S. Paul's Churchyard; for the rest of his life he appears to have been only a stationer. John Skot, who printed at four different addresses in the city of London between 1521 and 1537, worked partly for De Worde, partly on his own account, printing upwards of thirty books for himself, a few of them legal, the rest popular English books.

Two printers began to issue books in 1523. Robert Bankes, who turned out a few popular books in his first six years, was then silent for a time, and reappears in the religious controversies of 1539-42, and Robert Redman, who seems to have followed in Pynson's footsteps both in S. Clement's Without Temple Bar and at the sign of the George. In his office of Royal Printer Pynson was succeeded by Thomas Berthelet, or Bartlet, who had probably worked with him for upwards of ten years before starting on his own account in Fleet Street at the sign of Lucrece in 1528. We know of altogether about 400 pieces of printing from his press, but a large proportion of these consists of editions of the Statutes and Proclamations. For the Proclamations some of Berthelet's bills survive, and we learn that he charged a penny a piece for them, and imported his paper from Genoa. With his official printing must be reckoned his editions of the *Necessary Doctrine of a Christian Man*, issued with the royal sanction on 29 May, 1543. In order to produce sufficient copies of this he printed it simultaneously eight times over, all eight editions bearing the same date. Of the books which he printed on his own account the place of honour must be given to his handsome edition of Gower's *Confessio Amantis* in an excellent black-letter type in 1532, and the various works of Sir John Eliot, all of which came from his press.

On the accession of Edward VI Berthelet ceased to be Royal Printer, the post being given to Grafton. Berthelet died in September, 1555, leaving considerable property. He was buried as an Esquire with pennon and coat armour and four dozen scutcheons, and all the craft of printers, stationers, and booksellers followed him to his grave.

Richard Grafton, who succeeded Berthelet as Royal Printer, had a very chequered career. He was originally a member of the Grocers' Company, and, in conjunction with Edward Whitchurch and Anthony Marler of the Haberdashers' Company, superintended the printing of the English Bible of 1537, probably at Antwerp, and that of 1539 by François Regnault at Paris. When Bible-printing was permitted in England Grafton and Whitchurch shared between them the printing of the six editions of the Great Bible during 1540 and 1541. But when Cromwell, Earl of Essex, the chief promoter of Bible-printing, was beheaded, Grafton was himself imprisoned. In 1544, on the other hand, he and Whitchurch obtained an exclusive patent for printing Primers, and before Henry VIII's death Grafton was appointed printer to the Prince of Wales. Thus when Edward became king Grafton displaced Berthelet as Royal Printer, and henceforth had time for little save official work. Five editions of the Homilies and seven of Injunctions, all dated 31 July, 1547, were issued from his presses; in 1548 he published Halle's *Union of Lancaster and York* and several editions of the Order of Communion and Statutes; in 1549 came two Bibles and five editions of the first Prayer Book of Edward VI; in 1550 a reprint of Halle and an edition of Marbeck's Book of Common Prayer noted; in 1551 Wilson's *Rule of Reason;* in 1552 six editions of the second Prayer Book of Edward VI, and more Statutes. Proclamation-work, of course, went on steadily throughout the reign, and on Edward's death Grafton printed the enormously long document by which the adherents of Lady Jane Grey tried to justify her claim to the Crown. He did his work very handsomely, but on the triumph of Mary, though he impartially printed a proclamation for her nine days after "Queen Jane's," he naturally lost his post and might easily have lost his head also. For the rest of his life he was mainly occupied in writing his chronicle. But he printed a Book of Common Prayer in 1559, and (according to Herbert) a Bible in 1566. He died in 1573.

While Grafton was the King's printer for English books, the post of Royal Printer in Latin, Greek, and Hebrew had been conferred in 1547 on Reginald or Reyner Wolfe. Wolfe, who had come to England from Gelderland, was at first a bookseller, and was employed by various distinguished persons as a letter-carrier between England and Germany. When he set up as a printer in 1542, with type which he seems to have obtained from a relative at Frankfort, he was employed by the great antiquary, John Leland, and by John Cheke, Professor of Greek at Cambridge, for whom he printed in 1543 two Homilies of S. Chrysostom in Greek and Latin, this being the first Greek work printed in England. During Edward VI's reign he does not seem to have been given much to do in Latin, Greek, or Hebrew, but printed Cranmer's *Defence of the Sacrament* and *Answer unto a Crafty Cavillation*. After keeping quiet during Mary's reign he enjoyed the patronage of Elizabeth and Archbishop Parker, and lived, like Grafton, till 1573.

Though he never worked on a large scale, Wolfe certainly raised the standard of printing in England. In John Day it is pleasant to come to a native Englishman who did equally good work, and that in a larger way of business. Day was a Suffolk man, born in 1522 at Dunwich, a town over which the sea now rolls. He began printing in partnership with William Seres as early as 1546, but, save some fairly good editions of the Bible, produced nothing of importance during this period. His first fine book, published in 1559, is *The Cosmographicall Glasse*, a work on surveying, by William Cunningham. This has a woodcut allegorical border to the titlepage, a fine portrait of Cunningham, a map of Norwich, and some good heraldic and pictorial capitals. Its text is printed throughout in large italics. The book thus broke away entirely from the old black-letter traditions of

English printing, and could compare favourably with the best foreign work. Day printed other folios in this style, and in some of them instead of a device placed a large and striking portrait of himself. In 1563 he printed the first edition of *Acts and Monumentes of these latter and perillous days touching matters of the Church*, better known as *Foxe's Book of Martyrs*. This is a book of over two thousand pages, and is plentifully illustrated with woodcuts of varying degrees of merit. Day by this time had attracted the patronage of Archbishop Parker, and in 1566 printed for him a book called *A Testimony of Antiquitie, showing the auncient fayth of the Church of England touching the sacrament of the body and bloude of the Lord here publikely preached and also receaved in the Saxons tyme, above 600 yeares agoe*. For this sermon, attributed to Archbishop Aelfric, some Anglo-Saxon type, the first used in England, was specially cut. Later on Day printed at Lambeth Palace Parker's *De Antiquitate Britannicae Ecclesiae*. He also printed Ascham's *Scholemaster* and other important works. He appears, moreover, to have possessed a bookbinding business, or at least to have had binders in his employment who invented a very striking and dignified style of binding. Altogether, Day is a man of whom English bookmen may well be proud. He died in 1584.

Richard Tottell was another printer of some importance. The son of an Exeter man, he began printing about 1553, and early in his career received a patent which gave him a monopoly of the publication of law books. These, to do him justice, he printed very well, and he also published a number of works of literary interest. Chief among these, and always associated with his name, is the famous *Songs and Sonnets* of Wyatt and Surrey and other Tudor poets, edited by Nicholas Grimald, but often quoted, for no very good reason, as *Tottell's Miscellany*. To his credit must also be placed editions of Lydgate's *Falles of Princes*, Hawes's *Pastime of Pleasure*, Tusser's *Five Hundreth Points of Good Husbandry*, the works of Sir Thomas More in 1458 folio pages, Gerard Legh's *Accedens of Armoury*, numerous editions of Guevara's *Diall of Princes*, as translated by Sir Thomas North, and a version of Cicero's *De Officiis*, by Nicholas Grimald. In 1573 Tottell petitioned unsuccessfully for a monopoly of paper-making in England for thirty years, in order to encourage him to start a paper-mill. He lived till 1593.

Henry Denham (1564–89), Henry Bynneman (1566–83), and Thomas Vautrollier (1566–88), and the latter's successor, Richard Field, were the best printers of the rest of the century. Denham was an old apprentice of Tottell's, who gave him some important books to print for him. Herbert remarks of him: " He was an exceeding neat printer, and the first who used the semicolon with propriety." Among his more notable books were Grafton's *Chronicle* (for Tottell and Toy, 1569), editions of the Olynthiac orations of Demosthenes in English (1570) and Latin (1571), *An Alvearie or quadruple dictionarie containing foure sundrie tongues, namelie, English, Latine, Greeke, and French*, with a pleasing titlepage showing the royal arms and a beehive (1580), Thomas Bentley's *The Monument of Matrons: containing seuen seuerall Lamps of Virginitie*, a work in praise of piety and Queen Elizabeth (1582), Hunnis's *Seuen Sobs of a Sorrowfull Soule for Sinne*, a metrical version of the penitential psalms (1585), and the second edition of Holinshed's *Chronicles* (1587).

Henry Bynneman, though not so high in Archbishop Parker's favour as John Day, was yet recommended by him to Burghley in 1569, and deserved his patronage by much good work. He printed an English version of Epictetus, Dr. Caius's *De Antiquitate Cantabrigiensis Academiæ* (1568), a handsome book with the text in italics, according to the fashion of the day, Van der Nooät's *Theatre of Voluptuous Worldlings* (1569), a Latin text of Virgil believed to be the first printed in

220

England (1570), the *Historia Brevis* of Thomas Walsingham (1574), a handsome folio, several books by Gascoigne and Turberville, the first edition of Holinshed's *Chronicles* (1577, published by John Harrison), and a few books in Greek.

Thomas Vautrollier, a French refugee, set up a press at Blackfriars, at which he printed several editions of the Prayer Book in Latin (*Liber Precum Publicarum in Ecclesia Anglicana*), and of the New Testament in Beza's Latin version, for which latter he was granted a ten years' privilege in 1574. In 1579 he printed two very notable works, Fenton's translation of the History of Guicciardini and Sir Thomas North's *Plutarch*, the latter being one of the handsomest of Elizabethan books. In 1580 and again in 1584 he went to Edinburgh, printing several books there in 1584 and 1585. His second visit is said to have been due to trouble which came upon him for printing the *Spaccio della Bestia Triomphante* of Giordano Bruno. His press at Blackfriars continued to work during his absence. His daughter Jakin married Richard Field, who succeeded to his house and business in 1588, and continued his excellent traditions.

A company of stationers had existed in London since 1403, and in 1557 this was reconstituted and granted a Royal Charter. The object of the Crown was to secure greater control over printing, so that no inconvenient criticisms on matters of Church or State might be allowed to appear. The object of the leading printers and booksellers, who formed the court of the company, was to diminish competition, both illegitimate and legitimate. Both objects were to a very considerable degree attained. The quarter of a century which followed the grant of a charter witnessed a great improvement in the English standard of book production. Up to this time it seems probable that few English printers, who had not the royal patronage, had found their craft profitable. Caxton no doubt did very well for himself—as he richly deserved. He enjoyed the favour of successive kings, and received good support from other quarters. We may guess, moreover, that both as translator and publisher he kept his finger on the pulse of well-to-do book-buyers to an extent to which there is no parallel for the next two centuries. No one else in England possessed this skill, and certainly no one else enjoyed Caxton's success. The Act of Richard III permitting unrestricted importation of books quickly killed the presses at Oxford and St. Albans, which could not compete with the publications of the learned printers of Italy, France, and Switzerland. Until more than half-way through the reign of Elizabeth the united output of books from Oxford and Cambridge amounted to less than a couple of score. For more than twenty years after Caxton's death there was no undoubted Englishman as a master printer. Mr. Gordon Duff has lately published[1] the assessments of some of the chief stationers and printers from the Lay Subsidy Rolls of 1523-4. By far the highest of them is the £307 at which was assessed John Taverner, a stationer who is only otherwise known as having bound some books for the Royal Chapel, and who was wise enough not to meddle with printing. Wynkyn de Worde, most commercial of printers, was assessed at £201 11s. 1d.; a practically unknown stationer named Neale at £100; Pynson, who was Royal Printer and did really good work, at £60; three other stationers, one of whom printed (Henry Pepwell), at £40 apiece; Julyan Notary at £36 6s. 8d.; other printers at £10 (Robert Redman), £6 13s. 4d. (John Rastell), and £4 (Robert Wyer). It is tolerably clear that there was absolutely no inducement to an English stationer to take up printing. In 1534 Henry VIII repealed the Act of 1484, on the plea that native printing was now so good that there was less need to import books from abroad, the King's real reason, no doubt, being to make it easier to check the importation of heretical works. Mr. Duff has written of the King's action:

[1] In *The Library*, second series, Vol. IX, pp. 257-81.

PRINTING IN ENGLAND (1476-1580)

" The fifty years of freedom from 1484 to 1534 not only brought us the finest specimens of printing we possess, but compelled the native workman in self-protection to learn, and when competition was done away with his ambition rapidly died also. Once our English printing was protected, it sank to a level of badness which has lasted, with the exception of a few brilliant experiments, almost down to our own day."[1]

As a rule, whatever Mr. Duff writes about English printing is incontrovertible, but this particular pronouncement seems curiously unfounded. Whether we consider what they printed or how they printed it, the work of the English presses from 1535-57 is better, not worse, than the work of the corresponding period, 1512-34. There is nothing in the earlier period to compare with the Great Bibles, and the books of Berthelet and Reyner Wolfe are fairly equal to those of Pynson. If we take 1557 as a fresh point of departure, the books issued from then to about 1580 present a still more remarkable advance. While the work of the rest of Europe deteriorated, that of England, in the hands of such men as Day, Denham, and Bynneman, improved, and alike for their typography, their illustrations and decorations and their scholarship, they surpass those of any previous period since the days of Caxton, and deserve far more attention from collectors than they have yet received.

[1] "The Printers, Stationers, and Bookbinders of Westminster and London, 1476-1535" (last paragraph).

CHAPTER XIII

ENGLISH BOOKS PRINTED ELSEWHERE THAN AT LONDON

DURING the fifteenth century presses were set up in more than fifty places in Germany, in more than seventy in Italy, in nearly forty in France, in more than twenty in the Netherlands, in twenty-four in Spain, in only three (counting London and Westminster as one) in England. In London and Westminster over 330 books are known to have been printed ; in Oxford and St. Albans only twenty-five. The reason for this paucity of provincial printing in England must be found by the social historian. The beginning of the sixteenth century brought no change in the facts. For thirty years from March, 1487, there was no printing-press at Oxford. In December, 1517, a Latin commentary on the Posterior Analytics of Aristotle appeared with the imprint "Academia Oxonie," and in four subsequent books, printed in 1518, the printer of this gave his name as Johannes Scolar. A fragment of a sixth book has lately been found at the British Museum. In 1519 Scolar's place was taken by Carolus Kyrforth, who printed a *Compotus*, or small arithmetic book. A prognostication by Jaspar Laet may have been printed apparently either by Scolar or Kyrforth. After the appearance of these eight books there was no more printing at Oxford until a press was started there in 1585 by Joseph Barnes, under the auspices of the University. The last book of the Schoolmaster-printer appeared at St. Albans in 1486, and after this there was no more printing there until 1534. In that year, at the request of Abbot Catton, a printer named John Hertfort, or Herford, printed there *The*

Hys ys the boke of the generacio of Jesus Christ the sonne of David/The sonne also of Abra Cha. ❡Abraham begatt Isaac: Isaac begatt Jacob: Jacob begatt Judas and hys bre= Judasbegat Phares: (thren: and Zaram of thamar: Phares begatt Esrom: Esrom begatt Aram: Aram begatt Aminadab:

Aminadab begatt naassan:
Naasson begatt Salmon:
Salmon begatt boos of rahab:
Boos begatt obed of ruth:
Obed begatt Jesse:
Jesse begatt david the kynge:
❡David the kynge begatt Solomon/of her that was the Solomon begatt roboam: (wyfe of ury:
Roboam begatt Abia:
Abia begatt asa:
Asa begatt iosaphat:
Josaphat begatt Joram:
Joram begatt Osias:
Osias begatt Joatham:
Joatham begatt Achas:
Achas begatt Ezechias:
Ezechias begatt Manasses:
Manasses begatt Amon:
Amon begatt Josias:
Josias begatt Jechonias and his brethren about the tyme of the captivite of babilen
❡After they were led captive to babilen/ Jechonias begatt

[marginal notes:]

✳ Abraham and David are fyrst rehearsid/ because that christe was chefly promysed vnto them.

Saynct mathew leveth out certeyne generacions/ z describeth Christes linage from solomo/after the lawe of Moses/ but Lucas descrybeth it accordyng to nature/fro nathan solomos brother. For the lawe calleth them a mannes childre which hys broder begatt of his wyfe lefte behynde hym after his dethe. deu. xxv. c.

glorious lyfe and passion of seint Albon. Robert Catton was succeeded as abbot by Richard Stevenage, and in the years 1536–8 three religious books were printed for him by Hertfort, who also printed an Arithmetic and two other books on his own account, making seven books in all. Then, in October, 1539, John Hertfort fell under suspicion of having printed a "little book of detestable heresies," [1] and the Abbot had to send him to London. The abbey itself was suppressed by the King the same year, and Hertfort, deprived of his patron, had no inducement to return. He is next heard of as printing in London in 1544.

At York a *Directorium* was printed by Hugo Goes, and there is a seventeenth century reference to a *Donatus minor* and *Accidence* from his press. Three small books are also known to have been printed by Ursyn Mylner in 1514 and 1516. Previous to this, in or about 1507, an *Expositio hymnorum et sequentiarum* for use at York had been printed at Rouen by Pierre Violette for a stationer named Gerard Freez (also known as Gerard Wandsforth), who died in 1510. This Gerard Freez had a brother Frederick, who is described not only as a bookbinder and stationer, but as a printer, and may therefore have printed books which have perished without leaving any trace behind them. But the only extant York books of the sixteenth century are the *Directorium* of 1507, two small service-books of 1513, and a little grammatical work in 1516. After this there was no more printing in York until 1642.

At Cambridge a stationer named John Laer, of Siberch, i.e. Siegburg, near Cologne, settled, in or about 1520, and acted as publisher to an edition of Croke's *Introductiones in Rudimenta Græca*, printed at Cologne by Eucharius Cervicornus. After this, in 1521 and 1522, Siberch himself printed nine small books at Cambridge, the first of them being a Latin speech by Henry Bullock addressed

---

[1] Mr. Duff is no doubt right in his suggestion that this is *A very declaration of the bond and free wyll of man : the obedyence of the gospell and what the gospell meaneth*, of which a copy, with colophon, "Printed at Saint Albans," is in the Spencer Collection at the John Rylands Library. This increases Hertfort's total to eight.

to Cardinal Wolsey. Among the other books was a Dialogue of Lucian's (περὶ διψάδων), for which Siberch had to use some Greek type, and a work on letter-writing (*De conscribendis epistolis*) by Erasmus, with whom he seems to have been on friendly terms. After 1522 no more books were printed at Cambridge until 1583.

At Tavistock in 1525 a monk named Thomas Richard printed a translation of Boethius's *De Consolatione Philosophiae* for "the ryght worschypful esquyer Mayster Robert Langdon." Nine years later, in 1534, the same press printed the *Statutes* concerning the Devonshire Stannaries or Tin Mines. These are the only two early books known to have been printed at Tavistock.

At Abingdon in 1528, John Scolar, presumably the same man who had previously worked a few miles off at Oxford, printed a Portiforium or Breviary for the use of the monastery. No other early book is known to have been printed there.

From 1539, when John Hertfort was summoned from St. Albans, to the end of the reign of Henry VIII, we know of no provincial printing in England. But on the accession of Edward VI the extreme Protestants who had fled from England to the Netherlands, Germany, and Switzerland, came flocking back, and some of them seem to have stopped at Ipswich. Two, or perhaps three printers, all in the Protestant interest, worked there in the first few months of the new reign. The first of these, Anthony Scoloker, printed seven books at Ipswich in 1547 and 1548, and then went on to London. The second, John Overton, brought over with him from Wesel the text of Bishop Bale's Latin bibliography of the Illustrious Writers of Britain, printed there by Theodoricus Plateanus, otherwise Dirick van der Straten, and may or may not have printed at Ipswich two additional sheets, which he dated there 31 July, 1548.[1] The third printer, John Oswen,

---

[1] Mr. Duff plausibly suggests that Overton's name in the colophon was merely a device for surmounting the restrictions on the circulation in England of books printed abroad.

printed at Ipswich eleven tracts, mostly controversial, in or about 1548, and then removed to Worcester.

On his arrival at Worcester late in 1548, or early in 1549, John Oswen obtained a special privilege from Edward VI for printing service-books for use in the Principality of Wales, and produced there three editions of the first Prayer Book of Edward VI and a New Testament. Besides these, from 1549 to 1553 he printed eighteen other books, mostly of controversial theology, calling himself in his imprints "Printer appoynted by the Kinges Maiestie for the Principalitie of Wales and the Marches of the same." On the accession of Mary, it being no longer safe to print Protestant theology, Oswen's press ceased working.

At Canterbury in 1549 John Mychell, or Mitchell, who had moved there after producing a few books in London, printed an English psalter, "poynted as it shall be songe in churches." During Edward's reign Mychell printed at Canterbury altogether some twenty books and tracts, mostly more or less controversial treatises on the Protestant side. On the accession of Mary he ceased publishing till 1556, when his press was employed by Cardinal Pole to print his Articles of Visitation.

The next year, by the charter granted to the Stationers' Company, printing outside London was forbidden, the prohibition being subsequently relaxed in favour of the two Universities, although it was nearly thirty years before they availed themselves of their right. In the previous eighty years only about a hundred books[1] had been produced at the provincial presses, and in the year in which the charter was granted it can hardly be said that any press outside London was in existence. The new regulation stood in the way of development, but it was a development for which there seems to have been little demand. We may see some slight confirmation of this

---

[1] Those recorded by Mr. E. G. Duff in his Sandars Lectures on "The English Provincial Printers, Stationers, and Bookbinders to 1557," by my reckoning number 114.

view in the fact that during Elizabeth's reign there was very little secret printing, though there had probably been a good deal under Mary. The three Elizabethan secret presses which have been chronicled were:

(1) A Puritan press which printed various tracts on Church government, written by Thomas Cartwright. These were printed secretly in 1572 and 1573, first at Wandsworth, afterwards at Hempstead, near Saffron Walden, in Essex. The press was seized in August, 1573, and the type handed to Henry Bynneman, who, the next year, used it to reprint Cartwright's attack, interpolating Whitgift's replies in larger type.

(2) A Jesuit press which printed for Edmund Campion and Robert Parsons in 1580 and 1581, first at Greenstreet House in East Ham, afterwards at Stonor Park, near Henley. The press was managed by Stephen Brinckley, who was ultimately captured and imprisoned for nearly two years.

(3) The Puritan travelling press, from which issued the famous Martin Marprelate tracts in 1588 and 1589. Some of these were printed in East Molesey, in Surrey; others in the house of Sir Richard Knightley at Fawsley, near Daventry, others in that of Roger Wigston of Wolston Priory, between Coventry and Rugby. The chief printer of them was Robert Waldegrave, who eventually fled first to La Rochelle, where he may have printed one of the tracts, and then to Edinburgh, where he became a printer of some importance.

While there was thus very little secret printing in England, exiled Protestants, Catholics, and Nonconformists all in turn made frequent recourse to foreign presses, and apparently succeeded in circulating their books in England. Religious repression, however, though the chief, was not the only cause of English books being printed abroad. From a very early time the superior skill of foreign printers had procured them many commissions to print service-books for the English market, alike on account of their greater accuracy, their experience in printing in red and black, and the more attractive illustrations which they had at their disposal. Not long after 1470 a Sarum Breviary was printed abroad, possibly at Cologne. Caxton employed George Maynyal, of Paris, to print a Missal (and probably a *Legenda*) for him in 1487, and Johann Hamman or Herzog printed a Sarum Missal in 1494 as far away as Venice. When the Paris printers and publishers had won the admiration of all Europe by their pretty editions of the Hours of the Blessed Virgin, they competed with each other for the English market. Early in the sixteenth century Wolfgang Hopyl printed some magnificent Sarum Missals and also an Antiphoner and *Legenda*, besides some very fine editions of Lyndewood's Constitutions. Breviaries, Missals, and Primers were also poured out for English use by François Regnault, and in lesser numbers by nearly a dozen other Paris firms, and Martin Morin and other printers plied the same trade at Rouen, while Christoffel van Remunde, of Endhoven, was busy at Antwerp. The predominance of the foreign editions of these books over those printed in England may be estimated from the fact that of 105 Sarum service-books printed before 1540 in the possession of the British Museum, one was printed at Basel, one at Venice, eleven at Rouen, twelve at Antwerp, as many as fifty-six at Paris, and only twenty-four in England.[1]

In addition to service-books, a good many of the smaller Latin grammatical works were printed for the English market in France and the Low Countries, their destination being occasionally stated, but more often inferred from the appearance in them of English explanations of Latin words or phrases. A few attempts were also made to issue popular English works in competition with those produced at home. The most formidable of these rivalries was that of Gerard Leeu at Antwerp, who,

---

[1] This reckoning was made in 1896, but the proportion has not been substantially altered.

after printing three entertaining books *(The History of Jason, Knight Paris and the Fair Vienne,* and the *Dialogue of Salomon and Marcolphus),* embarked on a more important work, *The Chronicles of England,* and might have seriously injured the home trade had he not met his death in a quarrel with a workman while the *Chronicles* were still on the press.[1]

Soon after 1500 another Antwerp printer, Adriaen von Berghen, in addition to Holt's *Lac Puerorum,* published the commonplace book of a London merchant which passes under the name of *Arnold's Chronicle,* and is famous as containing the earliest text of the *Nutbrown Maid.* A little later still, Jan van Doesborch was at work at the same place, and between 1505 and 1530 produced at least eighteen popular English books, including *Tyll Howleglas, Virgilius the Magician, Robin Hood,* and an account of recent discoveries entitled, "Of the new landes and of the people found by the messengers of the kynge of portyngale named Emanuel."

Doesborch's books are poorly printed and illustrated, but his texts are not noticeably worse than those in contemporary editions published in England. The reverse is the case with two English books produced (1503) by the famous Paris publisher, Antoine Vérard, *The traitté of god lyuyng and good deying* and *The Kalendayr of Shyppars.* These have the illustrations which book-lovers prize so highly in the *Kalendrier des Bergers* and *Art de bien viure et de bien mourir,* but the translations seem to have been made by a Scot, only less ill equipped in Scottish than in French. In a third translation, from Pierre Gringore's *Chasteau de Labeur,* Vérard was more fortunate, for the *Castell of Labour* was rendered into (for that unpoetical period) very passable verse by Alexander Barclay. Vérard, however, had no cause to congratulate himself, for both Pynson and De Worde reprinted Barclay's translation with copies of the woodcuts, and the other two

---

[1] The colophon to the *Chronicles* which commemorates Leeu has already been quoted (p. 81).

books in new translations, so that in future he left the secular English market alone.

It may be supposed that the Act of 1534, restricting the importation of foreign books into England, finally put an end to competition of the kind which Leeu, Vérard, and Doesborch had attempted. But isolated English books have continued to appear abroad down to our own day, and form a miscellaneous, but curious and interesting appendix in the great volume of the English book trade. From 1525 onwards, however, until nearly the end of the seventeenth century, compared with the masses of theological books alternately by Protestant and Roman Catholic English exiles, printed in the Low Countries, Germany, Switzerland, and France, the output of secular work sinks into insignificance. The stream begins with Tyndale's New Testament, of which a few sheets were printed at Cologne (see Plate XXVIII), two editions at Worms, and half a dozen or more at Antwerp before it was suffered to appear in England.

The first English Bible is believed to have been printed (1535) by Christopher Froschauer at Zurich, the second (1537) at Antwerp, the third (1539) was begun at Paris and completed in England. Besides their New Testaments, Tyndale and George Joy published a good many controversial works at Antwerp. In the next generation the city became one of the strongholds of the Romanist exiles after the accession of Elizabeth, and Hans de Laet, John Fouler, Willem Sylvius, and Gillis van Diest the younger were frequently called on in 1564-6 to provide paper and print for Stapleton, Harding, William Rastell, and the other antagonists of Bishop Jewel.

In 1528 and the following year books by Tyndale, Roy, and Frith appeared purporting to be printed by "Hans Luft at Malborowe in the land of Hesse." A later book with this imprint has been shown by Mr. Sayle to have been printed at Antwerp; whether these earlier works were really produced at Marburg, or, as has been conjectured, at Cologne, or again at Hamburg, is

231

still uncertain. In the 'forties and 'fifties Christopher Froschauer printed several English Protestant books at Zurich, including *A faythfull admonycion of a certen trewe pastor and prophete sent unto the germanes*, translated from Luther's *Warnunge*, with the pleasing imprint "at Grenewych by Conrade Freeman in the month of may 1554." In the 'fifties, again, Jean Crespin and other Geneva printers worked for John Knox, and the Geneva New Testament was produced there in 1558 and the Bible in 1560. In the 'sixties, as we have seen, many treatises attacking Bishop Jewel were issued at Antwerp, others appeared at Louvain, and about the same time (1566), at Emden, G. van der Erven was printing for exiled Puritans some of their diatribes against the "Popish aparrell" (i.e. the surplice) which Elizabeth prescribed for the English Church.

In 1574 we encounter at Amsterdam a curious group of nine little books "translated out of Base-Almayne into English," in which Hendrik Niclas preached the doctrines of the "Family of Love." From that time onwards a good deal of theological literature on the Protestant side was published by Amsterdam presses. Richard Schilders at Middelburg was also an extensive publisher of this class of book. Presses at Leyden and Dort made similar contributions, but on a smaller scale. On the Roman Catholic side the head-quarters of propagandist literature, as we have seen, were at first at Antwerp and Louvain, at both of which places John Fouler had presses. In the 'eighties the existence of the English college at Rheims caused several Catholic books to be printed there, notably the translation of the New Testament which was made in the college itself. For like reasons much Catholic literature was published from 1602 onwards at St. Omer, and from 1604 onwards at Douai. Books of the same class, though in smaller numbers, appeared also at Paris and Rouen.

Individually the books from the presses we have been naming, both on the Romanist and the Puritan side, are

232

unattractive to look at and dull to read. Collectively they form a very curious and interesting episode in English bibliography, which deserves more study than it has yet received, though Mr. Sayle has made an excellent beginning in his lists of English books printed on the Continent in the third volume of his *Early English Printed Books in the University Library, Cambridge.* Since then Mr. Steele and Mr. Dover Wilson have made important contributions to the subject, but much still remains to be done.

It was doubtless the existence of these foreign safety-valves which rendered the course of English printing after the grant of a charter to the Stationers' Company so smooth and uneventful.[1] Two violations of the terms of the charter were winked at or authorized, in some way not known to us, by the Crown. The first of these was the printing of a few books for the use of foreign refugees by Antony de Solempne at Norwich. Most of these books were in Dutch, but in 1569 Antony Corranus, previously pastor of the Spanish Protestant congregation at Antwerp, published through de Solempne certain broadside tables *De Operibus Dei* in Latin, French, Dutch, and English, of which copies only of the first and second have been traced. In 1570 another English broadside commemorated the execution at Norwich of Thomas Brooke. Archbishop Parker seems to have resented the publication, unexamined, of the *De Operibus Dei*, but de Solempne placed the royal arms and a loyal motto (Godt bewaer de Coninginne Elizabeth) on some of his books, and seems in some way or another to have secured the Queen's protection.

Mr. Allnutt, to whose exhaustive articles on "English Provincial Printing" in the second volume of *Bibliographica* all subsequent writers on the subject must needs be indebted, conscientiously includes among his

---

[1] Before the incorporation of the Company brought English printing more easily under supervision, at least a few books had been issued by English printers with spurious foreign imprints, of which the most impudent was "At Rome under the Castle of St. Angelo."

notes one on the edition of Archbishop Parker's *De Antiquitate Ecclesiae Britannicae* printed for him by John Day, in all probability at Lambeth Palace, where a small staff of book-fashioners worked under the archiepiscopal eye.   Eton is a good deal farther "out of bounds" than Lambeth, but the employment of the King's Printer, John Norton, and a dedication to the King saved Sir Henry Savile from any interference when he started printing his fine edition of the works of S. John Chrysostom in the original Greek.   The eight folio volumes of which this consists are dated from 1610 to 1613, and in these and the two following years five other Greek books were printed under Savile's supervision.   After this his type was presented to the University of Oxford, where a fairly flourishing press had been at work since 1585.

That printing at Oxford made a new start in 1585 was due no doubt to the example of Cambridge, which two years earlier had at last acted on a patent for printing granted by Henry VIII in 1534, the year, it will be remembered, in which restrictions were placed on the importation of foreign books on account of the proficiency in the art to which Englishmen were supposed to have attained.   In the interim Printers to the University seem to have been appointed, but it was not till 1583 that a press was set up, whereupon, as soon as a single book had been printed, it was promptly seized by the Stationers' Company of London as an infringement of the monopoly granted by their charter.   Although the Bishop of London seems to have backed up the Stationers, Lord Burghley (the Chancellor of the University) and the Master of the Rolls secured the recognition of the rights of the University.   Forty years later they were again attacked by the Stationers, and the Privy Council forbade the Cambridge printer to print Bibles, Prayer Books, Psalters, Grammars, or Books of Common Law, but in 1628 the judges pronounced strongly in favour of the full rights of the University, and the next year these were recognized with some modifications by the Privy Council.

Up to this time there had been three printers, Thomas Thomas (1583–8), John Legate (1588–1610), and Cantrell Legge (1606–29), the University Library possessing (in 1902) 34 books and documents printed by the first, 108 by the second, and 55 by the third, or a total of 197 for a period of forty-six years. From 1628 to 1639 the majority of Cambridge books bear no individual names on them, but have usually the imprint "Cantabrigiæ, ex Academiæ celeberrimæ typographeo." But Thomas and John Buck and Roger Daniel, in various combinations, were responsible for a good many publications.

While Burghley was Chancellor of Cambridge, Dudley, Earl of Leicester, held the Oxford Chancellorship, and doubtless felt that, charter or no charter, it concerned his honour to see that his University should be allowed all the privileges possessed by the other. Under his auspices a press was started late in 1584 or early in 1585 by Joseph Barnes, an Oxford bookseller, to whom the University lent £100 to enable him to procure the necessary equipment, and on Leicester's visiting the University on 11 January, 1585, a *Carmen gratulatorium* in four elegiac couplets was presented to him, printed on an octavo leaf at the new press. The first book to appear was a *Speculum Moralium Quaestionum in uniuersam Ethicen Aristotelis*, by John Case, a former fellow of S. John's, with a dedication to Leicester by the author and another by the printer. In the latter the promise was made "ea solum ex his prælis in lucem venient que sapientum calculis approbentur & Sybille foliis sint veriora," but the remaining publications of the year were a polemical treatise by Thomas Billson, two issues of a Protestant adaptation of the *Booke of Christian exercise appertaining to Resolution*, by Robert Persons, the Jesuit, and two sermons. In 1586 no fewer than seventeen books were printed (a number not again attained for several years), and among them was an edition of six homilies of S. Chrysostom, "primitiæ typographi nostri in græcis literis preli." After this the press settled down to an average production of from eight to a dozen books a year, including a fair number of classical texts and translations, with now and then a volume of verse which brings it into connection with the stream of Elizabethan literature. Among the more interesting books which it produced, mention may be made of the *Sixe Idillia* of Theocritus (1588), poems by Nicholas Breton and Thomas Churchyard (1592), Richard de Bury's *Philobiblon* (1599), the *Microcosmus* of John Davies of Hereford (1603), Captain John Smith's *Map of Virginia, with a description of the Countrey* (1612), and Burton's *Anatomy of Melancholy* (1621). In the 'twenties of the seventeenth century the average annual output was still only 14; in the 'thirties, under the fostering care of Laud, it had risen as high as 25. In 1641 it was but 19. Then, on the outbreak of the Civil War, the King came to Oxford, and under the stress of official publications and royalist controversy the numbers shot up to about 147 in 1642, followed by 119 in 1643, about 100 in 1644, and 60 in 1645. Then they become normal again, and in 1649 under the Parliamentary *régime* sink as low as seven. These statistics are taken from the various works of Mr. Falconer Madan, mentioned in our bibliography, and from the same source we learn that until the nineteenth century the annual average of production, calculated by periods of ten years, never exceeded thirty-two.

Similar causes to those which brought about the sudden increase in the Oxford output in 1642 led to the establishment of presses at Newcastle and York. In 1639, when Charles I marched against the Scots, his headquarters were at Newcastle, and the Royal Printer, Robert Barker,[1] printed there a sermon by the Bishop of Durham, the *Lawes and Ordinances of Warre*, and some proclamations. In March, 1642, again Barker was

---

[1] Robert Barker himself was imprisoned for debt in the King's Bench at London in 1635, and died there in 1646. What is here written applies to his deputy, who may have been his son of the same name.

in attendance on the King at York, and printed there *His Majesties Declaration to both Houses of Parliament*, in answer to that presented to him at Newmarket, and some thirty-eight other pieces. Another London printer, Stephen Bulkley, was also given employment, and in the years 1642–4 printed at York some twenty-eight different pieces. Bulkley also attended the King at Newcastle in 1646, when he was in the hands of the Scots, and remained printing there and at Gateshead until the Restoration, when he returned to York, where a Puritan press had in the meantime been set up by Thomas Broad.

Charles I left York on 16 August, 1642, and six days later the Royal Standard was raised at Nottingham. *His Majesties Instructions to his Commissioners of Array*, dated " at our Court at Nottingham, 29th August, 1642," were printed by Barker at York. Two days later the King ordered that the press should be brought to Nottingham, but we next hear of Barker at Shrewsbury, where he served the King's immediate needs, and then remained at work for the rest of the year and the greater part of 1643 reprinting Oxford editions and publishing other royalist literature. After the capture of Bristol for the King on 2 August he removed once more and printed there during 1644 and 1645.

During the confusion of the Civil War an Exeter stationer, Thomas Hunt (the local publisher of Herrick's *Hesperides*), had a book printed for him—Thomas Fuller's *Good Thoughts in Bad Times*—which is described in the dedication as the " First Fruits of the Exeter Presse," and another is said to have been printed there in 1648. But we hear of no other presses being set up. After the Restoration printing was allowed to continue at York. Otherwise provincial printing outside the Universities was once more non-existent. The arrival of William of Orange caused some broadsides to be printed at Exeter in 1688, and in the same year Thomas Tillier printed at Chester, not only *An account of a late*

Horrid and Bloody Massacre in Ireland on a single leaf, but also a handsome folio, *The Academy of Armory*, for Randall Holme, who rewarded him for any risk he may have run by devising for him a fancy coat. Nevertheless, despite the change of Government, the Act of Parliament restricting printing to London, Oxford, Cambridge, and York was not allowed to expire till 1695. A press was set up at Bristol the same year. Plymouth and Shrewsbury followed in 1696, Exeter in 1698, and Norwich in 1701, the first provincial newspaper, *The Norwich Post*, dating from September in that year. By 1750 about seventy-five provincial towns possessed presses, cities and small country places starting them at haphazard, not at all in the order of their importance. The dates for some of the chief are as follows (all on the authority of Mr. Allnutt): 1708, Newcastle-upon-Tyne; 1709, Worcester; 1710, Nottingham; 1711, Chester; 1712, Liverpool; 1715, Salisbury; 1716, Birmingham; 1717, Canterbury; 1718, Ipswich, Leeds, and Taunton; 1719, Manchester and Derby; 1720, Northampton; 1721, Coventry and Hereford; 1723, Reading; 1731, Bath; 1737, Sheffield; 1745, Stratford-on-Avon; 1748, Portsmouth.

As a side-consequence of the lapsing of the Licensing Act in 1695, it became possible for any private person to buy a printing press, hire a journeyman printer, and start printing any books he pleased. Several private presses were thus set up during the second half of the eighteenth century, the most famous of them being that of Horace Walpole at Strawberry Hill, near Twickenham. Walpole started in 1757 by printing two of the Odes of his friend Gray, and at intervals during the next twenty-seven years printed several of his own works, and a few other books, of which an edition of Grammont's *Mémoires* was the most important. Walpole's example was followed by George Allan, M.P. for Durham, and Francis Blomefield, the historian of Norfolk; also in the nineteenth century by Thomas Johnes, who printed his translation of Froissart in four large quarto volumes at his own house at Hafod in Cardiganshire in 1803-5, and followed them up with a Joinville in 1807 and a Monstrelet in 1810. Between 1813 and 1823 Sir Egerton Brydges caused a number of interesting literary reprints to be issued for him in limited editions from a press in or near his house at Lee Priory in Kent. The work of both these presses, like that of Walpole's, was perhaps equal to the best commercial printing of its day, but was not superior to it, and perhaps the same may be said of the few reprints manufactured, in still more jealously limited editions, by E. V. Utterson between 1840 and 1843 at Beldornie House, Ryde. Sir Thomas Phillipps, who printed numerous antiquarian documents between 1822 and 1862 at Middle Hill in Worcestershire, and between 1862 and 1872 at Cheltenham, set even less store by typographical beauty and accuracy. The other private presses of the first half of the nineteenth century are not more interesting, though that of Gaetano Polidori at Park Village East, near Regent's Park, 1840-50, has become famous as having printed Gabriel Rossetti's *Sir Hugh the Heron* in 1843, and Christina Rossetti's first volume of verse four years later, Polidori being the grandfather of the young authors on their mother's side.

Passing north of the Tweed, where the most formidable competitors of the London printers now abide, we find the first Scottish press at work at Edinburgh in 1508. In September of the previous year Andrew Myllar, a bookseller who had gained some experience of printing at Rouen, and Walter Chapman, a merchant, had been granted leave to import a press, chiefly that they might print an Aberdeen Breviary, which duly appeared in 1509-10. The books which anticipated it in 1508 were a number of thin quartos, *The Maying or Disport of Chaucer*, dated 4 April, the *Knightly Tale of Golagros and Gawane*, dated 8 April, the *Porteous of Noblenes*, "translated out of franche in scottis be

Maistir Andrew Cadiou," dated 20 April, and eight undated pieces, three of them by Dunbar (*The Goldyn Targe*, *The Flyting of Dunbar and Kennedy*, and the *Twa Marrit Wemen and the Wedo*, with other poems), the others being the *Ballad of Lord Barnard Stewart*, *Orpheus and Eurydice*, the *Buke of Gude Counsale*, *Sir Eglamoure of Artoys*, and *A Gest of Robyn Hode*. All these have survived (some of them much mutilated) in a single volume, and it is at the reader's pleasure to decide whether they represent the harvest of some careful person who bought up all Chapman and Myllar's fugitive pieces, or are merely the remnants of a much larger output. The Aberdeen Breviary, which the printers were encouraged to produce by protection against the importation of Sarum books from England or abroad, is really handsomely printed in black and red. At the end of one of the four or five copies of it now known is an addendum, the *Officium Compassionis Beatae Virginis* (commemorated on the Wednesday in Holy Week), which bears the colophon "Impressum Edinburgi per Johannem Story nomine & mandato Karoli Stule," which Scottish bibliographers assign to about 1520. A fragment of a *Book of the Howlat* may belong to the same period. Thus although Scottish writers, such as John Vaus and Hector Boece of Aberdeen, had to send their books to France to be printed, it is possible that presses were at work in Edinburgh or elsewhere in Scotland, of which nothing is now known.

The next printer of whom we have certain information is Thomas Davidson, who in February, 1541 (1542), produced a handsome edition of *The New Actis and Constitutionis of Parliament maid be the Rycht Excellent Prince Iames the Fift*. This was his only dated book, but he issued also a fine edition of *The hystory and croniklis of Scotland*, translated by "Johne Bellenden, Archdene of Murray, chanon of Ros," from the Latin of Hector Boece, and some smaller works.

The next Scottish printer is John Scot, whom the

best authorities, despite the fact that he is first heard of in Edinburgh in 1539, refuse to identify with the John Skot who printed in London from 1521 to 1537. Whoever he was, he had no very happy existence, as notwithstanding some efforts to please the Protestant party, the work he did for the Catholics twice brought him into serious trouble. His first dated book, Archbishop Hamilton's *Catechism*, did not appear till 29 August, 1552, and was printed not at Edinburgh, but at St. Andrews. How he had been employed between 1539 and this date we have no means of knowing. At St. Andrews Scot printed Patrick Cockburn's *Pia Meditatio in Dominicam Orationem* (1555), and probably also Lauder's *Dewtis of Kingis* (1556). Scot also printed controversial works on the Catholic side by the Abbot of Crosraguell (Quentin Kennedy) and Ninian Winzet, and for the opposite party *The Confessione of faith Professit and Belevit be the Protestantes within the Realme of Scotland* (1561). He issued also two editions (1568 and 1571) of the works of Sir David Lindesay, while his undated books include some of Lindesay's single poems.

Since John Scot printed mainly on the Catholic side, the Protestant General Assembly in December, 1562, started a printer in opposition to him, Robert Lekpreuik, lending him " twa hundreth pounds to help to buy irons, ink and papper and to fie craftesmen for printing." He had previously, in 1561, like Scot, printed the *Confession of the Faith*, also Robert Noruell's *Meroure of an Chr[i]stiane* and an *Oration* by Beza. The grant allowed him was in connection with an edition of the Psalms, which eventually appeared in 1565, together with the *Form of Prayer and Ministration of the Sacraments used in the English Church at Geneva* and the Catechism (dated 1564). Lekpreuik continued active till 1574, and after an interval issued three books in 1581 and perhaps one in 1582. In Mr. Aldis's List he is credited with ninety-one publications (mostly controversial) as against four assigned to Davidson and fifteen to Scot. During 1571 he printed at Stirling, and the next two years at St. Andrews. Like Scot, he found printing perilous work, his intermission after the beginning of 1574 being due to imprisonment.

Thomas Bassandyne, who had previously published books at Edinburgh, began printing there in 1572. He produced but ten (extant) books and documents in all, but his name is famous from its connection with the first Scottish Bible, of which he produced the New Testament in 1576, the Old Testament being added, and the whole issued by his successor, Alexander Arbuthnot, in 1579. Besides the Bible, only five books were printed by Arbuthnot. Between 1574 and 1580 twenty-six were produced by John Ross, and on his death Henry Charteris, a bookseller, took over his material, and by the time of his death in 1599 had printed forty more. But the best Edinburgh work towards the end of the century was produced by two craftsmen from England, Thomas Vautrollier, who produced ten books in 1584-6, and Robert Waldegrave (1590-1603), who had to flee from England for his share in the Marprelate tracts, and during his thirteen years in Edinburgh issued 119 books.

When Joseph Ames was desirous of obtaining information about early printing in Ireland he applied to a Dr. Rutty, of Dublin (apparently a Quaker), who could only furnish the name of a single book printed there before 1600, this being an edition of the Book of Common Prayer, which states that it is " Imprinted by Humphrey Powell, printer to the Kynges Maiesti, in his Highnesse realme of Ireland dwellyng in the citie of Dublin in the greate toure by the Crane. Cum Privilegio ad imprimendum solum. Anno Domini MDLI." We know from the records of the English Privy Council that Humphrey Powell, an inconspicuous English printer, was granted £20 in July, 1550, " towards his setting up in Ireland," and this Prayer Book was doubtless the first fruits of his press. Powell remained in Dublin for fifteen years, but the only other products of his press still in existence are two proclamations, one issued in 1561 against Shane O'Neill, the other in 1564 against the O'Connors, and *A Brefe Declaration of certein Principall Articles of Religion*, a quarto of eight leaves set out by order of Sir Henry Sidney in 1566.

In 1571 John O'Kearney, Treasurer of St. Patrick's, was presented with a fount of Irish type by Queen Elizabeth, and a Catechism by him and a broadside poem on the Last Judgment, by Philip, son of Conn Crosach, both in Irish type, are still extant. But there seems to be no trustworthy information as to where they were printed, though it was probably at Dublin.

An Almanac, giving the longitude and latitude for Dublin, for the year 1587, appears to have been printed at London. But in 1595 William Kearney printed a Proclamation against the Earl of Tyrone and his adherents in Ireland "in the Cathedrall Church of the Blessed Trinitie, Dublin."

We reach continuous firm ground in 1600 when John Francke, or Franckton (as he called himself in 1602 and thenceforward), printed one or more proclamations at Dublin. In 1604 Franckton was appointed King's Printer for Ireland, and he continued at work till 1618, when he assigned his patent to Felix Kyngston, Matthew Lownes, and Thomas Downes. Some four-and-twenty proclamations and upwards of a dozen books and pamphlets from his press are extant, some of them in Irish type. In 1620 the office of Printer-General for Ireland was granted for a period of twenty-one years to Kingston, Lownes, and Downes, all of them members of the London Stationers' Company, and the usual imprint on the books they issued is that of the Company (1620–33) or Society (1633–42) of Stationers. They seem to have appointed an agent or factor to look after their interests, and the last of these factors, William Bladen, about 1642 took over the business.

The earliest allusion to books printed in what afterwards became the United States of America occurs in the diary of John Winthrop, Governor of Massachusetts Bay, for March, 1639: "A printing house was begun at Cambridge by one Stephen Daye, at the charge of Mr. Glover, who died on sea hitherward. The first thing which was printed was the freemen's Oath; the next was an almanac made for New England by Mr. William Pierce, mariner; the next was the Psalms newly turned into metre." The Mr. Glover here mentioned was the Rev. Joseph Glover, rector of Sutton in Surrey from 1628 to 1636, who, after collecting funds for the benefit of Harvard College at Cambridge, Mass., sailed with his family from England in the summer of 1638, but died on the way. His widow (Elizabeth Glover), shortly after her arrival, married the Rev. Henry Dunster, the first President of Harvard, and thus, as had happened in Paris, the first press in America was set up in a college under clerical auspices. Stephen Day, the printer whom Glover had brought from England, is naturally supposed to have been a descendant of John Day, the great Elizabethan printer, but of this there is no evidence. He obtained some grants of land in consideration of his services to the colony, but did not greatly thrive, and in 1648, or early in 1649, was superseded by Samuel Green. Of the specimens of his press mentioned by Governor Winthrop the *Oath of a Freeman* and the *Almanac* have perished utterly. Of the " Bay Psalter," or the " New England Version of the Psalms," as it was subsequently called, at least eleven copies are known to be extant, of which five are stated to be perfect.[1] It is a small octavo of 148 leaves, disfigured by numerous misprints, but with passable presswork. The translation was made by the Massachusetts clergy, who prefixed to it "A discourse declaring not only the lawfullnes but also the necessity of the heavenly ordinance of singing Scripture Psalmes in the Churches of God." Its titlepage bears the name neither of printer nor of place, but merely

---

[1] The assertion by Mr. Charles Evans (*American Bibliography*, p. 3) that one of these, "the Crowninshield copy, was privately sold by Henry Stevens to the British Museum for £157 10s.," despite its apparent precision, is an exasperating error.

" Imprinted 1640." There is no doubt, however, that it was produced by Day at Cambridge, whereas the edition of 1647 appears to have been printed in London.

The Massachusetts records make it probable that Day printed several books and documents now lost. An imperfect copy of Harvard Theses with the imprint "Cantabrigiæ Nov. Ang., Mens. 8 1643" is the next production of his press still extant. After this comes an historical document of some interest: "*A Declaration of former passages and proceedings betwixt the English and the Narrowgansets, with their confederates, wherein the grounds and iustice of the ensuing warre are opened and cleared.* Published by order of the Commissioners for the United Colonies. At Boston the 11 of the sixth month 1645." Another broadside of Harvard Theses (for 1647) and a couple of almanacs for 1647 and 1648, the first of which has the imprint "Cambridge Printed by Matthew Daye and to be solde by Hez . Usher at Boston . 1647 ", are the only other remnants of this stage of the press. Of Matthew Day nothing more is known.

Samuel Green appears to have taken over Day's business without any previous technical training, so that it is thought that Day may have helped him as a journeyman. The first book ascribed to Green is:

A Platform of Church Discipline gathered out of the word of God : and agreed upon by the Elders : and Messengers of the Churches assembled in the Synod at Cambridge in New-England. To be presented to the Churches and Generals Court for their consideration and acceptance in the Lord. The Eighth Moneth, Anno 1649. Printed by S.G. at Cambridge in New-England and are to be sold at Cambridge and Boston Anno Dom. 1649.

His next extant piece of work is an almanac for 1650, his next the third edition (the second, as noted above, had been printed at London in 1647) of the Bay Psalter, "printed by Samuel Green at Cambridge in New-England, 1651." This was followed in 1652 by Richard Mather's *The Summe of Certain Sermons upon Genes.*

15. 6, a treatise on Justification by Faith, and then Green seems to have begun to busy himself with work for the Corporation in England for the Propagation of the Gospel amongst the Indians in New England, or Corporation for the Indians, as it is easier to call it. A second press was sent over to enable this work to be undertaken, and a Primer by John Eliot ("the Apostle to the Indians") was printed in 1654, and the Books of Genesis and Matthew the next year, all three in the Indian language, all three now known only from records. The same destruction has befallen an Indian version of some of the Psalms mentioned as having been printed in 1658, but of another Indian book of the same year, Abraham Peirson's *Some helps for the Indians, shewing them how to improve their natural reason to know the true God, and the true Christian Religion*, two issues have been preserved, one in the New York Public Library, the other at the British Museum. Another edition, dated the next year, is also at the Museum, though it has escaped the notice of Mr. Evans, the author of the latest "American Bibliography." By this time the Corporation for the Indians had sent over a skilled printer, Marmaduke Johnson, to aid Green in his work. Unfortunately, despite the fact that he had left a wife in England, Johnson flirted with Green's daughter, and this conduct, reprehensible anywhere, in New England brought down on him fines of £20 and a sentence of deportation, which, however, was not carried out. Johnson's initials appears in conjunction with Green's in *A Brief Catechism containing the doctrine of Godlines*, by John Norton, teacher of the Church at Boston, published in 1660, and the two men's names in full are in the Indian New Testament of 1661 and the complete Bible of 1663. Of the New Testament it is conjectured that a thousand, or perhaps fifteen hundred copies, were printed, of which five hundred were bound separately, and forty of these sent to England. How many copies were printed of the Old Testament is not known, but

of the complete Bible some forty copies are still extant in no fewer than eight variant states produced by the presence or absence of the Indian and English titlepages, the dedication, etc., while of the New Testament about half as many copies may be known.

During the progress of the Indian Bible Green had continued his English printing on his other press, and had produced among other things *Propositions concerning the subject of Baptism* collected by the Boston Synod, and bearing the imprint "Printed by S.G. for Hezekiah Vsher at Boston in New England 1662." Printing at Boston itself does not appear to have begun until 1675, when John Foster, a Harvard graduate, was entrusted with the management of a press, and during that and the six following years printed there a number of books by Increase Mather and other ministers, as well as some almanacs. On his death in 1681 the press was entrusted to Samuel Sewall, who, however, abandoned it in 1684. Meanwhile, Samuel Green had continued to print at Cambridge, and his son, Samuel Green junior, is found working by assignment of Sewall and for other Boston booksellers. In 1690 his brother Bartholomew Green succeeded him, and remained the chief printer at Boston till his death in 1732.

At Philadelphia, within three years of its foundation in 1683, a *Kalendarium Pennsilvaniense, or America's Messinger: being and* [sic] *almanack for the year of grace 1686*, by Samuel Atkins, was issued with the imprint, "Printed and sold by William Bradford, sold also by the Author and H. Murrey in Philadelphia and Philip Richards in New York, 1685," and in the same year there was published anonymously Thomas Budd's *Good Order established in Pennsilvania & New Jersey in America, being a true account of the country; with its produce and commodities there made.* In 1686 Bradford printed *An Epistle from John Burnyeat to Friends in Pensilvania* and *A General Epistle given forth by the people of the Lord called Quakers;* in 1687 William Penn's *The excellent privilege of liberty and property being the birth-right of the free-born subjects of England*; in 1688 a collection including Böhme's *The Temple of Wisdom*, Wither's *Abuses Stript and Whipt*, and Bacon's *Essays*, edited by Daniel Leeds. In 1689 Bradford began work-ing for George Keith, and three years later he was im-prisoned for printing Keith's *Appeal from the Twenty Eight Judges to the Spirit of Truth and true Judgement in all faithful Friends called Quakers.* In consequence of this persecution Bradford left Philadelphia the next year and set up his press at New York. Reinier Jansen and Jacob Taylor are subsequently mentioned as printers at Philadelphia, and in 1712 Andrew Bradford, son of William, came from New York and worked there until his death in 1742. From 1723 he had as a competitor Samuel Keimer, and it was in Keimer's office that Ben-jamin Franklin began printing in Philadelphia. His edition of a translation of Cicero's *Cato Major on Old Age*, by J. Logan of Philadelphia, is said to have been the first rendering of a classic published in America.

Meanwhile, William Bradford had set up his press in New York in 1693, and obtained the appointment of Government Printer. His earliest productions there were a number of official Acts and Proclamations, on which he placed the imprint, "Printed and Sold by William Brad-ford, Printer to King William and Queen Mary, at the City of New York." In 1700 he was apparently em-ployed to print an anonymous answer to Increase Mather's *Order of the Gospel*, and a heated controversy arose as to whether the refusal of Bartholomew Green to print it at Boston was due to excessive "awe" of the President of Harvard or to a more praiseworthy objection to anony-mous attacks. Bradford remained New York's only printer until 1726, when Johann Peter Zenger set up a press which became notable for the boldness with which it attacked the provincial government. Such attacks were not regarded with much toleration, nor indeed was the press even under official regulation greatly beloved by authority. In 1671 Sir William Berkeley, Governor of Virginia, in an official document remarked : " I thank God we have not free schools nor printing ; and I hope we shall not have these hundred years. For learning has brought disobedience and heresy and sects into the world ; and printing has divulged them and libels against the government. God keep us from both." Eleven years later (21 February, 1682) there is an entry in the Virginian records : " John Buckner called before the Ld Culpeper and his council for printing the laws of 1680, without his excellency's license, and he and the printer ordered to enter into bond in £100 not to print anything hereafter, until his majesty's pleasure shall be known." As a result there was no more printing in Virginia till about 1729, nor are any other towns than those here mentioned known to have possessed presses during the seventeenth century, the period within which American books may claim the dignity of incunabula.

CHAPTER XIV

ENGLISH WOODCUT ILLUSTRATIONS

A FEW illuminated manuscripts of English workmanship and a few with illustrations in outline have come down to us from the fifteenth century, but amid the weary wars with France and the still wearier struggles of Yorkists and Lancastrians, the artistic spirit which had been so prominent in England in the thirteenth and fourteenth centuries seems to have died out altogether. Until the reign of Queen Elizabeth, or perhaps we should rather say until the advent of John Day, few English books were illustrated, and of these few quite a large proportion borrowed or copied their pictures from foreign originals. Nevertheless, English illustrated books are rightly sought after by English collectors, and though we may wish that they were better, we must give the best account of them we can.

As we shall see in a later chapter, there is some probability that an engraving on copper was specially prepared for the first book printed by Caxton, *The Recuyell of the Histories of Troye*. For the present, however, we must concern ourselves only with illustrations on wood, or on soft metal cut in relief after the manner of wood, a difference of more interest to the technical student than to book-lovers. The first English books thus illustrated appear in or about 1481, the year in which Jean Du Pré began the use of cuts in Paris. England was thus fairly well to the front in point of time ; it is the quality which is to seek. The first of these illustrated books was probably an undated edition of the *Mirrour of the World*, a translation of a French version of a Latin *Speculum* or *Imago mundi*. Besides some woodcut diagrams copied

kynde there as J leue a suffycient scole and a true of alle these
whoos soule reste in euerlastyng pees.as J hope he be ful hyhe
in blysse Joyned and knytte wythout departynge to his spouse
by parfyt vse of the best parte that he chese here wyth Mary:
Of the whyche parte he graunte vs felaushyp Jhesus our lord
god.Amen.

¶Of the reysyng of lazar.& other two dede bodyes.Ca.xxxiiij

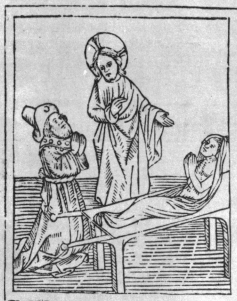

Among all the myra
cles that oure lorde
Jhesu Cryste wrought
here in erthe.the reysynge
of lazar is princypally cō
mended. and souerapnly
is to be consydered not
only for the souerayn my
racle it self. But also for
many notable thynges.
that befelle in that myra
cle and dyuerse mysterp
es:the whyche saynt Au
gustyn clergeally treateth
by long processe vpon the
same gospel.Of the why
che som what J shalle touche in party and more ouer as the gra
ce of oure lorde Jhesus wylle sende wytte partepnynge to the
purpos.¶And for as mykel as the gospel maketh mynde
of thre dede bodyes reysed by our lord Jhesu fro dethe to lyf/ of
the whyche two the fyrste is not spoken of specyally in thys tre
tees before.therfore it semeth conuenyent to thys purpos som
what touche of hem in thys place/as the forsayd saynt Austyn
dothe.And fyrste we shal vnderstande & haue in mynd that as

XXIX. WESTMINSTER, CAXTON, c. 1488

BONAVENTURA. MEDITATIONES. (PART OF SIG. K 5 RECTO)

CHRIST RAISING THE DAUGHTER OF JAIRUS

from drawings found in the French manuscripts, this has ten little cuts, seven of the masters of the seven liberal arts, one of the author, and two of the Creation. Two of the cuts illustrating the arts were used again almost at once in Caxton's third edition of the *Parvus et Magnus Cato*, a book of moral instruction for children in a series of Latin distichs. In 1481 also Caxton ornamented the second edition of the didactic treatise, *The Game and Play of the Chess* (from the Latin of Jacobus de Cessolis), with sixteen woodcuts, representing the characters after which the different pieces and pawns were called. The pictures are clumsy and coarsely cut, comparing miserably with the charming little woodcuts in the Italian edition printed at Florence, but they illustrate the book, and may conceivably have increased its sales. In any case, Caxton seems, in a leisurely way, to have set about producing some more, since by or about 1484 appeared three of his most important illustrated books, the *Golden Legend*, the second edition of Chaucer's *Canterbury Tales*, and an *Aesop*. The *Golden Legend* is ornamented with eighteen large and thirty-two smaller woodcuts ; the *Aesop* with a full-page frontispiece and one hundred and five smaller cuts ; the *Canterbury Tales* with a large cut of the Pilgrims seated at a round table, and with some twenty smaller pictures of the different story-tellers on their horses, some of these being used more than once. For the *Aesop*, like many other foreign publishers, Caxton sent his illustrators to the designs made for the Zainers at Augsburg and Ulm, and quickly imitated all over Germany, and the copies he obtained are merely servile and so clumsy as occasionally to attain to unintended humour. Foreign influence is also evident in some at least of the cuts in the *Golden Legend;* on the other hand, we may be sure that the device of the Earl of Arundel on leaf 3 verso, a horse galloping past a tree, must have been made in England. Original, too, of necessity, were the illustrations to the *Canterbury Tales*, for which no foreign models could have been found. But the succession of pilgrims, each decked with a huge string of praying-beads and mounted on a most ungainly horse, is grotesque in its cumulation of clumsiness, though when we find that the miller really has got a kind of bagpipe, we recognize that the illustrator had at least read his text.

Apparently Caxton himself realized that these English-made woodcuts were a failure, for the only two important illustrated books which he issued after this, the *Speculum Vitae Christi*, printed about 1488 (see Plate XXIX), and the *Fifteen Oes* of a year or two later, both seem to be decorated with cuts of Flemish origin. The *Fifteen Oes* (a collection of fifteen prayers, each beginning with O), though I have called it important, is so mainly as proving that Caxton must have printed a Horae of the same measurements (of which it may, indeed, have formed a part), illustrated with a set of very spirited woodcuts, undoubtedly imported from Flanders and subsequently found in the possession of Wynkyn de Worde. That the cuts in the *Speculum Vitae Christi* are also Flemish is a degree less certain, but only a degree. Some of these were used again in the *Royal Book*, the *Doctrinal of Sapience*, and the *Book of Divers Ghostly Matters*. But the seven books which we have named are the only ones for which Caxton troubled to procure sets of cuts, and of these seven sets, as we have seen, one was certainly and another probably imported, one certainly and another probably copied, and only three are of English origin, and these the rudest and clumsiest.

While our chief native printer made this poor record his contemporaries did no better. Lettou and Machlinia used no woodcuts which have come down to us save a small border, which passed into the possession of Pynson; for use at Oxford two sets of cuts were imported from the Low Countries, one which Mr. Gordon Duff thinks was originally designed for a *Legenda Aurea*, the other clearly meant for a Horae. These were used together in the Oxford edition of Mirk's *Liber Festivalis*, and the cut of the author of the *Legenda Aurea* (Jacobus de Voragine) is used for Lyndewood in an edition of his *Constitutions*. At St. Albans some poor little cuts were used in the *Chronicles of England*, but from the point of view of illustration the anonymous schoolmaster-printer is chiefly memorable for having printed some cuts of coat-armour in the "Book of St. Albans" (*The Boke of Haukyng, Huntyng and also of Cote-armuris*) in colours.

Wynkyn de Worde inherited Caxton's stock of wood-cuts, and early in his career used some of them again in reprints of the *Golden Legend* and *Speculum Vitae Christi*, and in his larger Horae used the full set of cuts which, while in Caxton's hands, is only known from those which appear in the *Fifteen Oes*. About 1492 he pur-chased some ornamental capitals (Caxton had only used a single rather graceful rustic A) and one or more cuts from Govaert van Os of Gouda. In his 1494 edition of Walter Hylton's *Scala Perfectionis* (the first book in which he put his name) he used a woodblock consisting of a picture of Christ suckled by His mother with a long woodcut inscription, part of which reads "Sit dulce nomen domini nostri ihesu christi et nomen genitricis virginis marie benedictum," the whole surrounded by a graceful floral border. In 1495 came Higden's *Poly-chronicon* with a few woodcut musical notes, the "hystorye of the deuoute and right renommed lyues of holy faders lyuynge in deserte" (usually quoted as the *Vitas Patrum*), with one large cut used six times and forty small ones used as 155, and about the same time a handsome edition of Bartholomaeus Anglicus's *De proprietatibus rerum*, with large cuts (two-thirds of the folio page) prefixed to each of the twenty-two books, apparently copied partly from those in a Dutch edition printed at Haarlem in 1485, partly from the illustrations (themselves not original) in a French edition printed at Lyon, of which Caxton, who finished the translation on his death-bed, had made use. In 1496, in reprinting the *Book of St. Albans* De Worde added a treatise on *Fishing with an angle*, to which he prefixed a cut of a happy angler hauling up a fish which will soon be placed in a well-filled tub which stands beside him on the bank. This is quite good primitive work and was sufficiently appreciated to be used for numerous later editions, but soon after this De Worde employed a cutter who served him very badly, mangling cruelly a set of rather ambitious designs for the *Morte d'Arthur* of 1498 (several of them used again in the *Recuyell* of 1503), and also some single cuts used in different books. For the next half-dozen years De Worde relied almost exclusively on old cuts, but at last found a competent craftsman who enabled him to bring out in January, 1505–6, an English version of the *Art de bien vivre et de bien mourir* with quite neat reductions of the pictures in Vérard's edition of 1492. It was, no doubt, the same workman who copied in 1506 the Vérard-Pigouchet cuts in Pierre Gringore's *Chasteau de Labeur* as translated by Alexander Barclay, but from the frequent omission of backgrounds it is obvious that in these he was hurried, and they are by no means so good as those in the 1505 edition by Pynson with which De Worde was enviously hastening to compete. The *Calendar of Shepherds* was another translation from the French, illustrated with copies of French cuts, while in the prose *Ship of Fools*, translated by Henry Watson from a French version of the German *Narrenschiff* of Sebastian Brant, Basel originals were reproduced probably from intermediate copies. But when in 1509 Henry VII died, De Worde for once seems to have let his craftsman do a bit of original work for a title-cut to a funeral sermon by Bishop Fisher. In this (see Plate XXX) the bishop is shown preaching in a wooden pulpit, immediately below which is the hearse covered by a gorgeous pall on which lies an effigy of the dead king, while beyond the hearse stands a crowd of courtiers. It is evident that perspective was not the artist's strong point, as the pavement seems climbing up the wall and the shape of the hearse is quite indeterminate, but the general effect of the cut is neat and pleasing. That it is an English cut is certain. A

¶ This sermon folowynge was compyled & sayd in the Cathedrall chyrche of saynt Poule within ÿ cyte of London by the ryght reuerende fader in god John bysshop of Rochester/the body beynge present of the moost famouse prynce kynge Henry the .vij. the .x. day of Maye/the yere of our lorde god . M . CCCCC.ix. whiche sermon was enprynted at the specyall requeſt of ÿ ryght excellent prynceſſe Margarete moder vnto the sayd noble prynce and Counteſſe of Rychemonde and Derby.

few months later Bishop Fisher preached another funeral sermon, over Henry VII's aged mother, Margaret Duchess of Richmond, and when De Worde economically wished to use the same woodcut on the titlepage of his edition of this, there was a craftsman on the spot able to cut out the royal hearse from the block and plug in a representation of an ordinary one, and the similarity of touch shows that this was done by the original cutter.

As we have already noted in Chapter XII, Wynkyn de Worde was singularly unenterprising as a publisher, and although he lived for nearly a quarter of a century after the accession of Henry VIII, during all this time he printed no new book which required copious illustration. On the other hand, he was a man of fixed habits, and one of these habits came to be the decoration of the titlepage of nearly every small quarto he issued with a woodcut of some kind or other, the title itself being sometimes printed on a riband above it. When a new picture was absolutely necessary for this purpose it was forthcoming and generally fairly well cut, but a few stock woodcuts, a schoolmaster holding a birch for grammatical books, a knight on horseback for a romance, etc., were used again and again, and often the block was picked out (we are tempted to say "at random," but that would be an exaggeration) from one of the sets already described, which De Worde had commissioned in more lavish days.

One of Richard Pynson's earliest books was an edition of Chaucer's *Canterbury Tales* with about a score of woodcuts of the pilgrims obviously influenced by those in Caxton's second edition, but in no way an improvement on them. It is true that not only is the miller again allowed his bagpipe, but a little mill is placed in the corner of the cut to identify him beyond doubt. On the other hand, the knight's horse is bedecked with the cumbrous skirts used in the tilt-yard, but which would have become sadly draggled ere much progress had been made along the miry road to Canterbury. The clerk, moreover, is made to carry a bow as if, instead of having his mind set on Aristotle, he were of the lusty sort that loved to get venison where they should not. Round most of the cuts there is a heavy edge of black, as if from an untrimmed block, which does not improve their appearance. Altogether they are poor work, and it was doubtless his recognition of this that caused Pynson in future to rely so largely on the purchase or imitation of foreign blocks. For his edition of Lydgate's *Falles of Princes*, a verse rendering of Boccaccio's *De casibus illustrium virorum*, issued in 1494, he procured the woodcuts made for the fine French edition (*De la ruine des nobles hommes*), printed at Paris by Jean Du Pré in 1483. Before 1500 he brought out an *Aesop*, copying as usual the German cuts. In 1505 he printed Alexander Barclay's version of Pierre Gringore's *Chasteau du Labeur* with cuts closely and fairly skilfully copied from those in the Pigouchet-Vérard editions. In 1506 he went further and procured from Vérard the blocks for a new edition of the *Kalendar of Shepherds*, which, however, he caused to be retranslated, with sundry remarks on the extraordinary English of the version published by Vérard. In 1509 he produced in a fine folio Barclay's free rendering of Brant's *Narrenschiff*, illustrating this English *Ship of Fools* with 117 cuts copied from the originals. In 1518 he procured from Froben some border-pieces for small quartos, one showing in the foot-piece a boy carried on the shoulders of his fellows, another an elephant, a third Mutius Scaevola and Porsenna.

If Pynson had dealt largely in illustrated books the borrowings and copyings here recited might seem insignificant. He published, however, very little English work which can be set against them, and even of the cuts which pass for English the native origin is not always sure. I should be sorry to pledge myself, for instance, as to the provenance of some neat but rather characterless column-cuts in his edition of the *Speculum Vitae Christi*

The preface of Alexander Barclay preest/ vnto the right hye and mighty prince: Thomas Duke of Northfolke.

Reuerēdissimo in Christo patri ac dño: dño Ioanni Veysy exonień episcopo Alexander Barclay presbyter debita cum obseruantía. S.

EMINI me superioribus annis cū adhuc sacelli regij presul esses: pastor vigilantissime: tuis suasionibus incitatū: vt Crispi Salustij hystoriā (quā Iugurthynū bellū dictitant) e romana linguā

Ight mighty/ hye/ and magnificent prince: mpne hūble serupce/ due vnto pour grace. And the behement affection which I haue vnto pour honour and ppetuall fame/ impelleth me often tymes to de= upse/ and to reuolue in mpnde: what serupce/ or pleasure mp symplenesse might

XXXI. LONDON, PYNSON, c. 1520

BARCLAY'S VERSION OF SALLUST'S JUGURTHA. THE TRANSLATOR
AND THE DUKE OF NORFOLK. (REDUCED)

(fifteenth century). The title-cut to the *Traduction and Mariage of the Princesse* (Katherine), printed in 1501, is almost certainly English in its heaviness and lack of charm, but despite the fact that they must have been produced in London we can hardly say as much of the two far prettier pictures which adorn the *Carmen* of Petrus Carmelianus on the treaty of marriage between the future Charles V and the Princess Mary (1508). In the first of these the ambassadors are being received by Henry VII, in the second by the Princess who is attended by her maids, and the latter is perhaps the first English book-illustration with any touch of grace. Unluckily there is a half Spanish, half Low-Country look about it, which suggests that some member of the ambassadors' suite with an artistic turn may at least have supplied the design, so that one hesitates to claim it too vigorously as English work. We may be more confident about the one good cut (the rest are a scratch lot) in the 1513 edition of Lydgate's *The hystory sege and dystruccion of Troy*. In this Henry V is shown seated in a large room, with his suite, while Lydgate in his black habit as a Benedictine presents him with his book. There is a general resemblance between this and another good piece of work, the picture in Alexander Barclay's translation of Sallust's *Jugurtha* (undated) of this other black monk offering his book to the Duke of Norfolk (see Plate XXXI). Probably both were from the same hand. It may be noted that the cut of Barclay was used again in the *Myrrour of good maners conteyning the iiii. vertues called cardynall compyled in latin by Domynicke Mancyn*, of which he was the industrious translator. In Pynson's 1516 edition of Fabyan's *Chronicle*, besides some insignificant column-cuts of kings and some decorative heraldic work, there is an excellent picture of a disembarkation. In other books we find cuts of a schoolmaster with his pupils, of an author, of a woman saint (S. Bridget, though used also for S. Werburga), etc.

Towards the end of his career in the collection of

Chaucer's works (1526) and reprint of Lydgate's *Falles of Princes* (1527), Pynson drew on his stock of miscellaneous blocks rather than allow works with which illustrations had become associated to go forth undecorated.[1] But with his purchase of the border-pieces from Froben in 1518, it would seem that he more or less definitely turned his back on pictorial illustration. Mr. Gordon Duff has shown that a change comes over the character of his books about this time, and has suggested that during the latter years of his life his business was to some extent in the hands of Thomas Berthelet, who succeeded him as King's Printer. Berthelet himself in the course of his long and prosperous career eschewed illustrations altogether, while he took some trouble to get good capitals and had a few ornamental borders. It is thus hardly too much to say that from 1518 for some forty years, until in 1559 John Day published Cunningham's *Cosmographicall Glasse*, book-illustration in England can only be found lurking here and there in holes and corners. In 1526 Peter Treveris issued the *Grete Herbal* with numerous botanical figures ; in 1529 John Rastell printed his own *Pastime of People* with huge, semi-grotesque cuts of English kings ; a few of Robert Copland's books and a few of Robert Wyer's have rough cuts of no importance. But when we think of Pynson's edition of Lord Berners' *Froissart*, of Berthelet's of Gower's *Confessio Amantis*, of Godfray's *Chaucer*, and of Grafton's edition of Halle's *Chronicle*, all illustratable books and all unillustrated, it is evident that educated book-buyers, wearied of rudely hacked blocks, often with no relevance to the book in which they were found, had told the printers that they might save the space occupied by these decorations, and that the reign of the primitive woodcut in English books, if it can be said ever to have reigned, was at an end.

---

[1] He had apparently returned the blocks borrowed from Du Pré for the *Falles of Princes*, as none of them is used in 1527, although one or two are copied. I have not met with all the Chaucer illustrations, and it is possible that a few of these are new.

This emphatic discouragement of book-illustrations during so many years in the sixteenth century was perhaps the best thing that could have happened—next to an equally emphatic encouragement of them. There can have been no reason in the nature of things why English book-illustrations should continue over a long period of time to be third-rate. A little help and a little guidance would probably have sufficed to reform them altogether. Nevertheless it can hardly be disputed that as a matter of fact they were, with very few exceptions, third-rate, the superiority of Pynson's to Wynkyn de Worde's being somewhat less striking than is usually asserted. In the absence of the needed help and guidance it was better to make a sober dignity the ideal of book-production than to continue to deface decently printed books by the use of job lots of column cuts. The borders and other ornaments used by Berthelet, Reyner Wolfe, and Grafton, the three principal firms of this period, are at least moderately good. All three printers indulged in the pleasing heresy of pictorial or heraldic capitals, Wolfe in the *Homiliae duae* of S. Chrysostom (1543), Grafton in Halle's Chronicle entitled *The Union of the Families of Lancaster and York* (1548), and Berthelet in some of his later proclamations. As regards their devices, Grafton's punning emblem (a tree grafted on a tun), though in its smallest size it may pass well enough, was not worthy of the prominence which he sometimes gave it; but Wolfe's "Charitas" mark, of children throwing sticks at an apple tree, is perhaps the most pleasing of English devices, while Berthelet's "Lucrece," despite the fact that her draperies have yielded to the Renaissance temptation of fluttering in the wind rather more than a Roman lady would have thought becoming at the moment of death, is of its kind a fine piece of work. As for pictures, from which Berthelet, as far as I remember, was consistent in his abstinence—Wolfe and Grafton were wisely content to make an exception in favour of Holbein, a little medallion cut after his portrait of Sir Thomas Wyatt adorning Wolfe's edition of Leland's *Naeniae*

(1542), and Grafton owing to him the magnificent title-page to the Great Bibles in which Cranmer and Cromwell, with a host of other worthies, are seen distributing Bibles under the superintendence of Henry VIII. After the fall of Cromwell his armorial bearings were cut out of the block, a piece of petty brutality on a level with that which compelled owners of Prayer Books and Golden Legends to deface them by scratching out the word "pope" and as much as they could of the service for the day of that certainly rather questionable saint, Thomas à Becket.

In 1548 we come across a definitely illustrated book, Cranmer's *Catechism*, published by Walter Lynne, with a delicately cut titlepage[1] showing figures of Justice, Prudence, and Victory, and also the royal arms, and in the text numerous small Biblical pictures, two of which are signed "Hans Holbein," while others have been rashly attributed to Bernard Salomon. In 1556 we find Heywood's *Spider and the Fly* illustrated not only with various woodcuts of spiders' webs, but with a portrait of the author stiff and ungainly enough in all conscience, but carrying with it an impression of lank veracity (see Plate XXXII). About this time, moreover, William Copland was issuing folio and quarto editions of some of the poems and romances which had pleased the readers of the first quarter of the century, and some of these had the old cuts in them. It is evident that illustrations would have come back in any case—book-buyers can never abstain from them for long together. But it is only fair to connect this return with the name of John Day, who made a strenuous effort, which only just failed of success, to bring up book-illustration to the high level at which he was aiming in printing. Day had issued a few books during the reign of Edward VI, notably a Bible with an excellent pictorial capital showing the promoter of the edition, Edmund Becke, presenting a copy of it to the King. As a staunch Protestant he had been in some danger under Queen Mary, but with the accession of

[1] Used again the same year in a treatise by Richard Bonner.

260

XXXII. LONDON, T. POWELL, 1556

HEYWOOD. THE SPIDER AND THE FLY. PORTRAIT OF HEYWOOD

Elizabeth he came quickly to the front, thanks to the help of Archbishop Parker, and the edition of *The Cosmographicall Glasse* of William Cunningham, which he issued in 1559, is thus, as we have already suggested, a real landmark in English book-production. In addition to its fine types, this book is notable for its woodcut diagrams and pictorial capitals, ornamental titlepage, large map of Norwich and, most important of all, a strong and vigorous portrait of the author, his right hand on a globe, a *Dioscorides* with a diagram of a rose lying open before him, and a wooded landscape being seen in the distance. The whole is enclosed in an oval frame, round which runs a Greek motto cut in majuscules, Η ΜΕΓΑΛΗ ΕΥΔΑΙΜΟΝΙΗ ΟΥΔΕΝΙ ΦΘΟΝΕΙΝ ("the great happiness is to envy no man"), with the author's age, "ÆTATIS 28" at the foot. The portrait measures about 6 inches by $4\frac{1}{2}$, and occupies the whole folio page. It is only too probable that it was the work not of a native Englishman, but of some Dutch refugee, but here at last in an English book was a piece of living portraiture adequately cut on wood, and with better luck it should have been the first of a long series. John Day himself did his best to promote a fashion by prefixing a small portrait of Becon to that author's *Pomander of Prayer*, 1561, and having a much larger one of himself cut the next year, "ÆTATIS SVÆ XXXX," as the inscription tells us, adding also his motto, "LIEFE IS DEATHE AND DEATH IS LIEFE", the spelling in which suggests a Dutch artist, though Dutch spelling about this time was so rampant in England that we may hope against hope that this was English work. The oval portrait is surrounded with strap-work ornament, another fashion of the day, and at the foot of this are the initials I. D. On one interpretation these would lead us to believe not only that the work is English, but that Day himself was the cutter. But bindings from his shop are sometimes signed I. D. P. (Ioannes Day pegit), and we must hesitate before attributing to him personal skill not only in printing, but in binding and wood-cutting as well.

The portrait itself is taken side-face and shows a cropped head, keen eye, and long beard, the neck being entirely concealed by a high coat-collar within which is a ruff. The ground to the front of the face is all in deep shadow, that at the back of the head is left white, a simple contrast which perhaps makes the general effect more brilliant. Day used this portrait as a device in some of his largest folio books—for instance, his three-volume edition of Becon's works (1560–4) and Foxe's *Book of Martyrs* (1563).

The full title of the *Book of Martyrs*, which we have now reached, is *Actes and Monuments of these latter and perillous dayes, touching matters of the Church, wherein ar comprehended and described the great persecutions and horrible troubles, that have bene wrought and practised by the Romishe Prelates, especially in this Realm of England and Scotlande, from the yeare of our Lorde a thousande unto the tyme nowe present.* It bears an elaborate title-page showing Protestants and Catholics preaching, Protestants being burnt at the stake contrasted with Catholics offering the sacrifice of the Mass, and finally the Protestant martyrs uplifted in heaven, while the Catholic persecutors are packed off to hell. The text is very unevenly illustrated, but the total number of woodcuts even in the first edition (1563) is very considerable, and as many new pictures were added in the second (1570), the book was certainly the most liberally illustrated with cuts specially made for it which had yet been produced in England. One or two of the smaller cuts, mostly the head of a martyr praying amid the flames, are used several times; of the larger cuts only a very few are repeated, and, considering the monotonous subject of the book, it is obvious that some trouble must have been taken to secure variety in the illustrations. A few of these occupy a whole page, that illustrating the Protestant legend of the poisoning of King John by a fanatic monk being divided into compartments, while others showing some of the more important martyrdoms are

262

ambitiously designed. The drawing of some of the later pictures is coarse, but on the whole the designs are good and with a good deal of character in them. The cutting is careful and painstaking, but hardly ever succeeds in making the picture stand out boldly on the page, so that the general effect is grey and colourless. As to the personality of the designers and cutters we know nothing. Day at one time was anxious to get leave to keep more than the permitted maximum of four foreigners in his employment, but we have really no sufficient ground for arguing either for an English or a foreign origin for these illustrations.

A few years after this, in 1569, when the new edition of the *Book of Martyrs* was in preparation, Day issued another illustrated book : *A christall glasse of christian reformation, wherein the godly maye beholde the coloured abuses used in this our present tyme.* Collected by *Stephen Bateman*, better known as the "Batman uppon Bartholomew," i.e. the editor by whom the *De Proprietatibus Rerum* of Bartholomaeus Anglicus was "newly corrected, enlarged, and amended" in 1582. The *Christall glasse of christian reformation* is a dull book with dull illustrations, which are of the nature of emblems, made ugly by party spirit. A more interesting book by the same author and issued in the same year was *The travayled Pylgrime, bringing newes from all partes of the worlde*, to which Bateman only put his initials and which was printed not by Day, but by Denham. This, although I cannot find that the fact has been noted, is largely indebted both for its scheme and its illustrations to the *Chevalier Délibéré* of Olivier de la Marche, though the woodcuts go back not to those of the Gouda and Schiedam incunabula, but to the Antwerp edition of 1555, in which these were translated into some of the most graceful of sixteenth century cuts. Needless to say, much of the grace disappears in this new translation, although the cutting is more effective than in the *Book of Martyrs*.

Besides these two books by Stephen Bateman, 1569

saw the issue of the first edition of one of John Day's most famous ventures, *A Booke of Christian Prayers, collected out of the ancient writers and best learned in our time, worthy to be read with an earnest mind of all Christians, in these dangerous and troublesome daies, that God for Christes sake will yet still be mercifull vnto vs.* From the presence on the back of the titlepage of a very stiff portrait of the Queen kneeling in prayer (rather like a design for a monumental brass), this is usually quoted as *Queen Elizabeth's Prayer Book.* It was reprinted in 1578 (perhaps also earlier), 1581, and 1590, and the later editions, the only ones I have seen, ascribe the compilation to R. D., i.e. Richard Day, John Day's clergyman son. The book is in appearance a kind of Protestant Horae, having borders to every page divided into compartments as in the Paris editions, showing scenes from the life of Christ, the cardinal virtues and their opposites, the works of charity, and a Dance of Death. Compared with the best, or even the second best, of the Horae of Pigouchet or Kerver, the book looks cold and colourless, but the rarity of the early editions shows that it must have been very popular.

The only other book issued by Day with borders to every page was the (supposititious) *Certaine select prayers gathered out of S. Augustines Meditations, which he calleth his selfe-talks with God,* which went through several editions, of which the first is dated 1574. This is a much less pretentious book, the borders being decorative instead of pictorial, but it makes rather a pretty little octavo. Another 1569 book which has cuts is the edition of Grafton's *Chronicle* of that year, printed by Henry Denham, but as the cuts look like a "job" lot, possibly of German origin, and are only placed at the beginnings of sections in the short first book, while all the history from 1066 onwards is left unillustrated, this speaks rather of decadence than progress.

In 1581, towards the close of his career, Day was employed to print John Derrick's *Image of Ireland,*

264

XXXIII. LONDON, C. BARKER, 1575

TURBERVILLE. BOOKE OF FAULCONRIE. QUEEN ELIZABETH HAWKING

giving an account of Sir Henry Sidney's campaign against the Irish "wood-karnes." In some few copies this work is illustrated with eight very large woodcuts, the most ambitious in some respects that had ever been attempted in England. The first four are wretchedly cut ; the last four, showing Sir Henry's battle with the rebels and his triumphal return, are both well designed and well executed.

Meanwhile, other printers and publishers had produced a few more illustrated books in the 'seventies. Thus in 1575 Henry Bynneman had printed Turberville's *Booke of Faulconrie* for Christopher Barker. The numerous excellent illustrations of hawks (and probably those of dogs also) are taken from French books, but there is a fairly vigorous picture of Queen Elizabeth hawking attended by her suite, badged, back and front, with large Tudor roses, and this (see Plate XXXIII) looks like English work. In a much later edition—that of 1611— it is curious to note that the portrait of the Queen was cut out and one of James I substituted.

In 1576 a rather forbidding woodcut portrait of George Gascoigne was printed (by R. Smith) in that worthy's *Steele Glas*. In 1577 came a very important work, the famous *Chronicle*, begun on a vast scale by Reyner Wolfe and completed for England, Scotland, and Ireland by Raphael Holinshed, now published by John Harrison the elder. This has the appearance of being much more profusely illustrated than the *Book of Martyrs* or any other English folio, but as the cuts of battles, riots, executions, etc., which form the staple illustrations, are freely repeated, the profusion is far less than it seems. The cuts, moreover, are much smaller than those in Foxe's *Martyrs*. As a rule they are vigorously designed and fairly well cut, and if it had come fifty years earlier the book would have been full of promise. But, as far as pictorial cuts in important books are concerned, we are nearing the end. In 1579 H. Singleton published Spenser's *Shepheardes Calender* with a small cut of no great merit at the head of each "æglogue," and in the same year Vautrollier illustrated North's *Plutarch* with insignificant little busts which derive importance only from the large ornamental frames, stretching across the folio page, in which they are set. Woodcuts did not cease to be used after this date. They will be found in herbals (but these were mainly foreign blocks), military works, and all books for which diagrams were needed. They continued fashionable for some time for the architectural or other forms of borders to titlepages, some of them very graceful, as, for instance, that to the early folio editions of Sidney's *Arcadia;* also for the coats of arms of the great men to whom books were dedicated. They are found also at haphazard in the sixpenny and fourpenny quartos of plays and romances, and many of the old blocks gradually drifted into the hands of the printers of ballads and chapbooks, and appear in incongruous surroundings after a century of service. But I cannot myself call to mind any important English book after 1580 for which a publisher thought it worth his while to commission a new set of imaginative pictures cut on wood, and that means that woodcut illustration as a vital force in the making of books had ceased to exist. They needed good paper and careful presswork, and all over Europe paper and presswork were rapidly deteriorating. They cost money, and book-buyers apparently did not care enough for them to make them a good investment. The rising popularity of copper engravings for book-illustration on the Continent probably influenced the judgment of English book-lovers, and although, as we shall see, copper engraving was for many years very sparingly used in England save for portraits, frontispieces, and titlepages, woodcuts went clean out of fashion for some two centuries.

CHAPTER XV

ENGRAVED ILLUSTRATIONS

THE good bookman should have no love for "plates," and to do them justice bookmen have shown commendable fortitude in resisting their attractions, great as these often are. As a form of book-decoration the plate reached its highest development in the French *livres-à-vignettes* of the eighteenth century, the charm of the best bookwork of Moreau, Eisen, and their fellows being incontestable. It would, indeed, have argued some lack of patriotism if French book-lovers had not yielded themselves to the fascination of a method of book-illustration which had thus reached its perfection in their own country, and they have done so. But as he reads the enthusiastic descriptions of these eighteenth century books by M. Henri Béraldi, a foreign book-lover may well feel (to borrow the phrase which Jonson and Herrick used of the over-dressed ladies of their day) that the book itself has become its "own least part." A book which requires as an appendix an album of original designs, or of proofs of the illustrations, or (worse still) which has been mounted on larger paper and guarded so that these proofs or designs can be brought into connection with the text, is on its way to that worst of all fates, the Avernus of extra illustration or Graingerism. When it has reached this, it ceases to be a book at all and becomes a scrap-album of unharmonized pictures.

Lack of means may make it easy for a bookman to resist the temptation to supplement the illustrations in a book with duplicates in proof or any like extravagances, but even then few books which have plates in them fail to bring trouble. If the plates are protected with "flim-

267

sies," the owner's conscience may be perturbed with doubts as to whether these may lawfully be torn out. If there are no flimsies, the leaf opposite a plate often shows a set-off from it and is sometimes specially badly foxed. Moreover, not being an integral part of the book, the plate presents problems to publishers and binders which are too often left unsolved. It ought to be printed on paper sufficiently wide to allow of a flap or turn-over, so that the leaf can be placed in the quire and properly sewn. But the flap thus left is not pretty, and unless very thin may cause the book to gape. Thus too often the plate is only glued or pasted into its place, with the result that it easily comes loose. Hence misplacements, imperfections, and consequent woe.

It is the charm of the earlier books illustrated with incised engravings that the impressions are pulled on the same paper as the rest of the book, very often on pages bearing letterpress, and almost always, even when they chance to occupy a whole page, the back of which is left blank, as part of the quire or gathering. The price, however, which had to be paid for these advantages was a heavy one, the trouble not merely of double printing, as in the case of a sheet printed in red and black, but of double printing in two different kinds, one being from a raised surface, the other from an incised. It is clear that this trouble was found very serious, as both at Rome and Florence in Italy, at Bruges in the Low Countries, at Würzburg and Eichstätt in Germany, and at Lyon in France, the experiment was tried independently and in every case abandoned after one or two books had been thus ornamented.

At Rome, after the failure of his printing partnership with Pannartz, Conrad Sweynheym betook himself to engraving maps to illustrate an edition of Ptolemy's *Cosmographia*, and this was brought out after his death by Arnold Buckinck, 10 October, 1478. Thirteen months earlier Nicolaus Laurentii, of Breslau, had published at Florence the *Monte Santo di Dio* of Antonio

XXXIV. FLORENCE, NICOLUS LAURENTII, 1477

BETTINI. MONTE SANTO DI DIO. CHRIST IN GLORY. (REDUCED)

Bettini, with two full-page engravings and one smaller one. The first of these shows the ladder of Prayer and the Sacraments up which, by the virtues which form its successive rungs, a cassocked youth is preparing to climb to heaven, where Christ stands in a mandorla supported by angels. The second plate is given up entirely to a representation of Christ in a mandorla, both drawing and engraving being excellent, and the little angels who are lovingly upholding the frame being really delightful (see Plate XXXIV). The third picture, printed on a page with text, is smaller than these and represents the pains of hell.

When a second edition of the *Monte Santo di Dio* was needed in 1491 the copperplates were replaced by woodcuts, a fact which may remind us that not only the trouble of printing, but the small number of impressions which could be taken from copperplates, must have been a formidable objection to their use in bookwork. But at the time the first edition may well have been regarded as a success. If so, it was an unlucky one, as Nicolaus Laurentii was thereby encouraged to undertake a much more ambitious venture, an annotated *Divina Commedia* with similar illustrations, and this, which appeared in 1481, can only be looked on as a failure. No space was left at the head of the first canto, and the engraving was printed on the lower margin, where it is often found cruelly cropped. In subsequent cantos spaces were sometimes left, sometimes not, but after the second the engravings are generally founded printed on separate slips and pasted into their places, and in no copy do they extend beyond canto xix. They used to be assigned to Botticelli, but the discovery of his real designs to the *Divina Commedia* has shown that these of 1481 were only slightly influenced by them.

In Germany the only copper engravings found in fifteenth century books are the coats of arms of the Bishops and Chapters of Würzburg and Eichstätt in the books printed for them at these places by Georg and

Michel Reyser respectively. In order more easily to persuade the clergy of these dioceses to buy properly revised service-books to replace their tattered and incorrect manuscript copies, the Bishops attached certain "indulgences" to their purchase, and as a proof that the recital of these was not a mere advertising trick of the printer permitted him to print their arms at the foot of the notice. These arms, most charmingly and delicately engraved, are found in the Würzburg Missals of 1481 (this I have not seen) and 1484, and the "Agenda" of 1482 (see Plate XXXV), and no doubt also in other early service-books printed by Georg Reyser. The Eichstätt books of his kinsmen Michel are similarly adorned—for instance, the *Statuta Synodalia Eystettensia* of 1484, though neither the design nor the engraving is so good. In how many editions by the Reysers these engraved arms appeared I cannot say, as the books are all of great rarity; but by 1495, if not earlier, they had been abandoned, for in the Würzburg *Missale Speciale* of that year we find the delicate engraving replaced by a woodcut copy of nearly four times the size and less than a fourth of the charm.

The only French book of the fifteenth century known to me as possessing copper engravings is a very beautiful one, the version of Breidenbach's *Peregrinatio ad Terram Sanctam*, by Frère Nicole le Huen, printed at Lyon by Michel Topie and Jacob Heremberck in 1488, and adorned with numerous excellent capitals. In this all the cuts in the text of the Mainz editions are fairly well copied on wood, but the large folding plans of Venice and other cities on the pilgrims' route are admirably reproduced on copper with a great increase in the delicacy of their lines.

We come now to a book bearing an earlier date than any of those already mentioned, but not entitled to its full pride of place because it is doubtful to what extent the engravings connected with it can be reckoned an integral part of it. This is the French version of Boccaccio's *De casibus illustrium virorum* ("Des cas des nobles

imp̃mẽdos nr̃oꝛ põtificat⁹ꝛ capl̃i
inl̃igniꝕs decozaꝛet Datũ iciuitate
nr̃a herbñ · Anno dñi M·cccc·lꝛꝛ
lecũdo· Dñica Trinitatis.

XXXV. WÜRZBURG, G. REYSER, 1482

WÜRZBURG AGENDA. (END OF PREFACE)

hommes "), printed at Bruges by Colard Mansion and dated 1476. As originally printed there was no space left for any pictorial embellishments; but in at least two copies the first leaf of the prologue has been reprinted so as to leave room for a picture; in another copy, which in 1878 belonged to Lord Lothian, spaces are left also at the beginning of each of the nine books into which the work is divided, except the first and sixth, and all the spaces have been filled with copper engravings coloured by hand; in yet another copy there is a space left also at the beginning of Book VI. According to the monograph on the subject by David Laing (privately printed in 1878), the subjects of the engravings are :—

(1) Prologue, the Author presenting his work to his patron, Mainardo Cavalcanti.
(2) Book I. Adam and Eve standing before the Author as he writes.
(3) Book II. King Saul on horseback, and lying dead.
(4) Book III. Fortune and Poverty.
(5) Book IV. Marcus Manlius thrown into the Tiber.
(6) Book V. The Death of Regulus.
(7) Book VI. Not known.
(8) Book VII. A combat of six men.
(9) Book VIII. The humiliation of the Emperor Valerian by King Sapor of Persia.
(10) Book IX. Brunhilde, Queen of the Franks, torn asunder by four horses.

From the reproductions which Laing gives in his monograph it is evident that the engraver set himself to imitate the style of the contemporary illuminated manuscripts of the Bruges school, and that he used his graver rather to get the designs on to the paper than with any real feeling for the characteristic charm of his own art. My own inclination is to believe that we must look on these plates as a venture of Colard Mansion's rather in his old capacity as an illuminator, anxious to decorate a few special copies, than as a printer intent on embellishing a whole edition. The engravings may have been made at any time between 1476 and 1483, when they were clearly used as models by Jean Du Pré for his Paris edition, the wood-blocks for which, as we have seen, were subsequently sold or lent to Pynson. The variations in the number of spaces in different copies may quite as well be due to a mixing of quires as to successive enlargements of the plan, and the fact that more copies of the engravings have survived apart from than with the book draws attention once more to the difficulty found in printing these incised plates to accompany letterpress printed from type standing in relief.

There is still one more engraving connected with an early printed book to be considered, and though the connection is not fully established, the facts that the book in question was the first from Caxton's press, and that the engraving may possibly contain his portrait, invite a full discussion of its claims. The plate (see Frontispiece to Chapter I, Plate II) represents an author on one knee presenting a book to a lady who is attended by five maids-of-honour, while as many pages may be seen standing in various page-like attitudes about the room. A canopy above a chair of state bears the initials CM and the motto *Bien en aveingne*, and it is thus clear that the lady represents Margaret Duchess of Burgundy, and that the offering of a book which it depicts must have taken place after her marriage with Charles the Bold, 3 July, 1468, and before the latter's death at Nancy, 5 January, 1477. During the greater part of this time Caxton was in the service of the Duchess; the donor of the book is represented as a layman, and a layman not of noble birth, since there is no feather in his cap; he appears also to be approaching middle-age. All these points would be correct if the donor were intended for Caxton, and as we know from his own statement that before his *Recuyell of the histories of Troy* was printed he had presented a copy of it (in manuscript) to the Duchess, probably in or soon after 1471, until some more plausible original is proposed the identification of the donor with our first printer must remain at least probable. Unfortunately, although the unique copy of the engraving is at present in the Duke of Devonshire's copy of the *Recuyell*, it is certain that it is an insertion, not an original part of the book, and beyond a high probability that it has occupied its present position since the book was bound for the Duke of Roxburghe some time before his sale in 1812, nothing is known as to how it came there. A really amazing point is that although the connection of this particular copy with Elizabeth, queen of Edward IV, caused it to be shown at the Caxton Exhibition, until the appearance of Mr. Montagu Peartree's article in the *Burlington Magazine* for August, 1905, no notice had ever been paid to the engraving. Analogy with the *Boccaccio* suggests that Caxton had the plate made before he realized the difficulties of impression, and that some prints were separately struck from it and one of these pasted inside the binding of the Devonshire copy, whence it was removed to its present position when the book was rebound. It should be noted that the style of the engraving is quite unlike that of the *Boccaccio* prints, and suggests that Caxton procured it from a Dutch rather than a Bruges engraver, possibly with the aid of Veldener, from whom, or with whose help, according to Mr. Duff's suggestion, he procured his first type.

For over a quarter of a century after the engraving of the plans in the Lyon *Breidenbach* printers seem to have held aloof altogether from copperplates. In 1514 we find four engraved plans, of only slight artistic interest, printed as plates in a topographical work on *Nola* by Ambrogius Leo, the printer being Joannes Rubeus (Giovanni Rossi) of Venice. Three years later, in 1517, a really charming print is found (set rather askew in the Museum copy) on the titlepage of a thin quarto printed at Rome, for my knowledge of which I am indebted to my friend, Mr. A. M. Hind. The book is a *Dialogus*, composed by the Right Reverend Amadeus Berrutus, Governor of the City of Rome, on the weighty and still disputable question as to whether one should go on writing to a friend who makes no reply,[1] and the plate shows the four speakers, Amadeus himself, Austeritas, Amicitia, and Amor, standing in a field or garden outside a building. The figures, especially that of Austeritas, are charmingly drawn (see Plate XXXVI); the tone of the little picture is delightful, and it is enclosed in a leafy border, which reproduces in the subtler grace of engraved work the effect of the little black and white frames which surround the Florentine woodcuts of the fifteenth century.

With the *Dialogus* of Bishop Berrutus copper engravings as book-illustrations came to an end, as far as I know, for a period of some forty years. I make this statement thus blankly in the hope that it may provoke contradiction, and at least some sporadic instances be adduced. But I have hunted through descriptions of all the books most likely to be illustrated—Bibles, Horae, editions of Petrarch's *Trionfi* and Ariosto's *Orlando Furioso* and books of emblems, and outside England (the necessity of the exception is almost humorous) I have lighted on nothing.

We may, perhaps, trace the revival of engraved illustrations to the influence of Hieronymus or Jerome Cock, an Antwerp engraver, who in May, 1551, issued a series of plates from the designs of F. Faber, entitled *Praecipua aliquot Romanae antiquitatis ruinarum monimenta*, without any letterpress save the name of the subject engraved on each plate. Cock followed this up in 1556 with twelve engravings from the designs of Martin van Veen illustrating the victories of Charles V, which are also celebrated in verses in French and Spanish. He issued also various other series of Biblical and antiquarian plates, which do not concern us, and in 1559 a set of thirty-two illustrating the funeral of Charles V. For this, aided by a subsidy, Christopher Plantin acted as publisher, and we thus get a connection established

---

[1] "In quo precipue tractat: An amico sepe ad scribendum prouocato ut scribat, non respondenti sit amplius scribendum."

Dialogus que coposuit. R. P. D.

Dñs Amadeus Berrutus Epus Aug. Gubernator Rome
Dú esset in minoribus Tépore Julij.ij.
In quo precipue tractat:An amico sepe ad scribendum prouocato:
ut scribat:non respondenti sit amplius scribendum
Et hinc incidenter multa pulcra.

De Amicitia vera   De Amore honesto   De amicis veris
De Epitetis curie Romane z alioruz principum.De curialibus u5
minus vere ã facete scribit. Et plura nouoeg si ilo addit his
que Pius.ij.in de miseris curialium scripsit
Postea vero Gubernator factus a Leone .pp.x.multa pulcra acco
modate addidit:quibus docet quales esse debeãt
qui magistratibus publicis preponuntur.
Et in eo quatuor colloquutores seu colluctatorce introducuntur
Uidelicet.

Amadeus.   Austeritas.   Amicitia.   z Amor.

AMADEVS   AVSTERITAS   AMICITIA   AMOR

XXXVI. ROME, GABRIEL OF BOLOGNA, 1517

BERRUTUS. DIALOGUS. (TITLE)

between engraving and printing.   This did not, however, bear fruit at all quickly.   Plantin's four emblem-books of 1562, 1564, 1565, and 1566 were illustrated not with copper engravings, but with woodcuts ; so was his Bible of 1566, so were his earlier Horae.   That of 1565 has unattractive woodcut borders to every page and small woodcut illustrations of no merit.   In 1570 he began the use of engravings for his Horae, but in a copy in the British Museum, printed on vellum almost as thick as cardboard, he was reduced to pulling the pictures on paper and pasting them in their places.   In 1571 he illustrated the *Humanae salutis monumenta* of his friend Arias Montanus with some rather pretty copperplates, each surrounded with an effective engraved border of flowers and birds, but for a new Horae (on paper) in 1573, for which he had commissioned a set of full-page plates of some merit (printed with the text on their back), he had not troubled to procure borders.   Two years later he produced a really curious edition in which the engraved illustrations (some of them from the *Humanae salutis monumenta*) are surrounded with woodcut borders, and in many cases have red underlines, so that each page must have undergone three printings.[1]

Although woodcuts were considered sufficiently good for Plantin's Bible of 1566, for his great Polyglot it was indispensable to have titlepages engraved on copper, and to the first volume he prefixed no fewer than three, engraved by P. van der Heyden after designs by P. van der Borcht.   All of them are emblematical, the first symbolizing the unification of the world by the Christian faith and the four languages in which the Old Testament was printed in the Polyglott, the second the zeal of Philip II for the Catholic faith, the third the authority of the Pentateuch.   While some volumes had no frontispiece others contained a few illustrations, and the total

---

[1] It was probably from his Horae plates that Plantin illustrated the *Rerum Sacrarum Liber* of Laur. Gambara in 1577.   They are printed with the text and are of average merit.

number of plates was twenty-eight. Some of these were used again in Plantin's Bible of 1583, and Raphelengius, into whose possession the whole set passed in 1590, used sixteen of them three years later to illustrate the *Antiquitates Judaicae* of Arias Montanus.

For his Missals and Breviaries as for his Horae Plantin sometimes used woodcuts, sometimes copperplates. For his editions of the works of S. Augustine and S. Jerome (1577) he caused really fine portrait frontispieces to be engraved by J. Sadeler from the designs of Crispin van den Broeck. As regards his miscellaneous secular books he was by no means given to superfluous illustrations, and, as we have seen, continued to use woodcuts contemporaneously with plates. Probably his earliest secular engravings (published in 1566, but prepared some years earlier) are the anatomical diagrams in imitation of those in the Roman edition of *Valverde* mentioned below, to which he prefixed a better frontispiece than that of his model. In 1574 he produced a fine book of portraits of physicians and philosophers, *Icones veterum aliquot ac recentium medicorum philosophorumque*, in sixty-eight plates, with letterpress by J. Sambucus. The next year he issued another illustrated book, the *De rerum usu et abusu* of Bernardus Furmerius, sharing the expense of it with Ph. Gallus, a print-seller, for whom later on he published several books on commission. From 1578 onwards he printed for Ortelius, the great cosmographer. In 1582 he published the *Pegasides* of Y. B. Houwaert, in 1584 Waghenaer's *Spieghel der Zeevaerdt*, and other illustrated books followed. But none of them, little indeed that Plantin ever produced, now excite much desire on the part of collectors.

Of what took place in other countries and cities in the absence of even tentative lists of the books printed after 1535 anywhere except in England it is difficult to say. In 1560 an anatomical book translated from the Spanish of Juan de Valverde was published at Rome with engraved diagrams of some artistic merit and a rather poorly executed frontispiece. In 1566 "in Venetia appresso Rampazetto," a very fine book of impresas, or emblematical personal badges, made its appearance under the title *Le Imprese Illustre con espositioni et discorsi del Sor Ieronimo Ruscelli*, dedicated "al serenissimo et sempre felicissimo re catolico Filippo d'Austria." This has over a hundred engraved *Imprese* of three sizes, double-page for the Emperor (signed G. P. F.), full-pagers for kings and other princely personages, half-pagers for ordinary folk (if any owner of an *impresa* may be thus designated), and all these are printed with letterpress beneath, or on the back of them, and very well printed too. In another book of *Imprese*, published in this same year 1566, the text, consisting of sonnets by Lodovico Dolce, as well as the pictures, is engraved, or rather etched. This is the *Imprese di diuersi principi, duchi, signori, etc., di Batt^a Pittoni Pittore Vicentino*. It exists in a bewildering variety of states, partly due to reprinting, partly apparently to the desire to dedicate it to several different people, one of the British Museum copies being dedicated by Pittoni to the Earl of Arundel and having a printed dedicatory letter and plate of his device preceding that of the Emperor himself.

Another noteworthy Venetian book, with engraved illustrations, which I have come across is an *Orlando Furioso* of 1584, "appresso Francesco de Franceschi Senese e compagni," its engraved titlepage bearing the information that it has been "nuouamente adornato di figure di rame da Girolamo Porro," a little-known Milanese engraver, who had reissued Pittoni's *Imprese* in 1578. The illustrations are far too crowded with incident to be successful, and their unity is often sacrificed to the old medieval practice of making a single design illustrate several different moments of the narrative. Their execution is also very unequal. Nevertheless, they are of interest to English collectors since, as we shall see, they served as models for the plates in Sir John Harington's version of the *Orlando* in 1591. All of them are full-pagers, with text on the back, and the printer was also compliant enough to print at the head of each canto an engraved cartouche within which is inserted a type-printed "Argomento."

Of sixteenth century engraved book-illustrations in France I have no personal knowledge. In Germany, as might be expected, they flourished chiefly at Frankfort, which in the last third of the century had, as we have seen, become a great centre for book-illustration. Jost Amman, who was largely responsible for its development in this respect, illustrated a few books with copper engravings, although he mainly favoured wood. But it is the work of the De Brys, Theodor de Bry and his two sons Johann Israel and Johann Theodor, which is of conspicuous importance for our present purpose, for it was they who originated and mainly carried out the greatest illustrated work of the sixteenth century, that known to collectors as the *Grands et petits voyages*. This not very happy name has nothing to do with the length of the voyages described, but is derived from the fact that the original series which is concerned with America and the West Indies is some two inches taller (fourteen as compared with twelve) than a subsequent series dealing with the East Indies. For the idea of such a collection of voyages Theodor de Bry was indebted to Richard Hakluyt, whose famous book *The Principall Navigations, Voiages, and Discoveries of the English Nation*, published in 1589, was in preparation when De Bry was in England, where he worked in 1587-8. The first volume, moreover, was illustrated with engravings by De Bry after some of the extraordinarily interesting water-colour drawings made by an Englishman, John White, in Virginia, and now preserved in the British Museum.[1] This first part was published in Latin at Frankfort by J. Wechel in 1590 and a second edition followed the same

---

[1] They were bought to accompany the fine set of De Bry collected by Mr. Grenville, but have since been transferred to the Department of Prints and Drawings.

year.   A second part describing Florida followed in 1591, a third describing Brazil in 1592.   By 1602 nine parts had been issued, all at Frankfort, though by different publishers, the name of J. Feyrabend being placed on the fourth, and that of M. Becker on the ninth.   After an interval of seventeen years two more parts of the Latin edition (x. and xi.) were printed at Oppenheim "typis H. Galleri," and then an appendix to part xi. at Frankfort in 1620, where also were issued part xii. in 1624 and part xiii., edited by M. Merian, in 1634, this last being accompanied by an "Elenchus," or index-volume, to the whole series.   Parallel with this Latin series ran a German one with about the same dates.   One or two parts were also issued in French and at least one in English.   There is also an appendix of "other voyages" usually added, mostly French, and issued at Amsterdam, and of nearly every volume of the whole series there were several issues and editions, all of them with differences in the plates. The "Petits voyages" followed a similar course, beginning in 1598 and ending in 1628.   Although the engravings, many of which are placed unpretentiously amid the text, vary greatly alike in the interest of their subjects, the value of the original designs, and the skill of the engraving, taken as a whole they have given to these *Grands et petits voyages* a unique position among books of travel, and a small literature has grown up round them to certify the collector as to the best state of each plate and what constitutes a complete set.

While the illustrations to the Voyages formed their chief occupation, the De Brys found time to engrave many smaller plates for less important books.   Thus in 1593 Theodor de Bry issued an emblem book *Emblemata nobilitati et vulgo scitu digna* (text in Latin and German), in which each emblem is enclosed in an engraved border, mostly quite meaningless and bad as regards composition, but of a brilliancy in the "goldsmiths' style" which to lovers of bookplates will suggest the best work of Sherborn or French.   The plates marked B and D, illustrating

279

the lines "Musica mortales divosque oblectat et ornat" and "Cum Cerere et Baccho Veneri solemnia fiunt," are especially fine and the "emblems" themselves more pleasing than usual.

In 1595 there was printed, again with Latin and German text, a *Noua Alphabeti effictio, historiis ad singulas literas correspondentibus*. The *motif* is throughout scriptural. Thus for A Adam and Eve sit on the crossbar on each side of the letter, the serpent rests on its peak amid the foliage of the Tree of Knowledge. In B Abel, in C Cain is perched on a convenient part of the letter, and so on, while from one letter after another, fish, birds, fruit, flowers, and anything else which came into the designer's head hang dangling on cords from every possible point. Nothing could be more meaningless or lower in the scale of design, yet the brilliancy of the execution carries it off.

The year after this had appeared Theodor de Bry engraved a series of emblems conceived by Denis Le Bey de Batilly and drawn by J. J. Boissard. The designs themselves are poor enough, but the book has a pretty architectural titlepage, and this is followed by a portrait of Le Bey set in an ornamental border of bees, flowers, horses, and other incongruities, portrait and border alike engraved with the most brilliant delicacy (see Plate XXXVII). In the following year, again, 1597, the two younger De Brys illustrated with line engravings the *Acta Mechmeti Saracenorum principis*, and (at the end of these) the *Vaticinia Severi et Leonis* as to the fate of the Turks, also the *David* of Arias Montanus. The plates are fairly interesting, but in technical execution fall far below those of their father.

Turning now to England, we find engraving in use surprisingly early in some figures of unborn babies in *The Birth of Mankind*, translated from the Latin of Roesslin by Richard Jonas and printed in 1540 by Thomas Raynold, a physician, who five years later issued a new edition revised by himself, again with engravings.

Si Virtus, Doctrina, Usus Prudentia charum
Efficiunt summis regibus esse virum

DIONYSIVS LEBE?-BATILLIVS
PRÆSES REGI? AP. MEDICÆ

Ista tibi certe simul arrisere Bathylli
Qui partes tanti Regis in urbe geris.

XXXVII. FRANKFORT, DE BRY, 1596

LE BEY. EMBLEMATA. PORTRAIT OF AUTHOR BY T. DE BRY,
AFTER J. J. BOISSARD

In 1545 there appeared a much more important medical work, a *Compendiosa totius anatomie delineatio* professedly by Thomas Geminus, a Flemish surgeon and engraver attached to the English Court. In reality this was a rather shameless adaptation of the *De Fabrica Humani Corporis* of Vesalius (Basel, 1543), with engravings copied by Geminus from the woodcuts of his original. For us its chief interest lies in an elaborate engraved titlepage showing the royal arms surrounded by a wealth of architectural and strapwork ornament in the style, if not actually the work, of Peter Cock of Alost, as has been shown by Sir Sidney Colvin in the invaluable introduction to his *Early Engravings and Engravers in England* (1905). In 1553 an English translation of the anatomy was published by Nicholas Hyll, and in a second edition of this, printed in 1559, a rather heavy and stiff portrait of Elizabeth replaces the royal arms, which were burnished out to make room for it. Geminus subsequently produced a much larger portrait of the Queen, set in an architectural frame studded with emblematical figures, and a royal proclamation forbidding unauthorized " Paynters, Printers, and Gravers " to meddle with so great a subject seems to have been provoked by his handiwork.

In 1563 John Shute for his work on *The First and Chief Groundes of Architecture* produced four amateurish engravings to illustrate four of the five "orders," a woodcut being considered good enough for the fifth. In 1568 we find the first edition of the "Bishops'" Bible adorned with an engraved titlepage in the centre of which, in an oval, is a not unpleasing portrait of the Queen, holding sceptre and orb, set in a mass of strapwork, amid which are seated Charity and Faith with the royal arms between them, while below the portrait a lion and dragon support a cartouche enclosing a text. Besides this titlepage, attributed by Sir Sidney Colvin to Franciscus Hogenberg, before the book of Joshua there is an engraved portrait of Leicester, while the "Blessed is the man"

of the first Psalm is heralded by another engraved portrait which shows Lord Burghley holding in front of him
a great B. In 1573 Remigius Hogenberg, brother of
Franciscus, engraved after a picture by John Lyne a stiff
but rather impressive portrait of Archbishop Parker,
prefixed to some copies of his *De Antiquitate Ecclesiae
Britanniae*. The year before this the second edition of
the "Bishops'" Bible had been enriched with a decorative
engraved map of the Holy Land, and in 1574 Archbishop Parker employed John Lyne to engrave for the
De Antiquitate Academiae Cantabrigiensis of Dr. Caius
(printed by Day) a plate of the arms of the colleges,
a plan of the University schools, and a large map of the
town. In 1579 there appeared a work which had occupied the intermediate five years, a series of maps of
England from the drawings of Christopher Saxton, engraved by Augustine Ryther (like Saxton a native of
Leeds), Remigius Hogenberg and others, and with a fine
frontispiece showing the Queen seated in state beneath
an architectural canopy, which Sir Sidney Colvin thinks
may perhaps be the work of Ryther. Ryther was subsequently concerned with other maps, including the series
illustrating the defeat of the Armada (*Expeditionis
Hispanorum in Angliam vera descriptio*), and other
cartographers got to work who hardly concern us here.
Two long engraved rolls, the first by Marcus Gheraerts,
representing a procession of the Knights of the Garter
(1576), the second by Theodor de Bry, from the designs
of Thomas Lant, the funeral of Sir Philip Sidney (1587),
although most safely preserved when bound in book
form, can hardly be reckoned as books. Yet over the
latter I must stop to confess a dreadful sin of my youth,
when I jumped to the conclusion that the portrait on the
first page stood for Sidney himself, whereas it really
represents the too self-advertising Lant. That it appears
in the sky, above the Black Pinnace which bore home
Sidney's body, and itself bears the suggestive motto
"God createth, Man imitateth, Virtue flourisheth, Death

finisheth," may palliate but cannot excuse the crime which enriched an edition of *Astrophel and Stella* with a portrait, not of Sidney, but of the illustrator of his funeral.

Not until 1590, when Hugh Broughton's *Concent of Scripture* was accompanied by some apocalyptic plates engraved by Jodocus Hondius (subsequently copied by W. Rogers), do we come across what can really be called engraved illustrations in an English book, and these, which are of little interest, were speedily eclipsed the next year by Sir John Harington's *Orlando Furioso in English Heroical verse* with its engraved titlepage and forty-six plates. Of these the translator writes in his introduction :

As for the pictures, they are all cut in brasse, and most of them by the best workemen in that kinde, that haue bene in this land this manie yeares : yet I will not praise them too much, because I gaue direction for their making, and in regard thereof I may be thought partiall, but this I may truely say, that (for mine owne part) I have not seene anie made in England better, nor (in deede) anie of this kinde in any booke, except it were in a treatise, set foorth by that profound man, maister Broughton, the last yeare, upon the Reuelation, in which there are some 3. or 4. pretie figures (in octauo) cut in brasse verie workemanly. As for other books that I haue seene in this realme, either in Latin or English, with pictures, as Liuy, Gesner, Alciats emblemes, a booke *de spectris* in Latin, & (in our tong) the Chronicles, the booke of Martyrs, the book of hauking and hunting, and M. Whitney's excellent Emblems, yet all their figures are cut on wood, & none in metall, and in that respect inferior to these, at least (by the old proverbe) the more cost, the more worship.

The passage is of considerable interest, but hardly suggests, what is yet the fact, that, save for the addition on the titlepage of an oval portrait of the translator and a representation of his dog, all the plates in the book are closely copied from the engravings by Girolamo Porro in the Venice edition of 1584. The English titlepage was signed by Thomas Cockson. We are left to conjecture to whom Harington was indebted for the rest of the plates.

Although, as we shall see, from this time forward a great number of English books contain engraved work, those which can be said to be illustrated during the next sixty years are few enough, a study of Mr. A. M. Hind's very useful *List of the Works of Native and Foreign Line-Engravers in England from Henry VIII to the Commonwealth*,[1] tempting me to place the number at about a score. The year after the *Orlando Furioso* came another curious treatise by Hugh Broughton, not printed with type, but "graven in brasse by J. H.," whom Sir Sidney Colvin identifies with Jodocus Hondius, a Fleming who lived in England from about 1580 to 1594, and may have done the plates in the *Concent of Scripture* and some at least of those in the *Orlando*. Six years later (1598) we find Lomazzo's *Tracte containing the artes of curious Paintinge* with an emblematical titlepage and thirteen plates by Richard Haydock, the translator, four of the plates being adapted from Dürer's book on Proportion, and all of them showing very slight skill in engraving. In 1602 came Sir William Segar's *Honour, Military and Civil*, with eight plates showing various distinguished persons, English and foreign, wearing the robes and insignia of the Garter, the Golden Fleece, S. Michael, etc. Three of the plates are signed by William Rogers, the most distinguished of the English Elizabethan engravers, and the others are probably his also. Most of them are very dignified and effective in the brilliantly printed "first states" in which they are sometimes found, but ordinary copies with only the "second states" are as a rule disappointing.

The beginning of the reign of James I was directly responsible for one ambitious engraved publication, Stephen Harrison's *The Archs of Triumph erected in honor of the High and mighty prince James, the first of that name king of England and the sixt of Scotland, at his Maiesties Entrance and passage through his Honor-*

---

[1] Contributed to the work by Sir Sidney Colvin, *Early Engravers and Engraving in England*, already quoted.

able City & Chamber of London vpon the 15th day of march 1603 [1604] *Invented and published by Stephen Harrison Joyner and Architect and graven by William Kip.* Here an engraved titlepage, with dangling ornaments in the style of the De Bry alphabet, is followed by seven plates of the seven arches, the most notable of which (a pity it was not preserved) was crowned with a most interesting model of Jacobean London, to which the engraver has done admirable justice.

In 1608 came Robert Glover's *Nobilitas politica et civilis*, re-edited two years later by T. Milles as the *Catalogue of Honour*, with engraved illustrations (in the text) of the robes of the various degrees of nobility, attributed by Sir Sidney Colvin to Renold Elstracke, the son of a Flemish refugee, and also two plates representing the King in a chair of state and in Parliament. After this we come to two works illustrated by an English engraver of some note, William Hole, Tom Coryat's *Crudities* (1611), with a titlepage recalling various incidents of his travels (including his being sick at sea) and five plates (or in some copies, six), and Drayton's *Polyolbion* (1612, reissued in 1613 with the portrait-plate in a different state), with a poor emblematic title, a portrait of Prince Henry wielding a lance, and eighteen decorative maps of England. In 1615 we come to a really well-illustrated book, the *Relation of a Journey*, by George Sandys, whose narrative of travel in Turkey, Egypt, and the Holy Land, and parts of Italy, is accompanied with little delicately engraved landscapes and bits of architecture, etc., by Francis Delaram. The work of the decade is brought to a close with two print-selling ventures, the *Basiliωlogia* of 1618 and *Herωologia* of 1620. The former of these works describes itself as being " the true and lively effigies of all our English Kings from the Conquest untill this present : with their severall Coats of Armes, Impreses and Devises. And a briefe Chronologie of their lives and deaths. Elegantly graven in copper. Printed for H. Holland and are to be sold by Comp.[ton]

Holland over against the Exchange." The full set of plates numbers thirty-two, including eight additions to the scheme of the book, representing the Black Prince, John of Gaunt, Anne Boleyn, a second version of Elizabeth, Mary Queen of Scots, Anne of Denmark, Prince Henry, and Prince Charles. Fourteen of the plates, mostly the earlier ones, are signed by Elstracke, and Simon Passe and Francis Delaram each contributed four. It need hardly be said that they are of very varying degrees of authenticity as well as merit. Several of the later plates are found in more than one state.

With the second of the two ventures Henry Holland was also concerned, but the expenses of the book were shared by Crispin Passe and an Arnhem bookseller named Jansen. Its title reads: "Herωologia Anglica: hoc est clarissimorum et doctissimorum aliquot Anglorum qui floruerunt ab anno Cristi MD. usque ad presentem annum MDCXX." It is in two volumes, the first containing thirty-seven plates, the second thirty. Two of these represent respectively Queen Elizabeth's tomb and the hearse of Henry Prince of Wales. All the rest are portraits of the notable personages of the reigns of Henry VIII and his successors, some of them based on drawings by Holbein, the majority on earlier prints, and all engraved by William Passe (younger brother of Simon) and his sister Magdalena.

The next decade was far from productive of works illustrated with more than an engraved titlepage and a portrait, but in 1630 appeared Captain John Smith's *True Travels* with several illustrations, one of them by Martin Droeshout; in 1634–5 came Wither's *Emblems*, with plates by William Marshall, and in 1635 Thomas Heywood's *Hierarchie of the Blessed Angels*, with an engraved title by Thomas Cecill and plates representing the several orders, Seraphim, Cherubim, and Thrones being entrusted to John Payne, Dominations to Marshall, Powers and Principalities to Glover, Virtues to Droeshout, etc. Some of the plates record the name of the patron

286

XXXVIII. LONDON, J. MARRIOT, 1638

QUARLES. HIEROGLYPHIKES OF THE LIFE OF MAN. PAGE 22

ENGRAVED BY W. MARSHALL

who paid for them, another suggestion that it was money which stood most in the way of book-illustrating. In 1638 Marshall illustrated Quarles's *Hieroglyphikes of the Life of Man*, with engravings, most of which seem chiefly made up of a candle, but in one the candle is being extinguished by Death egged on by Time, and to this not very promising subject (Plate XXXVIII) Marshall, the most unequal engraver of his day, has brought some of his too rare touches of delicacy and charm. In 1640 Wenceslaus Hollar, whom Thomas Earl of Arundel had discovered at Cologne (he was born at Prague) and brought to England, published his charming costume book *Ornatus Muliebris Anglicanus*, and his larger work, *Theatrum Mulierum*, must have been almost ready when Charles I hoisted his standard at Nottingham, since it was published in 1643. After this the Civil War interfered for some time with the book trade.

While fully illustrated books were thus far from numerous in the half century which followed the *Orlando Furioso* of 1591, the output of engraved titlepages and portraits to be prefixed to books was sufficient to find work for most of the minor engravers. The earlier title-pages were mostly architectural and symbolical, their purport being sometimes explained in verses printed opposite to them, headed "The Mind of the Front." William Rogers engraved a titlepage to Gerard's *Herbal* (1597), which is never found properly printed, and others to Linschoten's *Discourse of Voyages into yᵉ East and West Indies* (1598), Camden's *Britannia* (1600—a poor piece of work), and Moffett's *Theatrum Insectorum*, this last having only survived in a copy pasted at the head of the author's manuscript at the British Museum. William Hole did an enlarged title for Camden's *Britannia* (1607), titles for the different sections of Chapman's *Homer*, a portrait of John Florio for the Italian-English dictionary which he was pleased to call *Queen Anna's New World of Words*, a charming title-page to a collection of virginal music known as *Parthenia*

287

(1611–12), another to Browne's *Britannia's Pastorals*, and much less happy ones to Drayton's *Polyolbion* (1612), and the *Works* of Ben Jonson (1616).

The best-known titlepages engraved by Renold Elstracke are those to Raleigh's *History of the World* (1614) and the *Workes of the Most High and Mightie Prince James* (1616), the latter a good piece of work which when faced, as it should be, by the portrait of the king by Simon van de Passe, makes the most decorative opening to any English book of this period. Passe himself was responsible for the very imaginative engraved title to Bacon's *Novum Organum* (1620), a sea on which ships are sailing and rising out of it two pillars with the inscription : "Multi pertransibunt et augebitur scientia" (Many shall run to and fro, and knowledge shall be increased). His son William, besides his work on the *Herwologia*, already mentioned, engraved a complicated title for Chapman's version of *The Batrachomyomachia* or Battle of the Frogs and Mice, humorously called *The Crowne of all Homer's Worckes*.

After 1620 the old architectural and symbolical title-pages began to be replaced by titles in compartments, in which a central cartouche is surrounded by little squares, each representing some incident of the book. Portraits of the author remained much in request, and nearly a hundred of these were done by William Marshall, who was employed also on about as many engraved titlepages. As has been noted, his work was strangely uneven, and he fully deserved the scorn poured on him by Milton for the wretched caricature of the poet prefixed to the *Poems* of 1645. Yet Marshall could at times do a good plate, as, for instance, that in Quarles's *Hieroglyphikes* already mentioned, a portrait of Bacon prefixed to the 1640 Oxford edition of his *Advancement of Learning* and the charming frontispiece to Brathwait's *Arcadian Princess*. Marshall at his worst fell only a little below the work of Thomas Cross ; at his best he rivalled or excelled the good work of Thomas Cecill and George Glover.

288

ENGRAVED ILLUSTRATIONS

After Cromwell's strong hand had given England some kind of settled government the book market revived, and some ambitiously illustrated books were soon being published. The too versatile John Ogilby, dancing-master, poet, and publisher, appeared early in the field, his version of the Fables of Aesop, "adorned with sculpture," being printed by T. Warren for A. Crook in 1651. The next year came Benlowe's *Theophila, or Love's Sacrifice*, a mystical poem, some copies of which have as many as thirty-six plates by various hands, with much more etching than engraving in them. In 1654 Ogilby produced his translation of Virgil, a great folio with plates dedicated to noble patrons by Pierre Lombart. Ogilby's other important ventures were the large *Odyssey* of 1665, and the Aesop's *Fables* of the same year, with plates by Hollar, D. Stoop, and F. Barlow, and two portraits of the translator engraved respectively by Pierre Lambert and W. Faithorne. Faithorne embellished other books of this period, e.g. the Poems of the " Matchless Orinda" (1667), with portraits, and publishers who could not afford to pay Faithorne employed R. White. The presence of a portrait by White in a copy of the first edition of Bunyan's *Pilgrim's Progress*, to which it was very far indeed from certain that it really belonged,[1] has once made the book sell for over £1400, but save for the sake of completeness his handiwork is not greatly prized by collectors, nor is there any English illustrated book of this period after the Restoration which is much sought after for the sake of its plates, although those of Ogilby's *Virgil* were sufficiently well thought of to be used again for Dryden's version in 1697.

Meanwhile, books with illustrations *en taille douce* were being issued in some numbers both at Paris and at Amsterdam. In the former city François Chauveau (1613–76), in the latter Jan and Casper Luyken are

---

[1] This was an early proof of the portrait which is found in a slightly different state in copies of the third edition, and seemed to be an insertion in the first edition rather than an integral part of it.

credited by Mr. Hind (*A Short History of Engraving and Etching*, 1908) with having produced "hosts of small and undistinguished plates," and these damning epithets explain how it is that even patriotic French collectors like Eugène Paillet and Henri Béraldi thought it wise to leave the illustrated books of the seventeenth century severely alone.

We meet the first advance guard of the brilliant French eighteenth century school of book-illustration in 1718, when a pretty little edition of *Les Amours de Daphnis et Chloé* (as translated by Bishop Amyot from the Greek of Longus) made its appearance with twenty-eight plates by Benoit Audran, after the designs of no less a person than the Regent of France, and duly labelled and dated "Philippus in. et pinx. 1714." The plates vary very much in charm, but that with the underline *Chloé sauve Daphnis par le son de sa flûte* certainly possesses it, and one of the double-plates in the book, *Daphnis prend ses oyseaux pendant l'Hyver pour voir Chloé*, is really pretty. We find no other book to vie with this until we come to a much larger and more pretentious one, the works of Molière in six volumes, royal quarto, published in 1734. This was illustrated with thirty-three plates, in the mixture of etching and engraving characteristic of the French school of the day, by Laurent Cars, after pencil drawings by François Boucher, and by nearly two hundred vignettes and tailpieces (not all different) after Boucher and others by Cars and François Joullain. Another edition of this in four volumes with Boucher's designs reproduced on a smaller scale was published in 1741 and reprinted three times within the decade.

After the Molière, books and editions which collectors take count of come much more quickly. There was an edition of Montesquieu's *Le Temple de Gnide* in 1742 (imprint: Londres), a *Virgil* in 1743 with plates by Cochin, engraved by Cochin père, the *Contes* of La Fontaine (Amsterdam, 1743-5) also illustrated by Cochin, Guer's *Moeurs et usages des Turcs*, with plates after

Boucher (1746), an edition of the works of Boileau in five volumes, with vignettes by Eisen and tailpieces by Cochin (1743-5), and in 1753 a *Manon Lescaut* (imprint: Amsterdam) with some plates by J. J. Pasquier, which are stiff, and others by H. Gravelot, which are feeble.

In the four-volume edition of the *Fables* of La Fontaine (1755-9) with illustrations after J. B. Oudry, we come to a very ambitious piece of work, handsomely carried out, which a book-lover may yet find it hard to admire. Oudry's designs are always adequate, and have more virility in them than is often found in the work of this school, and they are competently interpreted by a number of etchers and engravers, some of whom, it may be noted, worked together in pairs on the same plate, so that we find such signatures as "C. Cochin aqua forti, R. Gaillard cælo sculpsit," and "Gravé à l'eau forte par C. Cochin, terminé au burin par P. Chenu"—a very explicit statement of the method of work. But adequate as the plates may seem, if they are judged not as book-illustrations but as engravings, no one could rate them high, and as a book what is to be said of an edition of La Fontaïne's *Fables*, which fills four volumes, each measuring nearly nineteen inches by thirteen? The book-man can only regard such a work as a portfolio of plates with accompanying text, and if the plates as plates are only second rate, enthusiasm has nothing to build on.

We return to book-form in 1757, when Boccaccio's *Decamerone* was published in Italian (imprint: Londra) in five octavo volumes, with charming vignettes and illustrations mostly by Gravelot, although a few are by Boucher and Eisen. Gravelot, who was more industrious than successful as an illustrator, is seen here to advantage, and deserves some credit for having made his designs not less but more reticent than the stories he had to illustrate. This praise can certainly not be given to the famous 1762 edition of the *Contes* of La Fontaine, the cost of which was borne by the Fermiers-Généraux (imprint: Amsterdam). The *fleurons* by Choffard are throughout delightful and the plates are brilliantly engraved, but the lubricity of Eisen's designs is wearisome in the first volume and disgusting in the second, and possessors of the book are not to be envied. It is to be regretted that the next book we have to notice, the *Contes Moraux* of Marmontel (3 vols., 1765), has very little charm to support its morality, the plates after Gravelot being poor, while the head- and tailpieces, or rather the substitutes for them, are wretched. A much better book than either of these last is the edition in French and Latin of Ovid's *Metamorphoses* in four quarto volumes (1767-71), with plates after Boucher, Eisen, Gravelot, and Moreau, and headpieces by Choffard at the beginning of each book. The imprint, "A Paris, chez Leclerc, Quai des Augustins, avec approbation et privilège du Roi," prepares us to find that the designers have kept their licence within bounds, and many of the plates have a combined humour and charm which are very attractive. If I had to choose a single plate to show Gravelot at his best, I doubt if prolonged search would find any success more complete than that of the illustration to Book I, xi., *Deucalion et Pyrrha repeuplant la Terre, suivant l'Oracle de Themis* (see the frontispiece to this volume, Plate I), and though Eisen was a much better artist than Gravelot, his *Apollon gardant les troupeaux d'Admet, dans les campagnes de Messene* (II, x.) is certainly one of his prettiest pieces.

During the next few years illustrated books became the fashion, so that in 1772 Cazotte wrote *Le diable amoureux, nouvelle d'Espagne*, with the false imprint Naples (Paris, Lejay) and six unsigned plates, said to be by Moreau after Marillier, on purpose to ridicule the craze for putting illustrations into every book. In 1768 the indefatigable Gravelot had illustrated an edition of the works of Voltaire, published at Geneva, with forty-four designs. In 1769 *Les Saisons*, a poem by Saint Lambert, was published at Amsterdam, with designs by Gravelot and Le Prince and *fleurons* by Choffard. In

VII. BAISER.

LE BAISER DEVINÉ.

Un soir d'été, quand l'astre de Vénus
Verse un jour doux sur les fleurs rafraîchies,
Joue à travers les rameaux plus touffus,
Et sert l'Amour errant dans les prairies;
Thaïs, quittant l'ombre de ses berceaux,
Court respirer l'air serein des campagnes,
Et va chercher ses folâtres compagnes
Qui l'attendoient sur le bord des ruisseaux.

the same year there was published at Paris Meunier de Queslon's *Les Graces*, with an engraved title by Moreau, a frontispiece after Boucher, and five plates after Moreau. In 1770 came Voltaire's *Henriade* with ten plates and ten vignettes after Eisen, and more highly esteemed even than this, Dorat's *Les Baisers* (La Haye et Paris), with a frontispiece and plate and forty-four head- and tail-pieces, all (save two) after Eisen, not easily surpassed in their own luxurious style (see Plate XXXIX). In 1771 Gravelot, more indefatigable than ever, supplied designs for twenty plates and numerous head- and tailpieces for an edition of Tasso's *Gerusalemme Liberata*, and was honoured, as Eisen had been in the Fermiers-Généraux edition of La Fontaine's *Contes*, by his portrait being prefixed to the second volume. In 1772 a new edition of Montesquieu's *Le Temple de Gnide*, in which the text was engraved throughout, was illustrated with designs by Eisen, brilliantly interpreted by Le Mire, and Imbert's *Le Jugement de Paris* was illustrated by Moreau, with *fleurons* by Choffard. In 1773 *Le Temple de Gnide* was versified by Colardeau, and illustrated by Monnet, and selections from Anacreon, Sappho, Bion, and Moschus by Eisen, while Moreau and others illustrated the *Chansons* of Laborde in four volumes and the works of Molière in six. After this the pace slackened, and we need no longer cling to the methods of the annalist. Moreau illustrated Saint Lambert's *Les Saisons* and Fromageot's *Annales du règne de Marie Thérèse* (both in 1775), Marmontel's *Les Incas* (1777), the seventy-volume Voltaire (1784–9), *Paul et Virginie* (1789), and many other works, living on to illustrate Goethe's *Werther* in 1809; other books were adorned by Marillier, Cochin, Duplessis, Bertaux, Desrais, Saint Quentin, Fragonard, Gérard, and Le Barbier, and the fashion survived the Revolution and lingered on till about 1820.

We must go back now to England, where at the end of the seventeenth century the requirements of book-illustration were neglected, partly because of the growing

293

taste for a neat simplicity in books, partly because the chief English engravers all devoted themselves to mezzotint. A few foreigners came over to supply their place, and Michael Burghers, of Amsterdam, illustrated the fourth edition of *Paradise Lost*, a stately folio, in 1688, with plates which enjoyed a long life and were also imitated for smaller editions. Burghers also illustrated the Oxford almanacs, and supplied frontispieces to the Bibles and other large books issued by the University Press up to about 1720. Another Dutchman who came to England not much later (in about 1690) was Michael Van der Gucht, who worked for the booksellers, as his children did after him. How low book-illustration had fallen in England at the beginning of the eighteenth century may be seen by a glance at the wretched plates which disfigure Rowe's Shakespeare in 1709, the first edition on which an editor and an illustrator were allowed to work their wills. The year after this Louis Du Guernier came to England, and was soon engaged in the not too patriotic task of helping Claude Du Bosc to illustrate the victories of Marlborough. In 1714 he and Du Bosc were less painfully, though not very successfully, employed in making plates for Pope's *Rape of the Lock*. Du Bosc subsequently worked on the *Religious Ceremonies of all Nations* (1733), an English edition of a book of Bernard Picart's, and on plates for Rapin's *History of England* (1743), but he was far from being a great engraver. It is a satisfaction that the plates to the first edition of *Robinson Crusoe* (1719) were engraved by two Englishmen, and not very badly. Their names are given as "Clark and Pine," the Clark being presumably John Clark (1688–1736), who engraved some writing-books, and the Pine, John Pine (1690–1756), who imitated some designs by Bernard Picart to the book of Jonah in 1720, and may have been a pupil of his at Amsterdam.

It should, perhaps, have been mentioned that two years before *Crusoe* an English engraver, John Sturt

(1658–1730), produced a Book of Common Prayer, of which the text as well as the pictures was engraved. This is rather a curiosity than a work of art, the frontispiece being a portrait of George I made up of the Creed, Lord's Prayer, Ten Commandments, Prayer for the Royal Family, and Psalm xxi. written in minute characters, instead of lines. Sturt produced another engraved book, *The Orthodox Communicant*, in 1721.

In 1723 William Hogarth began what might have proved a notable career as a book-illustrator had not he soon found more profitable work. He illustrated the Travels of Aubry de la Mottraye in 1723, Briscoe's *Apuleius* (1724), Cotterel's translation of *Cassandra* (1725), Blackwell's *Compendium of Military Discipline* (1726), and (also in 1726) Butler's *Hudibras*, his plates to which, though grotesque enough, show plenty of character. For some years after this he worked on frontispieces, e.g. to Leveridge's *Songs* (1727), Cooke's *Hesiod* (1728), J. Miller's comedy, *The Humours of Oxford* (1729), Theobald's *Perseus and Andromeda* (1730), and in 1731 to a Molière, Fielding's *Tragedy of Tragedies*, and Mitchell's *Highland Fair*. But the success of his set of prints on "The Harlot's Progress" diverted him from bookwork, although many years after he contributed frontispieces to Vols. II and IV of *Tristram Shandy*, and in 1761 a head- and tailpiece (engraved by Grignion) to a Catalogue of the Society of Arts.

In 1733 Hubert Gravelot was invited from France by Du Bosc to help in illustrating Picart's *Religious Ceremonies*. He illustrated Gay's *Fables* in 1738, Richardson's *Pamela* in 1742, Theobald's *Shakespeare* in 1740, and, mainly after Hayman, Hanmer's in 1744–6. Neither of the sets of Shakespeare plates deserves any higher praise than that of being neat and pretty, but at least they were a whole plane above those in Rowe's edition.

The year after Gravelot came to England, in 1733, Pine produced the first volume of his *Horace*, engraved throughout, and with head- and tailpieces in admirable taste. The second volume followed in 1737, and in 1753 the first of an illustrated *Virgil* which Pine did not live to complete.

Besides his work on Hanmer's *Shakespeare*, Francis Hayman designed illustrations to Moore's *Fables of the Female Sex* (1744), which were well engraved, some of them by Charles Grignion, a pupil of Gravelot's, born in England (1717), but of foreign parentage. Hayman also illustrated the *Spectator* (1747), Newton's *Milton* (1749-52), and later on, with the aid of Grignion, Smollett's *Don Quixote* (1755), and Baskerville's edition of Congreve's *Poems* (1761). The plates to the earlier edition of *Don Quixote*, that of 1738, had been chiefly engraved by Gerard van der Gucht after Vanderbank, but two are by Hogarth.

Samuel Wale (died 1786), a pupil of Hayman, was also an illustrator, and in 1760 supplied Sir John Hawkins with fourteen drawings for his edition of Walton's *Angler*. These were engraved by the luckless W. W. Rylands, who was hanged for forgery in 1783, and the Walton thus produced is one of the prettiest and least affected of the illustrated books of its day (see Plate XL). Wale also drew designs for Wilkie's *Fables* (1768) and Goldsmith's *Traveller* (1774). He also worked for the magazines which about the middle of the century made rather a feature of engravings, often as headpieces to music. A few of the isolated books may be named, thus Paltock's *Peter Wilkins* (1750) was illustrated very well by Louis Peter Boitard, who had previously contributed numerous plates to Spence's *Polymetis*, and in 1751 supplied a frontispiece to each of the six books of the *Scribleriad* by R. O. Cambridge. Another book which, like *Peter Wilkins*, was concerned with flight, Lunardi's *Account of the first aerial voyage in England* (1784), has a portrait of the author by Bartolozzi and two plates. For Baskerville's edition of the *Orlando Furioso* (Birmingham, 1773) recourse was had to plates by De Launay, after Moreau and Eisen.

296

XL. LONDON, T. HOPE, 1760

WALTON. COMPLEAT ANGLER   W. W. RYLANDS AFTER S. WALE

CHAPTER XVI

MODERN FINE PRINTING

AFTER the Restoration, printing and the book trade generally in England became definitely modern in their character, and the printer practically disappears from view, his work, with here and there an exception, as in the case of Robert Foulis or John Baskerville, being altogether hidden behind that of the publisher, so that it is of Herringman and Bernard Lintott and Dodsley that we hear, not of Newcomb and Roycroft.

Notwithstanding this decline in the printer's importance, there was a steady improvement in English printing. As an *art* it had ceased at this time to exist. If a publisher wished to make a book beautiful he put in plates. If he wanted to make it more beautiful he put in more or larger plates. If he wanted to make it a real triumph of beauty he engraved the whole book, letterpress and all, as in the case of Sturt's Prayer Books and Pine's *Horace*. That a printer by the selection and arrangement of type, by good presswork and the use of pretty capitals and tailpieces, could make a book charming to eye and hand, without any help from an illustrator—such an idea as this had nearly perished. There was little loss in this, since if any artistic work had been attempted it would assuredly have been bad, whereas the craftsmen, when set to do quite plain work, gradually learnt to do it in a more workmanlike way. In this they were helped by certain improvements in printing which rendered the task of the pressman less laborious. In the middle of the seventeenth century William Blaew, of Amsterdam, invented an improved press, " fabricated nine of these new fashioned presses, set them all on a row in his Printing House and called each Press by the name of one of the Muses." Clearly Blaew was an enthusiast. His chronicler, Joseph Moxon, was a fairly good English printer, and his description of the equipment of a printing house in the second part of his *Mechanick Exercises* (1683) contains much information still interesting. We gather from Moxon that Blaew's improvements were slowly copied in England, and we know that the English printers still continued to buy their best founts from Holland. Thus when Bishop Fell, about 1670, was equipping the University Press at Oxford with better type, he employed an agent in Holland to purchase founts for him. English founts of which we have any reason to be proud date from the appearance about 1716 of William Caslon, who established a firm of type founders which has enjoyed a long and deservedly prosperous career.

The next move came from the north. Robert Foulis (the name was originally spelt Faulls), born in 1707, the son of a Glasgow maltster, had been originally apprenticed to a barber. He was, however, a man of bookish tastes, and, when already over thirty years of age, was advised to set up in business as a printer and bookseller. With his brother Andrew, five years younger than himself and educated for the ministry, he went on a book-buying tour on the Continent, and on his return started bookselling in 1741, and printed in that year Dr. William Leechman's *Temper, Character, and Duty of a Minister of the Gospel*, and four other books, including a Phaedrus and a volume of Cicero. In March, 1743, he was appointed Printer to the University of Glasgow, and his edition of *Demetrius Phalerus de Elocutione* in Greek and Latin was the first example of Greek printing produced at Glasgow. A *Horace* which was hung up in proof in the University, with the offer of a reward for every misprint detected (in spite of which six remained), followed in 1744, an *Iliad* in 1747, an edition of *Hardyknute* in 1748, and a *Cicero* in 1749. In 1750 as many

298

as thirty works were printed at the Foulis press. The next two years were mainly spent in touring on the Continent, and on his return Robert Foulis unhappily started an Academy of Art at Glasgow, which he had neither the knowledge nor the taste to direct successfully, and which sapped his energies without producing any valuable results. An edition of the Greek text of Callimachus in 1755 was rewarded by an Edinburgh society with a gold medal, and other Greek and Latin texts followed, including the *Iliad* in 1756, *Anacreon* in 1757, *Virgil* and the *Odyssey* in 1758, and *Herodotus* in 1761. Among the more notable later books of the firm were an edition of Gray's *Poems* in 1768, and a *Paradise Lost* in 1770. The younger brother died in 1775, and Robert, after a mortifying experience in London, where he sold the "old masters" he had bought as models for his Academy for less than a pound over the expenses incurred in the sale, followed him the next year. The two brothers had raised printing at Glasgow from insignificance to an excellence which equalled, and perhaps surpassed, the standard attained at London, Oxford or Cambridge, or, indeed, for the moment, anywhere in Europe. This was no small achievement, and their compatriots and fellow citizens may well show them honour. But they were content to work according to the best standards set by other men without making any positive advance upon them or showing any originality. They avoided the snare of bad ornaments by using none; their Greek types were modelled on the French royal types associated with the name of the Étiennes; their roman types exhibit no special excellence. Historically, their chief importance is that they proved that care and enthusiasm for fine printing was re-awakening, and that printers with high ideals would not lack support.

Meanwhile, in the English Midlands an interesting and creditable, though wrong-headed, attempt to improve on existing founts had been made by John Baskerville, a Worcestershire man, born in 1706, who worked at Birmingham, and in 1757 printed there in his own types a quarto edition of *Virgil* which attracted considerable notice. The merit of Baskerville's type is its distinctness; its fault is the reappearance in a slightly different form of the old heresy of Aldus, that what is good, or is thought to be good, in penmanship must necessarily be good in type. In imitation of the Writing-Masters Baskerville delighted in making his upstrokes very thin and his downstrokes thick, and his serifs—that is, all the little finishing strokes of the letters—sharp and fine. It is probable that his ideals were influenced in this direction by books like Pine's *Horace* (1733–7), in which, as already noted, the letterpress as well as the illustrations and ornament is engraved throughout. These contrasts of light and heavy lines would naturally please an engraver; but they have no advantage when transferred to type, only making the page appear restless and spotty. Contemporary opinion in England was no more than lukewarm in their favour. The *Virgil* procured Baskerville a commission from the University of Oxford to cut a Greek fount, but this was generally condemned, though it had the merit of being free from contractions. Editions of Milton's *Paradise Lost* and *Paradise Regained* (1758), and other classics, were more successful, and Baskerville was appointed printer to the University of Cambridge for ten years; but his profits were small, and when he died in 1775, in default of an adequate English offer, his types were sold to a French society for £3700, and used in printing a famous edition of the works of Voltaire (1785–9).

The most conspicuous exponent of Baskerville's methods was an Italian, Giovanni Battista Bodoni, born in Piedmont in 1740. Bodoni settled at Parma, and it was at Parma that he did most of his printing. Even more notably than Baskerville, he tried to give to the pages which he printed the brilliancy of a fine engraving. He used good black ink (which is to his credit), exaggerated the differences between his thick strokes and his thin, and left wide spaces between his lines so as to let the elegance of his type stand out as brilliantly as possible against the white paper. The judgment of the best modern printers is against these vivid contrasts and in favour of a more closely set page, the two pages which face each other being regarded as an artistic whole which should not be cut into strips by a series of broad white spaces. Bodoni's books, which used to be highly esteemed, are now perhaps unduly neglected, for his work in its own way, whether he used roman type, italics, or Greek, is very good, and his editions of *Virgil, Homer*, and the *Imitatio Christi* are very striking books, though built on wrong lines. Bodoni died at Padua in 1813.

While the names of Caslon, the brothers Foulis, and Baskerville in Great Britain, and of Bodoni in Italy, stand out from amid their contemporaries, the premier place in French book-production was occupied by members of the Didot family. The first of these was François Didot (1689–1757); his eldest son, François Ambroise (1730–1804), was a fine printer; his younger son, Pierre (1732–95), was also a typefounder and papermaker. In the third generation Pierre's son Henri (1765–1852) was famous for his microscopic type, while Pierre II (1760–1853), the eldest son of François Ambroise and nephew of Pierre I, printed some fine editions of Latin and French classics at the press at the Louvre; and his brother Firmin Didot (1764–1836) won renown both as a typefounder and engraver, and also as a printer and improver of the art of stereotyping, besides being a deputy and writer of tragedies. In the fourth generation, the two sons of Firmin Didot, Ambroise (1790–1876) and Hyacinthe, carried on the family traditions. Incidentally, Ambroise wrote some valuable treatises on wood-engraving and amassed an enormous library, which, when sold at auction in 1882–4, realized nearly £120,000.

With the names of Bodoni and the Didots we may link that of the German publisher and printer Georg Joachim Goeschen, grandfather of the late Viscount Goschen. He was born in 1752, died in 1828, and worked the greater part of his life at Leipzig. He brought out pretty illustrated editions, made experiments with Greek types, much on the same lines as Bodoni, and devoted his life to the improvement of printing and bookmaking and the spread of good literature, enjoying the friendship of Schiller and other eminent German writers.

Coming back to England, we may note the beginning of the Chiswick Press in 1789, the year of the French Revolution. Charles Whittingham was then only twenty-two (he had been born at Coventry in 1767), and for his first years as his own master he was content to print hand-bills and do any other jobbing work that he could get. He began issuing illustrated books in 1797, and after a time the care he took in making ready wood-blocks (the use of which had been revived by Bewick) for printing gained him a special reputation. From about 1811 to his death in 1840 he left one branch of his business in the city under the charge of a partner, while he himself lived and worked at Chiswick, whence the name the Chiswick Press by which the firm is still best known.

His nephew, Charles Whittingham the younger, was born in 1795, was apprenticed to his uncle in 1810 and worked with him until 1828. Then he set up for himself at Tooks Court off Chancery Lane, and came rapidly to the front, largely from the work which he did for William Pickering, a well-known publisher of those days.

On his uncle's death in 1840 the younger Whittingham inherited the Chiswick business also. Four years after this, in 1844, he led the way in the revival of old-faced types. The examples of Baskerville at home and of Bodoni and other printers abroad had not been without effect on English printing. Brilliancy had been sought at all costs, and in the attempt to combine economy with it the height of letters had been increased and their breadth diminished so that, while they looked larger, more of them could be crowded into a line. The younger Whittingham had the good taste to see that the rounder, more evenly tinted type, which Caslon had made before these influences had come into play, was much pleasanter to look at and less trying to the eyes. He was already thinking of reviving it when he was commissioned by Longmans to print a work of fiction, *So much of the Diary of Lady Willoughby as relates to her Domestic History and to the Eventful Period of the Reign of Charles the First*, and it occurred to him that the use of old-faced type would be especially in keeping with such a book. A handsome small quarto was the result, and the revival of old-faced type proved a great success.

Not content with reviving old type, the younger Whittingham revived also the use of ornamental initials, causing numerous copies to be cut for him from the initials used in French books of the sixteenth century. Some of these are good, some almost bad, or while good in themselves, suitable only for use with black-letter founts and too heavy for use with roman letter. Still the attempt was in the right direction, and the books of this period with the imprint of the Chiswick Press are worth the attention of collectors interested in the modern developments of printing. During the succeeding forty years there is little by which they are likely to be attracted save the issues of the private press kept and worked by the Rev. C. H. O. Daniel of Worcester College, Oxford, of which he is now Provost. While he was yet a lad Mr. Daniel had amused himself with printing, and a thin duodecimo is still extant entitled *Sir Richard's Daughter, A Christmas Tale of Olden Times*, bearing the imprint " Excudebat H. Daniel : Trinity Parsonage, Frome, 1852." In 1874 Mr. Daniel resumed his old hobby at Oxford, printing *Notes from a catalogue of pamphlets in Worcester College Library*, and in 1876 *A new Sermon of the newest Fashion by Ananias Snip*, of which the original is preserved in the library of Worcester College. It was, however, in 1881, by an edition of thirty-six copies of *The Garland of Rachel* " by divers kindly hands," that the Daniel Press won its renown. Rachel was Mr. Daniel's little daughter, and the eighteen contributors to her " Garland" included Frederick Locker, Robert Bridges, Austin Dobson, Andrew Lang, Edmund Gosse, John Addington Symonds, Lewis Carrol, W. Henley, and Margaret Woods. Each poet was rewarded by a copy in which his name was printed on the titlepage, and the " Garland " soon came to be regarded as a very desirable possession. Mr. Daniel subsequently printed numerous little books by interesting writers (Robert Bridges, Walter Pater, Canon Dixon, and others), and while neither his types nor his presswork were exceptionally good, succeeded in investing them all with a charming appropriateness which gives them a special place of their own in the affections of book-lovers.

Another venture in which a high literary standard was combined with much care for typography was *The Hobby-Horse*, a quarterly magazine edited by Herbert P. Horne and Selwyn Image between 1886 and 1892, after which it appeared fitfully and flickered out. The change in the type, the setting it close instead of spaced, and the new initials and tailpieces which may be noted at the beginning of Vol. III (1888), constituted a landmark in the history of modern printing of an importance similar to that of the return to old-faced type in *Lady Willoughby's Diary*. The progress of the movement can be followed (i) in the catalogue of the Exhibition of Arts and Crafts Exhibition Society, held at the New Gallery in the autumn of 1888, with an article on printing by Mr. Emery Walker ; (ii) in three books by William Morris, viz. *The House of the Wolfings, The Roots of the Mountains*, and the *Gunnlaug Saga*, printed under the superintendence of the author and Mr. Walker at the Chiswick Press in 1889 and 1890. In 1891 William Morris gave an immense impetus to the revival of fine printing by setting up a press at No. 16 Upper Mall, Hammersmith, close to his own residence, Kelmscott House. "It was the essence of my undertaking," he wrote subsequently, "to produce books which it would be a pleasure to look upon as pieces of printing and arrangement of type," and no one will be inclined to deny that the Kelmscott Press books fulfil this aim. The gothic type, whether in its larger or smaller size (the Troy type designed for the reprint of Caxton's *Recuyell of the Histories of Troy,* and the Chaucer type designed for the great *Chaucer*), will hold its own against any gothic type of the fifteenth century. The Golden type (designed for the reprint of Caxton's *Golden Legend*) cannot be praised as highly as this. " By instinct rather than by conscious thinking it over," Morris confessed, " I began by getting myself a fount of Roman type," and it is no unfair criticism of it to say that it betrays the hand of a man whose natural expression was in gothic letter forcing roman into yielding some of the characteristic gothic charm. The *Golden Legend* would have been a far finer book if it had been printed in the Chaucer type, and the Shelley, Keats, Herrick and other books which Morris printed in it to please F. S. Ellis or other friends cannot stand the test of comparison with *The Wood Beyond the World* and the other romances which he printed entirely to please himself. But whether he used his roman or his gothic type the exquisite craftsmanship which he put into all his books enabled Morris to attain his aim, and his wonderful borders and capitals crown them with the delight which this king of designers took in his work. No other printer since printing began has ever produced such a series of books as the fifty-three which poured from the Kelmscott Press during those wonderful seven years, and no book that has ever been printed can be compared for richness of effect with the Chaucer which was the crowning achievement of the Press.

Morris's example brought into the field a host of competitors and plagiarists and a few workers in the same spirit. By his side throughout his venture had stood Mr. Emery Walker, who had no small part in starting the whole movement, whose help and advice for more than twenty years have been freely at the service of any one who has shown any inclination to do good work, and who, whenever good work has been achieved, will almost always be found to have lent a hand in it. After Morris's death Mr. Walker joined with Mr. Cobden Sanderson in producing the Doves Press books, printed, all of them, in a single type, but that type a fine adaptation of Jenson's and handled with a skill to which Jenson not only never attained but never aspired. The first book printed in it was the *Agricola* of Tacitus, and this and Mr. Mackail's lecture on Morris and other early books are entirely without decoration. Woodcut capitals and borders, it was thought, had reached their highest possible excellence under the hand of William Morris, and since not progress but retrogression would be the certain result of any fresh experiments, decoration of this sort must be abandoned. The reasoning was perhaps not entirely cogent, since the decoration appropriate to the Doves type would hardly enter into any direct competition with Morris's gothic designs. Later on, however, it was more than justified by the use in the *Paradise Lost*, the Bible, and most subsequent books (these later ones issued by Mr. Sanderson alone) of very simple red capitals, which light up the pages on which they occur with charming effect.

Similar capitals on a less bold scale, some in gold, others in red, others in blue, are a conspicuous feature in the masterpieces of the Ashendene Press belonging to Mr. St. John Hornby. This was started by Mr. Hornby at his house in Ashendene, Herts, in 1894, and was for some time worked by Mr. Hornby himself and his sisters, with, as at least one colophon gratefully acknowledges, "some little help of Cicely Barclay," who subsequently, under a different surname, appears as a joint proprietor. The early books—the *Journals* of Joseph Hornby, *Meditations* of Marcus Aurelius, *Prologue* to the *Canterbury Tales*, etc.—are not conspicuously good, but in 1902, in a type founded on that used by Sweynheym and Pannartz at Subiaco, Mr. and Mrs. Hornby produced the first volume of an illustrated *Divina Commedia* which cannot be too highly praised. Its story is told in the red-printed colophon, the wording of which is very prettily turned:

Fine della prima Cantica appellata Inferno della Commedia di Dante poeta eccellentissimo. Impressa nella Stamperia Privata di Ashendene a Shelley House, Chelsea, per opera e spesa di St. John & Cicely Hornby coll' aiuto del loro cugino Meysey Turton. Le lettere iniziali sono l'opera di Graily Hewitt, le incisioni in legno di C. Keates secondo disegni fatti da R. Catterson Smith sopra gli originali dell' edizione di 1491. Finita nel mese di Dicembre dell' anno del Signore MCMII, nel quale dopo dieci secoli di bellezza cadde il gran Campanile di San Marco dei Veneziani.

The third type happily inspired by the example of Morris was the Greek type designed by Robert Proctor on the model of that used for the New Testament of the Complutensian Polyglott in 1514, with the addition of majuscules and accents, both of them lacking in the original. An edition of the *Oresteia* of Aeschylus in this type was being printed for Mr. Proctor at the Chiswick Press at the time of his death, and appeared in 1904. In 1908 it was followed by an edition of the *Odyssey* printed at the Clarendon Press. Like Morris's gothic founts, this Greek type may or may not be admired, but that it attains the effects at which it aims can hardly be denied. No page of such richness had ever before been set up by any printer of Greek.

To write of books printed in types which for one reason or another seem less successful than those already named is a less grateful task, but there are several designers and printers whose work approaches excellence, and who worked independently of Morris, though with less sure touch. Foremost among these must be placed Mr. Charles Ricketts,[1] whose Vale type, despite a few blemishes, is not very far behind the Golden type of the Kelmscott Press, and whose ornament at its best is graceful, and that with a lighter and gayer grace than Morris's,

[1] Like Proctor, Mr. Ricketts had no press of his own. His books were printed for him by Messrs. Ballantyne.

though it cannot compare with his for dignity or richness of effect. In a later type, called the Kinge's Fount from its use in an edition of *The Kinges Quair* (1903), Mr. Ricketts's good genius deserted him, for the mixture of majuscule and minuscule forms is most unpleasing.

The Eragny books printed by Esther and Lucien Pissarro on their press at Epping, Bedford Park, and the Brook, Chiswick, were at first (1894–1903, Nos. 1–16) printed by Mr. Ricketts's permission in the Vale type. In June, 1903, a "Brook" fount designed by Mr. Pissarro was completed, and *A Brief Account of the Origin of the Eragny Press* printed in it. Mr. Pissarro's books are chiefly notable for their woodcuts, which are of very varying merit.

In the United States, in addition to some merely impudent plagiarisms, several excellent efforts after improved printing were inspired by the English movement of which Morris was the most prominent figure. Mr. Clarke Conwell at the Elston Press, Pelham Road, New Rochelle, New York, printed very well, both in roman and black letter, his edition of the *Tale of Gamelyn* (1901) in the latter type being a charming little book. Mr. Berkeley Updike of the Merrymount Press, Boston, and Mr. Bruce Rogers during his connection with the Riverside Press, Boston, have also both done excellent work, which is too little known in this country. The artistic printing which Mr. Rogers did while working for the Riverside Press is especially notable because of the rich variety of types and styles in which excellence was attained.

SELECT BIBLIOGRAPHY

GENERAL WORKS

FERGUSON, J. *Some Aspects of Bibliography.* Edinburgh, 1900.

PEDDIE, R. A. *A List of Bibliographical Books published since the foundation of the Bibliographical Society in 1893 (Bib. Soc. Transactions,* vol. x., pp. 235–311). London, 1910.

BIGMORE and WYMAN. *A Bibliography of Printing.* With notes and illustrations, 2 vols. London, 1880.

REED, T. B. *A List of Books and Papers on Printers and Printing under the Countries and Towns to which they refer.* (Bibliographical Society.) London, 1895.

BIBLIOGRAPHICAL SOCIETY. *Transactions.* London, 1893, etc.

EDINBURGH BIBLIOGRAPHICAL SOCIETY. *Transactions.* Edinburgh, 1896, etc.

Le Bibliographe Moderne. Paris, 1897, etc.

Bibliographica. 3 vols. London, 1895–7.

Centrallblatt für Bibliothekswesen. Leipzig, 1888, etc.

The Library. London, 1889, etc.

Zeitschrift für Bücherfreunde. Bielefeld, 1897, etc.

BRUNET, J. C. *Dictionnaire de Géographie ancienne et moderne à l'usage du libraire et de l'amateur de livre. Par un Bibliophile.* Paris, 1870.
With notes on the introduction of printing into the places named.

CRANE, W. *Of the Decorative Illustration of Books Old and New.* Second edition. London, 1901.

DUFF, E. G. *Early Printed Books.* (*Books about Books.*) London, 1893. 8vo.

HUMPHREYS, H. N. *Masterpieces of the Early Printers and Engravers :* Series of facsimiles from rare and curious books, remarkable for illustrative devices, beautiful borders, decorative initials, printers' marks, and elaborate titlepages. Fol. London, 1870.

KRISTELLER, P. *Kupferstich und Holzschnitt in vier Jahrhunderten.* 4to. Berlin, 1905.

LANG, A.   *The Library.*   With a chapter on modern English illustrated books by Austin Dobson, London, 1881.
—— Second edition.   London, 1892.

LIPPMANN, F.   *Druckschriften des xv. bis xviii. Jahrhunderts in getreuen Nach-bildungen herausgegeben von der Direction der Reichsdruckerei unter Mitwir-kung von Dr. F. Lippmann and Dr. R. Dohme.*   Fol.   Berlin, 1884–7.

MORGAN, J. P.   *Catalogue of Early Printed Books from the libraries of William Morris, Richard Bennett, etc., now forming portion of the library of J. P. Morgan.*   [By S. Aldrich, E. G. Duff, A. W. Pollard, R. Proctor.]   3 vols.   Large 4to.   London, 1907.
With many facsimiles.

ROUVEYRE, E.   *Connaissances nécessaires à un bibliophile.*   10 vols.   Paris, 1899.

I.—COLLECTORS AND COLLECTING

ELTON, C. I. and M. A.   *The Great Book Collectors.*   London, 1893.

FLETCHER, W. Y.   *English Book-Collectors.*   London, 1902.

QUARITCH, B.   *Contributions towards a Dictionary of English Book Collectors.*   London, 1892–9.

DAVENPORT, C.   *English Heraldic Book-Stamps.*   London, 1909.
With biographical notes.

GUIGARD, J.   *Nouvel Armorial du Bibliophile.   Guide de l'amateur des livres armoriés.*   2 tom.   Paris, 1890.
With biographical notices of many French collectors.

Book Prices Current.   London, 1893, etc.

American Book Prices Current.   New York, 1895, etc.

LIVINGSTON, L. S.   *Auction Prices of Books.*   1886–1904.   4 vols.   New York, 1905.

LAWLER, J.   *Book Auctions in England in the Seventeenth Century.*   London, 1898.

ROBERTS, W.   *Catalogues of English Book Sales.*   London, 1900.
—— *Rare Books and their Prices.*   London, 1896.

WHEATLEY, H. B.   *Prices of Books:* An inquiry into the changes in the price of books which have occurred in England at different periods.   London, 1898.

BRUNET, J. C.   *Manuel du libraire et de l'amateur de livres, contenant 1ᵉ un nouveau dictionnaire bibliographique,* etc.   Cinquième Édition.   6 vols.   Paris, 1860–5.

GRAESSE, J. G. T.   *Trésor de livres rares et précieux: ou Nouveau Dictionnaire bibliographique.*   7 vols.   Dresde, 1859–69.
These two books mark the close of the fashion of General Collecting.

SELECT BIBLIOGRAPHY

II.—BLOCK-BOOKS

SOTHEBY, S. L. *Principia typographica.* The block-books issued in Holland, Flanders, and Germany during the fifteenth century, etc. 3 vols. Fol. London, 1858.

SCHREIBER, W. L. *Livres xylographiques et xylo-chirographiques. Fac-similés des livres xylographiques.* (*Manuel de l'amateur de la gravure sur bois et sur métal au xvᵉ siècle,* tomes 4, 7, 8.) 8vo and fol. Leipzig, 1895, 1900, 1902.

PILINSKI, A. *Monuments de la xylographie . . . reproduits en fac-similé sur les exemplaires de la Bibliothèque Nationale, précédés des notices par Gustave Pawlowski.* Fol. Paris, 1882–3.

> 1. Apocalypse.
> 2. Bible des Pauvres.
> 3. Ars Memorandi.
> 4. Ars Moriendi.
> 5. Oraison Dominicale.
> 6. Cantica Canticorum.

BIBLIA PAUPERUM. *Biblia pauperum. Nach dem Einzigen in 50 Darstellungen herausgegeben von P. Heitz, W. L. Schreiber.* 4to. Strassburg, 1903.

CUST, L. H. *The Master E. S. and the Ars Moriendi.* 4to. Oxford, 1898.

III. AND IV.—THE INTRODUCTION OF PRINTING— HOLLAND AND MAINZ

GROLIER CLUB. *A description of the Early Printed Books owned by the Grolier Club,* with a brief account of their printers and the history of typography in the fifteenth century. Fol. New York, 1895.

Quotes numerous early references to the invention of printing, and gives some facsimiles.

ENSCHEDÉ, C. *Laurens Jansz. Coster de uitvinder van de boekdrukkunst.* Haarlem, 1904.

—— *Technisch onderzoek naar de uitvinding van de boekdrukkunst.* Haarlem, 1901.

HESSELS, J. H. *Gutenberg: Was He the Inventor of Printing?* London, 1882.

—— *Haarlem the Birthplace of Printing, not Mentz.* London, 1887.

—— Article "Typography" in the *Encyclopædia Britannica.*

GUTENBERG GESELLSCHAFT. *Veröffentlichungen.* Mainz, 1902, etc. 4to.

> I. ZEDLER, G. *Die älteste Gutenbergtype.* 1902.
> II. SCHWENKE, P. *Die Donat- und Kalendertype.* 1903.
> III. *Das Mainzer Fragment vom Weltgericht. Der Canon Missae vom Jahre.* 1458.
> IV. ZEDLER. *Das Mainzer Catholicon.*
> V–VI. *Das Mainzer Fragment vom Weltgericht. Die Type B⁴² im Missale von 1493. Die Missaldrucke P. und Joh. Schöffers. Die Bucheranzeigen P. Schöffers.*
> VIII–IX. SEYMOUR DE RICCI. *Catalogue raisonné des premières impressions de Mayence (1445–67).*

FINE BOOks

FINE BOOKS

DZIATZKO, C. *Was wissen wir von dem Leben und der Person Joh. Gutenbergs?*
[1895.]
—— *Gutenberg's früheste Druckerpraxis auf Grund einer . . . Vergleichung des 42-zeiligen und 36-zeilgen Bibel.* (Sammlung, No. 4.) 1890.
HESSELS, J. H. *Gutenberg: Was He the Inventor of Printing?* London, 1882.
—— *The So-called Gutenberg Documents.* (Reprinted from *The Library*.) London, 1912.

V.—OTHER INCUNABULA

PANZER, G. W. *Annales Typographici ab artis inventæ origine ad annum MD. (ad annum MDXXXVI).* 11 vols. 4to. Norimbergæ, 1793–1803.
HAIN, L. *Repertorium Bibliographicum, in quo libri omnes ab arte typographica inventa usque ad annum MD. typis expressi ordine alphabetico vel simpliciter enumerantur vel adcuratius recensentur.* Stuttgartiæ et Tubingæ, 1826.
—— *Indices uberrimi operâ C. Burger.* Lipsiæ, 1891.
COPINGER, W. A. *Supplement to Hain's Repertorium Bibliographicum.* (Index by Konrad Burger.) 3 vols. London, 1895–1902.
REICHLING, D. *Appendices ad Hainii Copingeri Repertorium Bibliographicum. Additiones et emendationes.* 7 pt. Monachii, 1905–11.
PELLECHET, M. L. C. *Catalogue général des Incunables des bibliothèques publiques de France.* [Continued by M. L. Polain.] Vols. i.–iii. Paris, 1897, etc.
PROCTOR, R. *An Index to the Early Printed Books in the British Museum, with notes of those in the Bodleian Library, Oxford.* 2 vols. London, 1898.
BRITISH MUSEUM. *Catalogue of Books Printed in the Fifteenth Century, now in the British Museum.* Vols. i–ii. [Block-books and Germany, Mainz-Trier.] 4to. London, 1908, etc.
PROVIDENCE, R.I. ANNMARY BROWN MEMORIAL. *Catalogue of Books mostly from the Presses of the First Printers, showing the progress of printing with movable metal types through the second half of the Fifteenth Century.* Collected by Rush C. Hawkins. Catalogued by A. W. Pollard. 4to. Oxford, 1910.
BURGER, K. *Monumenta Germaniae et Italiae typographica. Deutsche und italienische Inkunabeln in getreuen Nachbildungen.* Parts 1–8. Fol. Berlin, 1892, etc.
GESELLSCHAFT FÜR TYPENKUNDE DES 15. JAHRHUNDERTS. *Veröffentlichungen.* Fol. Uppsala, 1907, etc.
TYPE FACSIMILE SOCIETY. *Publications.* (1900–4 edited by R. Proctor; 1904–8 by G. Dunn.) 4to. Oxford, 1900, etc.
WOOLLEY PHOTOGRAPHS. *Woolley Photographs. Photographs of fifteenth century types of the exact size of the originals, designed to supplement published examples, with references to Robert Proctor's Index of Books in the British Museum and Bodleian Library.* [Edited by George Dunn, with a list of the 500 photographs.] Fol. Woolley, 1899–1905.

SELECT BIBLIOGRAPHY

HAEBLER, K. *Typenrepertorium der Wiegendrucke.* 3 vols. Leipzig, 1905, etc. 8vo.

This supplies the measurement and some guide to the characteristics of every recorded fifteenth century type, with helps to the identification of the printers of unsigned books by means of the different forms of M, Qu, etc.

———

BERNARD, A. J. *De l'Origine et des Débuts de l'Imprimerie en Europe.* 2 vols. Paris, 1853.

Valuable for its numerous references to notes and dates in individual copies.

HAWKINS, RUSH C. *Titles of the First Books from the Earliest Presses established in different Cities, Towns, and Monasteries in Europe, before the end of the Fifteenth Century. With brief notes upon their printers.* 4to. New York, 1884.

———

CLAUDIN, A. *Histoire de l'imprimerie en France.* Vols. i.–iii. 4to. Paris, 1900, etc.

THIERRY-POUX, O. *Premiers monuments de l'imprimerie en France au xv⁰ siècle.* [40 sheets of facsimiles.] Fol. Paris, 1890.

HOLTROP, J. W. *Monuments typographiques des Pays-Bas au quinzième siècle.* [130 plates of facsimiles.] Fol. La Haye, 1868.

CAMPBELL, M. F. A. G. *Annales de la Typographie Néerlandaise au xv⁰ siècle.* (With four supplements.) La Haye, 1874 (1878–90).

FUMAGALLI, G. *Lexicon typographicum Italiae. Dictionnaire géographique d'Italie pour servir à l'histoire de l'imprimerie dans ce pays.* Florence, 1905.

HAEBLER, K. *Bibliografía ibérica del siglo 15.* La Haya, 1904.

—— *The Early Printers of Spain and Portugal.* [Bibliog. Soc. Illust. Monographs, 4.] 4to. London, 1897.

—— *Typographie ibérique du xv⁰ siècle. Reproduction en fac-similé de tous les caractères typographiques employés en Espagne et en Portugal jusqu'à 1500.* Fol. La Haye, 1902.

VI.—THE DEVELOPMENT OF THE PRINTED BOOK

POLLARD, A. W. *An Essay on Colophons.* With specimens and translations, by A. W. Pollard, and an introduction by R. Garnett (Caxton Club). Chicago, 1905.

—— *Last Words on the History of the Titlepage.* 4to. London, 1890.

ROBERTS, W. *Printers' Marks: A Chapter in the History of Typography.* London, 1893.

BÜCHERMARKEN. *Die Büchermarken oder Buchdrucker und Verlegerzeichen.* 4to. Strassburg, 1892, etc.

1. *Elsässische Büchermarken bis Anfang des 18. Jahrhunderts.* Herausgeg. von P. Heitz, 1892.

2. *Die Italienischen Buchdrucker- und Verlegerzeichen bis 1525.* Herausgeg. von P. Kristeller, 1893.

3. *Die Basler Büchermarken bis Anfang des 17. Jahrhunderts.* Herausgeg. von P. Heitz, 1895.

4. *Die Frankfurter Drucker und Verlegerzeichen bis Anfang des 17. Jahrhunderts.* Herausgeg. von P. Heitz, 1896.

5. *Spanische und Portugiesische Bücherzeichen des xv. und xvi. Jahrhunderts.* Herausgeg. von. K. K. Haebler, 1898.

6. *Kölner Büchermarken bis zum Anfang des xvii. Jahrhunderts.* Herausgeg. von Dr. Zaretzky, 1898.

7. *Genfer Buchdrucker, und Verlegerzeichen von xv. xvi. und xvii. Jahrhundert.* Von P. Heitz, 1908.

SILVESTRE, L. C. *Marques typographiques, ou recueil des monogrammes . . . des libraires et imprimeurs en France, depuis l'introduction de l'imprimerie jusqu'à la fin du xvie siècle.* Paris, 1853–67.

JENNINGS, O. *Early Woodcut Initials.* London, 1908.

VII.—EARLY GERMAN AND DUTCH ILLUSTRATED BOOKS

DODGSON, C. *Catalogue of early German and Flemish woodcuts preserved in the Department of Prints and Drawings in the British Museum.* Vols. i.–ii. London, 1903, 1911.

MUTHER, R. *Die deutsche Bücherillustration der Gothik und Frührenaissance (1460–1530).* 2 Bde. 4to. München, 1884.

SCHREIBER, W. L. *Catalogue des incunables à figures imprimés en Allemagne, en Suisse en Autriche-Hongrie et en Scandinavie, avec des notes critiques et bibliographiques.* (*Manuel de l'amateur de la gravure sur bois et sur métal au xve siècle*, tom. 5 & 6.) Leipzig, 1910.

COCKERELL, S. C. *Some German Woodcuts of the Fifteenth Century.* 4to. Hammersmith, 1897.

CONWAY, Sir W. M. *The Woodcutters of the Netherlands in the Fifteenth Century.* Cambridge, 1884.

VIII.—EARLY ITALIAN ILLUSTRATED BOOKS

LIPPMANN, F. *The Art of Wood-Engraving in Italy in the Fifteenth Century.* London, 1888.

POLLARD, A. W. *Italian Book-Illustrations, chiefly of the Fifteenth Century.* (Portfolio monographs, 12.) London, 1894.

KRISTELLER, P. *Early Florentine Woodcuts.* With an annotated list of Florentine illustrated books. London, 1897.

ESSLING, PRINCE D'. *Les Missels imprimés à Venise de 1481 à 1600. Description, illustration, bibliographie. Ouvrage orné de planches sur cuivre et de 250 gravures.* Fol. Paris, 1894.

——*Études sur l'art de la gravure sur bois à Venise. Les livres à figures vénitiens de la fin du 15e siècle et du commencement du 16e.* Fol. Paris, 1907, etc.

SELECT BIBLIOGRAPHY

IX.—EARLY FRENCH AND SPANISH ILLUSTRATED BOOKS

MURRAY, C. F. *Catalogue of a collection of early French Books in the library of C. Fairfax Murray.* Compiled by H. W. Davies. 4to. London, 1910.

VINDEL, P. *Bibliografía grafica:* Reproduccion en facsimil de portadas, retratos, colofones y otras curiosidades útiles á los bibliófilos, que se hallan en obras únicas y libros preciosos ó raros. 2 tom. Madrid, 1910.

1224 facsimiles of titlepages, illustrations, etc., of Spanish books, unfortunately neither well selected, nor well arranged, but still useful.

X.—LATER FOREIGN BOOKS

PROCTOR, R. *An index to the Early Printed Books in the British Museum. Part II. 1501–20.* Germany. London, 1903.

NIJHOFF, W. *Bibliographie de la typographie néerlandaise des années 1500 à 1540.* La Haye, 1901, etc.

—— *L'art typographique dans les Pays-Bas, 1500–1540:* Reproduction en fac-similé des caractères, typographiques, des marques d'imprimeurs, etc. Fol. La Haye, 1902, etc.

RENOUARD, A. A. *Annales de l'imprimerie des Aldes, ou histoire des trois Manuces, et de leurs éditions. Troisième édition, avec notes de la famille des Juntes, etc.* 3 vols. Paris, 1834.

—— *Annales de l'imprimerie des Estiennes ou histoire de la famille des Estiennes et de ses éditions.* 2e édition. Paris, 1843.

ROOSES, MAX. *Christopher Plantin, imprimeur anversois. Biographie et documents.* 2e édition. Fol. Anvers, 18o´.

WILLEMS, A. *Les Elzevier. Histoire et annales typographiques.* Bruxelles, etc., 1880.

GOLDSMID, E. M. *Bibliotheca curiosa.* A complete catalogue of all the publications of the Elzevir presses. Edinburgh, 1888.

XI.—SIXTEENTH CENTURY ILLUSTRATIONS

** Many of the books entered under VII, VIII, and IX relate also to this period.

BUTSCH, A. F. *Die Bücherornamentik der Renaissance, eine Auswahl stylvoller Titeleinfassungen, Initialen, Leisten, Vignetten und Druckerzeichen hervoragender italienischer, deutscher, und französischer Officinen aus der Zeit der Frührenaissance.* 4to. Leipzig, 1878.

XII.—ENGLISH PRINTING, 1476-1580

HAZLITT, W. C. *Handbook to the Popular, Poetical and Dramatic Literature of Great Britain, from the Invention of Printing to the Restoration.* London, 1867.

FINE BOOKS

HAZLITT, W. C. *Collections and Notes.* Three series with supplements. London, 1876–89.

—— *A General Index to Hazlitt's Handbook and his Bibliographical Collections, 1867–1889.* By G. T. Gray. London, 1893.

BRITISH MUSEUM. *Catalogue of Books in the Library of the British Museum printed in England, Scotland, and Ireland, and of Books in English printed abroad, to the year 1640.* [Mainly by G. W. Eccles.] 3 vols. London, 1884.

DUFF, E. G. *Catalogue of Books in the John Rylands Library, Manchester, printed in England, Scotland, and Ireland, and of Books in English printed abroad to the end of the year 1640.* 4to. Manchester, 1895.

SAYLE, C. E. *Early English Printed Books in the University Library, Cambridge, 1475–1640.* Cambridge, 1900–7.
The books are arranged under the printers.

AMES, J. *Typographical Antiquities :* Being an historical account of printing in England ; with some memoirs of our antient printers, and a register of the books printed by them, 1471–1600. With an appendix concerning printing in Scotland and Ireland to the same time. 4to. London, 1749.

—— Considerably augmented. . . . By W. Herbert. 3 vols. 4to. London, 1785–90.

—— Greatly enlarged, with copious Notes and Engravings by T. F. Dibdin. Vols. i.–iv. 4to. London, 1810–19.

DUFF, E. G. *English Printing on Vellum to the end of 1600.* (Bibliographical Society of Lancashire.) 4to. Aberdeen, 1902.

—— *A Century of the English Book Trade :* Short notices of all Printers, Stationers, Bookbinders, and others connected with it, 1457–1557. 4to. Bibliographical Society, London, 1905.

—— *The Printers, Stationers, and Bookbinders of Westminster and London, 1476–1535.* (Sandars Lectures.) Cambridge, 1896.

—— *Early English Printing :* A series of facsimiles of all the types used in England during the fifteenth century. Fol. London, 1896.

—— (and others.) *Handlists of English Printers, 1501–1557.* Parts 1–3. 4to. Bibliographical Society, London, 1896, etc.

ARBER, E. *A Transcript of the Registers of the Company of Stationers of London, 1554–1640.* 5 vols. 4to. London, 1875–94.

BLADES, W. *The Life and Typography of William Caxton.* 2 vols. 4to. London, 1861–3.

—— *Biography and Typography of Caxton.* London, 1882.

DUFF, E. G. *William Caxton.* (Caxton Club of Chicago.) 4to. Chicago, 1905.

RICCI, SEYMOUR DE. *A Census of Caxtons.* (Bibliographical Society, Illust. Monographs, 15.) London, 1909.

PLOMER, H. R. *A Short History of English Printing, 1476–1898.* (English Bookman's Library.) London, 1900.

REED, T. B. *History of the Old English Letter Foundries.* 4to. London, 1887.

SELECT BIBLIOGRAPHY

XIII.—EARLY PRINTING IN ENGLISH OUTSIDE LONDON

ALLNUTT, W. H. *English Provincial Presses.* (Bibliographica, Parts 5–7.) London, 1895.

DUFF, E. G. *The English Provincial Printers, Stationers, and Bookbinders to 1557.* (Sandars Lectures.) Cambridge, 1912.

BOWES, R. *A Catalogue of Books Printed at or relating to the University, Town and County of Cambridge, 1521–1893.* Cambridge, 1894.

MADAN, F. L. Oxford Books. Vol. 1. *The Early Oxford Press:* A Bibliography of Printing and Publishing at Oxford " 1468–1640."
—— —— Vol. 2. *Oxford Literature, 1450–1640, and 1641–1650.* Oxford, 1895, 1912.
—— *A Chart of Oxford Printing, " 1468"–1900.* With notes and illustrations. 4to. Oxford, 1903.
—— *A Brief Account of the University Press at Oxford.* With illustrations, together with a chart of Oxford printing. 4to. Oxford, 1908.

DAVIES, R. *A Memoir of the York Press.* With notices of Authors, Printers, and Stationers in the 16th, 17th, and 18th centuries. Westminster, 1868.

DOBSON, A. *Horace Walpole: A Memoir.* With an Appendix of Books Printed at the Strawberry Hill Press. New York, 1893.

ALDIS, H. G. *A List of Books Printed in Scotland before 1700, including those Printed furth of the realm for Scottish Booksellers.* With brief notes on the Printers and Stationers. 4to. Edinburgh Bibliographical Society, Edinburgh, 1904.

DICKSON, R., and EDMOND, T. P. *Annals of Scottish Printing: from the Introduction of the Art in 1507 to the beginning of the 17th Century.* 4to. Cambridge, 1890.

DIX, E. R. McC. *A List of Irish Towns and Dates of Earliest Printing in each.* Second edition. Dublin, 1909.
—— *The Earliest Dublin Printing.* With list of books, etc., printed in Dublin prior to 1601. Dublin, 1901.

GILBERT, SIR J. T. *Irish Bibliography.* Two papers. With an introduction, notes, and appendices by E. R. McC. Dix. Dublin, 1904.

WATKINS, G. T. *Bibliography of Printing in America:* Books, etc., relating to the history of printing in the New World. Boston, 1906.

EVANS, C. *American Bibliography.* . . . A Chronological Dictionary of all books, pamphlets, and periodical publications printed in the United States from 1639 to 1820. 4to. Chicago, 1903, etc.

THOMAS, J. *The History of Printing in America.* With a Biography of Printers, etc. Second edition. 2 vols. Albany, 1874.

RODEN, R. F. *The Cambridge Press, 1638–1692:* A history of the first printing press in English America, together with a bibliographical list of the issues. New York, 1905.

XIV.—ENGLISH WOODCUT ILLUSTRATIONS

CHATTO and JACKSON. *A Treatise on Wood Engravings:* Historical and Practical. Second edition. London, 1861.

LINTON, W. J. *The Masters of Wood-Engraving.* Folio. London, 1889.

XV.—ENGRAVED BOOKS—ILLUSTRATIONS

HIND, A. M. *A Short History of Engraving and Etching for the use of Collectors and Students.* With full bibliography, classified list, and index of engravers. Second edition, revised. London, 1911.

COLVIN, SIR S. *Early Engraving and Engravers in England, 1545–1695.* Fol. British Museum. London, 1905.

HIND, A. M. *List of the Works of Native and Foreign Line-Engravers in England from Henry VIII to the Commonwealth.* British Museum. London, 1905.
Reprinted from Sir S. Colvin's work.

COHEN, H. *Guide de l'amateur de livres à gravure du 18ᵉ siècle, 6ᵉ édition, augmentée par Seymour de Ricci.* Paris, 1912.

LEVINE, J. *Bibliography of the 18th Century Art and Illustrated Books.* London, 1898.

BÉRALDI, J. H. *Estampes et livres, 1872–1892.* 4to. Paris, 1892.
A catalogue of the compiler's own collection of French illustrated books.

XVI.—MODERN FINE PRINTING

STRAUS, R., and DENT, R. K. *John Baskerville: A Memoir.* 4to. Cambridge, 1907.

GOSCHEN, VISCOUNT. *The Life and Times of Georg Joachim Goeschen, Publisher and Printer of Leipzig, 1752–1828.* 2 vols. London, 1903.

WERELET, E. *Études bibliographiques sur la famille des Didot, imprimeurs, etc., 1713–1864.* (Extrait de l'Histoire du Livre en France.) Paris, 1864.

WARREN, A. *The Charles Whittinghams, Printers.* (Grolier Club.) New York, 1896.

MORRIS, W. *A Note by William Morris on his Aims in Founding the Kelmscott Press.* With a short description of the Press by S. C. Cockerell, and an annotated list of the books printed thereat. Hammersmith, 1898.

RICKETTS. *A Bibliography of the Books issued by Hacon and Ricketts.* (The Vale Press.) London, 1904.

STEELE, R. *The Revival of Printing.* London, 1912.

INDEX

INDEX

INDEX

INDEX

328

INDEX

Quinterniones, a name for manuscripts, 94

Quire, origin of the word, 94

Quiring in old books, 94 *sqq.*; collection by, 96 *sq.*

R-printer, the, of Strassburg, 60

Rappresentazioni, illustrated Florentine editions, 138

Rarity, effect on value of books, 7 *sq.*

Rastell, John, lawyer-printer, 215, 222, 258

— William, printed English plays, 215

Ratdolt, Erhard, early printer at Venice, 69; titlepage to his Calendar, 93; his decorative work at Venice, 125 *sq.*; at Augsburg, 106; colour-printing by, 129

Rawlinson, Richard, gives manuscripts to the Bodleian, 5

Raynold, Thomas, his ed. of the *Birth of Mankind*

Recuyell of the Histories of Troye, 206, 254; engraving in Chatsworth copy of Caxton's, 272

Redman, Robert, Pynson's successor, 216, 222

Red printing, difficulty of, 86, 228 *sq.*; colophons in, 92

Regiomontanus. *See* Müller

Reinhard, Johann. *See* Grüninger

Retza, Fran. de, block-book of his *Defensorium*, 27

Reuwich, Erhard, illustrator of Breidenbach's *Peregrinatio*, 108, 115 *sq.*

Reyser, Georg, first Würzburg printer, 64, 269 *sq.*

— Michel, first Eichstätt printer, 64, 269 *sq.*

Rheims, English Catholic books printed at, 232

Richard III, Statute permitting free importation of books into England, 209, 222

Richard, Thomas, printer at Tavistock, 226

Richel, Bernhard, early printer at Basel, his illustrated books, 109, 158

Ricketts, Charles, the Vale Press books, 307

Rodericus Zamorensis, illustrated editions of his *Speculum Humanae Vitae*, 104, 159, 162

Rodlich, Hieronymus, his illustrated books, 193

Rogers, Bruce, fine printer, 308

— William, engraver, 284, 287

Rolewinck, Werner, all his books printed by ther Hoernen, 62; Venice editions of his *Fasciculus Temporum*, 126; Seville ed., 161

Roman de la Rose, early editions of, 160

Roman type, 88–90

Rome, printing at, 65, 167; book-illustration at, 123, 268, 273, 276

Rome under the Castle of St. Angelo, spurious imprint, 233

Rood, Theodoricus, printer at Oxford, 76

Ross, John, Edinburgh printer, 242

Rouen early printing, 72, 146; English books, 225, 229

Ruppel, Berthold, of Hanau, Basel printer, 47, 60

Ruscelli, Jerononimo, his *Imprese*, 277

Rusch, Adolf, the R-printer, 60; roman type used by, 88

Rylands, W. H., engraver, 296

Ryther, Augustine, engraver, 282

Saint Albans, printing at, 76, 208, 224 *sq.*, 253

Saint Andrews, printing at, 241

Saint Omer, English Catholic books printed at, 232

Saluzzo, book-illustration at, 141

Sanctis, Hieronymus de, wood-cutter and printer at Venice, 127

Sanderson, Cobden, fine printing by, 306

Sandys, George, *Relation of a Journey*, 285

Santritter, Johann, illustrator and printer at Venice, 127

Saragossa, early printing at, 75; illustration, 162

Sarum service-books mostly printed abroad, 229; their importation into Scotland forbidden, 240

Savonarola, Girolamo, illustrated editions of his tracts, 133 *sq.*, 137

Savile, Sir Henry, his press at Eton, 234

Saxton, Christopher, maps by, 282

Sayle, C., his catalogue of English books in Cambridge University Library, 233

Schatzbehalter. *See* Stephan

329

INDEX

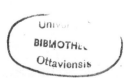